Round Hall Annotated Legislation Series

CRIMINAL JUSTICE (THEFT AND FRAUD OFFENCES) ACT, 2001

Cathal McGreal,

B.C.L., Barrister-at-Law

Note: The contents of this book have been substantially extracted from the *Irish Current Law Statutes Annotated* (ICLSA), Round Hall, Dublin, 2001.

THOMSON ROUND HALL
DUBLIN
2003

Published in 2003 by
Round Hall Ltd
43 Fitzwilliam Place
Dublin 2
Ireland

Typeset by
Gough Typesetting Services
Dublin

Printed by
Modus Media, Dublin

ISBN 1-85800-319-9

A catalogue record for this book
is available from the British Library

© Round Hall Ltd 2003

CRIMINAL JUSTICE (THEFT AND FRAUD OFFENCES) ACT, 2001

UNITED KINGDOM
Sweet & Maxwell
London

AUSTRALIA
Law Book Co.
Sydney

CANADA and USA
Carswell
Toronto

HONG KONG
Sweet & Maxwell Asia

NEW ZEALAND
Brookers
Wellington

SINGAPORE and MALAYSIA
Sweet & Maxwell Asia
Singapore and Kuala Lumpur

CRIMINAL JUSTICE (THEFT AND FRAUD OFFENCES) ACT, 2001

(2001 No. 50)

ARRANGEMENT OF SECTIONS

PART 1

PRELIMINARY

PART 2

THEFT AND RELATED OFFENCES

PART 3

HANDLING, ETC. STOLEN PROPERTY AND OTHER PROCEEDS OF CRIME

PART 4

FORGERY

PART 5

COUNTERFEITING

PART 6

CONVENTION ON PROTECTION OF EUROPEAN COMMUNITIES' FINANCIAL INTERESTS

PART 7

INVESTIGATION OF OFFENCES

PART 8

TRIAL OF OFFENCES

PART 9

MISCELLANEOUS

SCHEDULE 1

ENACTMENTS REPEALED

SCHEDULE 2

TEXT IN THE ENGLISH LANGUAGE OF THE CONVENTION DRAWN UP ON THE BASIS OF ARTICLE K.3 OF THE TREATY ON EUROPEAN UNION, ON THE PROTECTION OF THE EUROPEAN COMMUNITIES' FINANCIAL INTERESTS DONE AT BRUSSELS ON 26 JULY 1995

SCHEDULE 3

TEXT IN THE IRISH LANGUAGE OF THE CONVENTION DRAWN UP ON THE BASIS OF ARTICLE K.3 OF THE TREATY ON EUROPEAN UNION, ON THE PROTECTION OF THE EUROPEAN COMMUNITIES' FINANCIAL INTERESTS DONE AT BRUSSELS ON 26 JULY 1995

SCHEDULE 4

TEXT IN THE ENGLISH LANGUAGE OF THE PROTOCOL DRAWN UP ON THE BASIS OF ARTICLE K.3 OF THE TREATY ON EUROPEAN UNION TO THE CONVENTION ON THE PROTECTION OF THE EUROPEAN COMMUNITIES' FINANCIAL INTERESTS DONE AT BRUSSELS ON 27 SEPTEMBER 1996

SCHEDULE 5

TEXT IN THE IRISH LANGUAGE OF THE PROTOCOL DRAWN UP ON THE BASIS OF ARTICLE K.3 OF THE TREATY ON EUROPEAN UNION TO THE CONVENTION ON THE PROTECTION OF THE EUROPEAN COMMUNITIES' FINANCIAL INTERESTS DONE AT BRUSSELS ON 27 SEPTEMBER 1996

SCHEDULE 6

TEXT IN THE ENGLISH LANGUAGE OF THE PROTOCOL DRAWN UP ON THE BASIS OF ARTICLE K.3 OF THE TREATY ON EUROPEAN UNION, ON THE INTERPRETATION, BY WAY OF PRELIMINARY RULINGS, BY THE COURT OF JUSTICE OF THE EUROPEAN COMMUNITIES OF THE CONVENTION ON THE PROTECTION OF THE EUROPEAN COMMUNITIES' FINANCIAL INTERESTS DONE AT BRUSSELS ON 29 NOVEMBER 1996

SCHEDULE 7

TEXT IN THE IRISH LANGUAGE OF THE PROTOCOL DRAWN UP ON THE BASIS OF ARTICLE K.3 OF THE TREATY ON EUROPEAN UNION, ON THE INTERPRETATION, BY WAY OF PRELIMINARY RULINGS, BY THE COURT OF JUSTICE OF THE EUROPEAN COMMUNITIES OF THE CONVENTION ON THE PROTECTION OF THE EUROPEAN COMMUNITIES' FINANCIAL INTERESTS DONE AT BRUSSELS ON 29 NOVEMBER 1996

SCHEDULE 8

TEXT IN THE ENGLISH LANGUAGE OF THE PROTOCOL DRAWN UP ON THE BASIS OF ARTICLE K.3 OF THE TREATY ON EUROPEAN UNION, TO THE CONVENTION ON THE PROTECTION OF THE EUROPEAN COMMUNITIES' FINANCIAL INTERESTS DONE AT BRUSSELS ON 19 JUNE 1997

SCHEDULE 9

Text in the Irish language of the Protocol drawn up on the basis of Article K.3 of the Treaty on European Union, to the Convention on the protection of the European Communities financial interests done at Brussels on 19 June 1997

An Act to amend the law relating to stealing and related offences and their investigation and trial; to give the force of law to provisions of the Convention on the protection of the European Communities' financial interests done at Brussels on 26 July 1995 and the three Protocols to that Convention; and to provide for consequential and related matters.

[19th December, 2001]

Introduction and General Note*

It is said of larceny, the antecedent to theft, that "as the inadequacies of the law were exposed by the ingenuity of rogues, so the courts and, later, Parliament, extended the law to punish more sophisticated forms of dishonesty" (J.C. Smith); that law, it seems, has been extended just about as far is possible. Thus, we begin (almost) afresh with the law of theft, and hope that the ingenuity of rogues will not too quickly find inadequacies with it. More importantly it is hoped that it will no longer be the case, as it was in the past, that "[t]he courts achieved their purpose by extending the ambit of the original crime of larceny by means of fictitious and strained interpretations of the concepts which constitute the definition of that crime. ..." (*ibid.* at 1–01). This long awaited piece of legislation is the result of several analyses of the law relating to dishonesty, principally the Law Reform Commission's *The Law Relating to Dishonesty* and also the 1992 Report of the Government Advisory Committee on Fraud. The Criminal Justice (Theft and Fraud Offences) Act 2001 replaces many of the common law offences, with many other offences amended and hopefully improved upon. Despite the seeming breadth of changes effected, in reality the changes are generally not so fundamental as to offer anything new to the common law (especially as practiced by our common law neighbour); as one writer put it in the English context: "The modern trend is to replace ... expressions with more everyday language, but in many cases (*e.g.* the redefinition of forgery, or the replacement of larceny with theft) the change is one of terminology rather than substance." (*Arlidge & Parry*, 1–001). Going beyond the realm of the common law, the provisions of the Convention on the Protection of the European Communities' Financial Interests 1995 (and the three Protocols to that Convention) are given the force of Irish law and the Money Laundering Directive is broadened beyond the proceeds of drug trafficking. Finally, matters such as investigation and trial procedure in theft and fraud offences are dealt with to some extent, as are computer crime, forgery and counterfeiting.

The Act – genesis and background

In the traditional manner, the Irish draftsman had the benefit of recourse to the English legislative experience. The Law Reform Commission (LRC) quite understandably stated that "... we do not consider it unreasonable to learn from English Experience" (LRC 43/92, para. 13.6; we shall refer here to the English Theft Act 1968 as "the English Model"). But this willingness to learn and benefit from experience from an obvious source should not permit a tendency to facile and uncritical subscription to an example which is by no means perfect (it is ironic that on the last occasion of legislating in this field, not only did the draftsperson ignore home-grown suggestions for change, he or she also ignored weighty *English* criticisms of the English model; see LRC 23/87, para. 108; see also comments in General Note on s. 17 below). Thus, the re-conceptualisation of the protection of property

*Bibliography and key on page 137.

in criminal law finds its origin in the seminal English Theft Act 1968, with arguably some enlightenment also from the American Law Institute's Model Penal Code, *Model Penal Code*. Ireland, far from being the only jurisdiction to take such recourse to other country's laws has been more reluctant than some to adopt the variations from the English template. Among the jurisdictions to adopt the English Theft Act 1968 *verbatim* are Northern Ireland (Theft Act (NI) 1969), Hong Kong (Crimes (Theft) Act 1973) and Australia (various versions of the Victoria Theft Act), (see also Law Reform Commission of Canada, *Report 12, Theft and Fraud,* Ottawa 1979; for a comparative analysis, see Elliot, "Theft and Related Problems – England, Australia and the USA Compared" (1977) I.C.L.Q. 110).

The draftsman's explanatory memorandum cites numerous reasons for the passage of this Act, among them: the fact that a number of different offences existed to describe similar dishonest behaviour, the inadequacy of the former code to deal with dishonest behaviour generally and specific conduct such as the giving of false statements as to future intentions. The Act also caters for procedural changes in the investigation of theft offences and trial procedure, as well as protecting European Community interests from both fraud and corruption. Forgery, counterfeiting and money laundering also receive treatment under this Act, making it, with the Criminal Damage Act 1991, the most significant piece of criminal legislation with regard to property offences. But perhaps the greatest challenge the legislature faced was to attempt to classify the historical plethora of property offences into what purports to be a relatively neat classification of four types of offence, namely:
– Theft (and related offences), (Pt 2 of the Act);
– Handling Stolen Goods and Proceeds (Pt 3 of the Act);
– Forgery (Pt 4 of the Act); and
– Counterfeiting (Pt 5 of the Act).

Charlton lists 22 different "corresponding" property offences in Irish law prior to this enactment (the word "corresponding" is used tentatively in relation to s. 65 below). The new Act literally condenses, reforms or replaces the following offences in Pt 2 of the Act:
– simple larceny, larceny from the person, embezzlement, larceny by clerk or servant, fraudulent conversion, obtaining by false pretences, larceny by bailee, larceny by trick, obtaining credit by fraud and false accounting,
into the following:
– theft, making a gain or causing loss by deception, obtaining services by deception, unlawful use of a computer, false accounting, and suppression of documents,
whereas robbery, burglary, aggravated burglary, and possession of implements continue to feature in Pt 2 of the Act.

Appropriation of cultural or archaeological objects, corruption of public office, bribery, and cheating the public revenue are not dealt with under the Act (on the last of these, see David Ormerod, "Cheating the Public Revenue" [1998] Crim.L.R. 627). Tax cheating is legislated for in the Tax Acts. The statutory law in relation to both forgery and counterfeiting is entirely replaced with the repeal of prior statutes. The Act does not contain a provision for blackmail, which has interestingly been pre-empted by the Non-Fatal Offences Act 1997 (s. 11, demands for payment of debt causing alarm) and also by s. 17 of the Criminal Justice (Public Order) Act 1994, (demanding money with menaces).

A classification of offences leads to a consideration of the issue of alternative verdicts and interchangeability. In this regard there are two discernible tendencies — to be specific about the circumstances which constitute an offence, or to list generic offences and their correspondent penalty. The Larceny Act 1916 is an example of the latter. The English Theft Act chose the more specific alternative. New Zealand chose the generic approach and Australia an amended form of the English model. With this choice available it would appear that the Irish legislature opted generically. It did not (and, it submitted, wisely so) take on board the Law Reform Commission's recommendation for a catch-all offence of "dishonesty" which would have served as a fallback where the specific circumstances of a case did not fit the more particularised offences (see LRC 43/92, pp. 318 *et seq.*). This is not to say that the Courts may not choose to operate s. 4, the general theft provision — broad as it is — in this manner. S. 54(6) is an example of express authority (see, however, the right of accused persons and the need to prevent defendants escaping through improper charging (LRC 43-1992, pp. 313–315); see the comments of the Supreme Court in *People (DPP) v. Rock* [1994] I.L.R.M. 66:

> "... if the State decides not to prosecute a person for some aggravated form of larceny but decides to prosecute for simple larceny only, thus confining the case to a lower maximum sentence, I cannot see that such a course of action should be condemned as in any way contrary to the statute or, otherwise, bad in law".

With slightly inverted grammar, the Minister indicates the reason for the broad scope of s. 4 to be precisely its function of encapsulating the many offences it is meant to replace: "... the broadness of the new offence of theft obviates the necessity for the multiplicity of specific offences, such as larceny embezzlement, which co-exist at present" (527 *Dáil Debates* Col. 249). This is acceptable where it does not turn out to be a "blunderbuss" of interchangeability. There is a requirement, after all, to ensure consistency in sentencing and of maximum possible certainty (see Ormerod, *supra*).

The Irish Penal code, such as it is, has in the past created difficulties with "grafting" innovations from abroad to older legislation. This Act proposes a more comprehensive importation, reproducing many aspects of the English Theft Act 1968. Thus, "[w]hilst this achieves a close degree of correspondence between the two jurisdictions, which should, *inter alia*, facilitate easier extradition for the offence, it can be expected that considerable difficulties in interpretation will be faced" (McCutcheon, ICLSA, 1990/9–01, 9–01). This might be what McCutcheon calls our national legislative eccentricity, where the draftsman adopts formulas from abroad uncritically (see McCutcheon, "Revision of the Larceny Act" ICLJ 1991), but might also be the practical and simpler option both as regards jurisprudential analysis and where an evident lack of original legislative initiative exists.

The concept of theft

In 1968 our common law neighbour abandoned the term "larceny" and redefined such general (mis)behaviour by referring now to "theft" as "dishonest appropriation of property belonging to another with the intention of *permanently* depriving" (emphasis added). Some 34 years later, Ireland chose to abandon the larceny term (s.3) and define theft as "dishonest appropriation of property without the consent of its owner and with the intention of depriving" (note the absence of the word "permanently"). Despite the slightly different phraseology, the two-step "mental element" is the same:
(a)   there must be an *intention* to deprive, and
(b)   the appropriation must be *dishonest*.

The external elements are similar:
(a)   there must be some identifiable *property*,
(b)   this property must *belong to some* person other than the accused,
(c)   the accused must have *"appropriated"* this property, and
(d)   the appropriation is *without the consent* of the owner.

The former regime of the law of "larceny" was a code of consolidated laws premised upon an historical understanding of only certain forms of property (A.T.H. Smith, p. 13). The elusive nature of the precise meaning of "property" has necessitated a more comprehensive protection of property in criminal law. In choosing to frame our reform upon the template of the English Theft Act 1968, it was (and unfortunately continues to be) of particular importance that we refer to the experience and criticisms of that Act. However, one commentator in particular has said of the English Act that it has begun to show its age and that it is "in some places unprincipled and capricious" (Elliot & Allen, *Casebook on Criminal Law* (5th ed., 1989), p.674); Glazebrook went so far as to condemn the Act to an early and unlamented death (Glazebroook, "Thief or Swindler: Who cares?" [1991] 50 Camb. L.J. 389)! With such criticism, it is unfortunate that we chose to follow much of the troublesome terminology in that Act. In any event, it is crucial that we endeavour to learn from and attempt to avoid similar problems. We shall consider these criticisms with particular reference to the concept of dishonesty.

Criminal Justice (Theft and Fraud Offences) Act, 2001

The concepts of fraud, dishonesty and offences of deception

– Fraud

The concept of fraud is not defined in the Act despite being part of the title. It may tentatively and generically be couched in terms of effecting a breach of property rights by deception or without a claim of right. The Courts refer to it as an absence of a claim of right (*R v. Cockburn* [1958] 1 All E.R. 466). In *Halloway*, Parke B. refers to "wrongful and fraudulent" meaning "without claim of right" (3 Cox 241 at 244 (Cr Cas Res, 1849)). This was the basis of the meaning of inclusion of the concepts fraudulently *and* claim of right in the Larceny Act 1916 (and not, as suggested by the LRC, as a basis only for the latter). It is significant that this important dictum used the phrase "wrongful and fraudulent" because there is in this phrase a marriage of legalism and the layman's term which would later haunt common law jurisdictions for choosing "dishonesty" as a working concept upon which to found their law of theft. It has often been argued that fraud has been widened so as to confuse it with "dishonesty" (*People (Attorney General) v. Grey* [1944] I.R. 326; see also *People (DPP) v. O'Laughlin* [1979] I.R. 85). This "confusion", however, seems to be the very direction in which the law has evolved, not through expansion of the term "deception", but of "dishonesty". A marriage of fraudulent plus a claim of right into the term "dishonesty" is contemplated — dishonesty is defined in s. 2(1) as "a claim of right made in good faith". "Fraudulently" has now arguably been replaced with "dishonestly". A legal concept is replaced by a household word. Thus, the tendency is immediately away from legal analysis to a jury's debate of moral rights and wrongs. So, if it is accepted that a person appropriated property believing one has a right to it, this is not theft where it turns out to be the property of another. It is not theft because it is not a dishonest appropriation. However, a person may appropriate property in the belief that he or she has *no* legal right to it. This property may turn out, in fact, to actually be that person's property! He or she has acted dishonestly and possibly committed theft (see later), but has not acted fraudulently. Equally, a person may know full well that he or she is getting an extraordinary bargain when he or she receives stolen property and claim legal right of that purchase. This is dishonest but not fraudulent. The Irish case of *O'Loughlin* referred to above illustrates that a person may have a legal claim of right to an item but achieves appropriation by dishonest means, thereby achieving the very criteria which form the basis of this entire piece of legislation. Thus, dishonesty is understood to be a non-legal term (indeed, this seems to have been the reason why the English Criminal Law Revision Committee sought to introduce it; see LRC 43/94, para. 15.28).

There is something more in the alternative to dishonesty which requires not only moral culpability but also culpable behaviour in its factual *and* legal sense. It might be that it is fraud or deception which were the key terms — though deception might not be essential (Arlidge & Parry, 1–003; note that cognates of deception include imposition, insincerity fraud and duplicity (Oxford English Dictionary)). Deception may itself be determined by the notion of dishonesty. But dishonesty is arguably incongruent with the term fraud. Placing dishonesty, and not fraud or deception, at the heart of any definition can cause confusion. Dishonesty is internal as a concept. It is a *mens rea* criteria. Where an offence shows sufficient dishonesty, however, it will be tempting for courts to "fudge" the essential external element in order to secure conviction. But *actus reus* cannot merely be dispensed with because of an over-broad approach to the state of mind of the accused. Terms which *do* intimate some externalisation of one's intention, however, are deception and fraud. It is not at all clear whether "appropriation", in principle the *actus reus* element, always requires something active to be done (*AG's Reference (No. 1 of 1983)* [1985] Q.B. 182). This is not to suggest that deceit should stand alone but that it be considered an essential element of fraud, cast in the role of *actus reus* for the "protean concept" of fraud (we will see from ss. 6 and 7 below that some positive act is necessary in the context of deception). The essence then, of fraud, is composed of circumstances informed by the presence of these essential factors and not of dishonesty alone. The usefulness and centrality of the concept of fraud is clear from English case law which demonstrates that fraud is amenable to be applied to a host of cognate offences (see *Wai Yu-Tsang* [1992] 1 A.C. 269 and the cases referred to therein). Equally, the concept of fraud is generally applicable by recourse to the same definition of dishonesty in each case. Therefore, fraud should remain a crucial denomination of the wrongs we are here concerned with. It is submitted that deception should have been considered a more prominent part of the equation and not, as we shall see, a mere afterthought.

– Dishonesty

This writer's concerns about the use of the word dishonesty feature broadly in these annotations. They arise from a real failure of the courts, both here and in England, to reconcile wrongful conduct with wrongful intent. This failure is illustrated through a series of cases which includes our own comparatively innocuous decisions in *Morrissey* [1982] I.L.R.M. 487 and *Keating* [1989] I.L.R.M. 581, and leads through to the decisions of *Lawrence* [1972] A.C. 626, *Morris* [1983] 3 All E.R. 288, *Kaur* [1981] 2 All E.R. 430, *Philippou* [1989] Crim.L.R. 585, *Dobson* [1989] 3 All E.R. 927, and, ultimately, *Gomez* [1991] 4 All E.R. 394. These cases concern various scenarios which demonstrate clear inferences of dishonesty but fall short of clear authority on the actual positive transgression of the law (though the English law did not incorporate the new "absence of consent" requirement in s. 4). It is not merely the inconsistencies from one case to the next which show un undisciplined approach, it is the oscillation between acceding to factual inference (*Philippour, Keating* and *Morrissey*), on the one hand and the strict application of principle (*Morris* and *Kaur*) on the other. The law saw some hope of coming into focus (*Dobson*) but was cast back into "an appalling condition because of the incoherence of the cases" (Griew, p. 53 as cited LRC 43/92 139). The LRC expressed the view that "[i]nevitably the question of the *mens rea* of the accused has been allowed to seep into the analysis of the *actus reus.*" Lord Lane seemed to back-track on his own sensible advice that "the court should be astute not to find theft where it would be straining the language" (see Glanville Williams, *Textbook of Criminal Law* (2nd ed.), p. 819). It might be the LRC were correct in suggesting that these scenarios are more amenable to the law of attempt. They betray themselves, however, in agreeing with the ultimate result in these cases (LRC 43/92, 137–141); they may be included in the striking remarks of J.C. Smith:

> "*Morris*, whatever its flaws, did seem to offer an escape from the old weary round of cases adopting whatever meaning of theft would lead to the conviction of the particular dishonest defendant before the court, with obviously disastrous effects on the consistency and clarity of the law. The Criminal law has suffered from this approach for at least 150 years. ... The present case [Phillippou] suggests we may be falling back into the bad old ways. If it goes higher, please, House of Lords, stick to principle and do not pretend that the irreconcilable can be reconciled".

It is submitted that if we are dealing with an offence irreparably susceptible to overbroad application of the moral culpability with scant regard for the technical requirement of the offence – it must be that there is something wrong not just with the formula (which may have been patched up in the Irish version), but with the basis on which the formula is built and also the interpretive attitude which that formula inspires. *Actus reus* has never taken second place to intention in murder; why should it be otherwise for theft? But this is precisely what will happen without at least some effort and discipline to infuse the offence with positive, external manifestations of dishonesty. These, it is submitted, bear out in the well traversed epistemology of fraud and deception which offer just such infusions. The LRC has expressed the view that all that is required to capture the offending behaviour is the absence of a claim of right and the causing of financial prejudice and that deception is not required. It is submitted, however, that there is something furtive in the nature of these offences which cannot be inadvertent. Thus, something positive is required before theft arises. In Scotland, the offences of appropriation are confined by a requirement of deception. In our code, deception was merely an afterthought (see 546 *Dáil Debates* Col. 963), and yet this delimitation has for some time been considered helpful and workable not just by those who would defend an accused, but by those who seek to prosecute him. Mills QC, when heading the English Serious Fraud Squad Office favoured the enactment in England of a simple offence of fraud, as in Scotland (*The Times*, January 28, 1992; see the Irish Report of the Government Advisory Committee on Fraud 1992, para. 3.13).

Though not a legal observation, fraud is part of the title of this Act whereas dishonesty is not. Fraud and theft are the new catchwords in relation to this field of Irish criminal law; it is probably true to say that an Act entitled "dishonesty" would be too broad, as is an offence based upon it. Dishonesty might sit comfortably with jurors, but they *expect* something legal in their deliberations. The amenable "deception" seems to have been an afterthought of parliamentary debate (see 546 *Dáil Debates* Col. 963). The legislator for the European Union chose to allow fraud to take centre stage by defining it as "any act or omission relating to the use or presentation of false, incorrect or incomplete documents or statements"; such act or omission must have the effect of either (as to expenditure) misappropriation or wrongful retention of Community funds or (as to revenue) illegal diminution of Community resources (importantly, this definition chose to use a formula of act or omission *having as their effect* and then setting out three *mis*behaviours which by themselves must be assessed for moral culpability). In contrast, the Law Reform Commission not only endorsed the use of the notion of dishonesty, it recommended a catch-all offence of "dishonesty" which would have served as a fallback where the specific circumstances of a case did not fit the more particularised offences (see LRC 43/92, 318 *et seq.*). Of the three concepts: (1) fraud, (2) dishonesty, and (3) deception, it is clear that dishonesty is in favour. Dishonesty features in ss. 4, 6, 7, 8, 9, 10, 11 and 17, whereas deception only features in ss. 4, 6, 7 and 11 and in two of those only as an alternative to dishonesty. Thus, the formulation chosen by our legislature places central focus on dishonesty. To be more positive, one leading text describes dishonesty as: "[t]he factor that lends this protean concept [*i.e.* fraud] some semblance of unity [which] is not so much what is actually done, as the legal and moral *character* of what is done, the element of disregard for the rights of others and for ordinary standards of conduct" (Arlidge & Parry, 1–003).

– Offences of Deception

There was a time when *laissez-faire* attitudes in relation to business relations were so strong that it was legitimately asked "shall we indict one man for making a fool of another?" (*Jones* (1704) 91 E.R. 330). This was at a time when a criminal offence occurred only where there was a collective victim or a conspiracy to defraud or, more telling of the attitudes of the day, where the gain was made by cheating. These were common law offences. In 1757 the law took on the statutory formula of obtaining by false pretences. Thankfully there has been considerable sophistication on this attitude, consisting of complex developments in this very particular branch of what was once larceny and is now theft. Not alone has the offence been modified from the obtaining of property to making gain or causing loss, the original bifurcation from larceny was to create the offence of "larceny by trick" which did not quite cover situations where both possession and ownership were obtained. This gave rise to the statutory creation of obtaining by false pretences, most recently formulated in our law in s. 32 of the now repealed Larceny Act 1916. It is submitted, however, that even the level of codification now reached does not preclude overlap with the offence of theft. At least this is the position in relation to the English offence of obtaining by deception which in *Gomez* ([1993] A.C. 442) was quite clearly seen to overlap. The problem will be that a plea of *autrefois acquit/convict* is not available where confusion occurs (*Debhade* [1993] Q.B. 329). Deception will normally require both the mental and physical element. If we are to follow the English model, the jury must consider whether:

1. the complainant thought that the defendant expressly or impliedly *communicated* the existence of certain facts, and
2. the defendant *intended* to produce this belief (A.T.H. Smith, para. 17–15).

Practice will show whether communication may be inferred, as a matter of law, by certain clear and recognised types of conduct. It was held by Lord Diplock in *Charles* [1977] A.C. 177 that:

> "[b]y exhibiting to the payee a cheque card containing the undertaking by the bank to honour cheques drawn in compliance with the conditions endorsed on the back, and drawing the cheque accordingly, the drawer represents to the payee that he has actual authority from the bank to make a contract with the payee on the bank's behalf that it will honour the cheque on presentment for payment" (*cf.* Viscount Dilhorne at p. 186C).

Certainly secretive and entirely silent subterfuge cannot be deception as there is inherently no communication (A.T.H. Smith, para. 17–81).

The complex and broad provision which referred to obtaining by false pretences has now been broken up into particular offences. The person referred to as "another" need not necessarily be the victim and so the old offence of conspiracy to defraud can be fitted within the wording of s. 6. We see the important introduction of the specified component element of "dishonesty", which we have dealt with in s. 2. Again, the dishonesty need not be with reference to the person induced — though that person may be aware of the dishonesty, in which case he or she is also culpable. The old offence of conspiracy to defraud, which was vague and often unnecessary, is nowhere mentioned in the Act despite the LRC's recommendation that it be retained (Chap. 34). The section also refers to "making gain or causing loss" and thus departs from the notion of "obtaining property" (we note that s. 7 retains the term "obtaining services by deception"). The broad scope which is clear from the wording of the section would appear to avoid the limitations of the English section. Indeed the drafting of this very broad and conceptual offence was a confident move on the part of the draftsperson (upon recommendation by the LRC), especially given the failure of other jurisdictions to effectively operate the similar offence of "obtaining pecuniary advantage by deception". Though the particularity of the provision seems to be the emphasis on the positive act (or absence thereof) required of the victim, it would appear to encompass the English offence of obtaining property by deception and more particularly the difficult "obtaining a pecuniary advantage by deception".

The concept of property

S. 2 defines property as "money and all other property, real or personal, including things in action and other intangible property".

The definition of property in s. 2 is substantially a replication of s. 4(1) of the English Theft Act and is "not quite as circular as it seems: its effect is to import into the Act the ordinary legal concept of property anything that can belong to a person as property for the purpose of the Act" (Arlidge & Parry, para. 3–003; we note, however, that the Irish definition of theft does not include reference to "belonging to another").

The law of theft and fraud is essentially conceived for the protection of persons from offences to their property. The important point to note here is that it is the protection of persons and not the property itself. This is because the legal relationship involved is between persons and not *things* (A.T.H. Smith, p. 1). Things, of themselves, cannot have rights, nor can they owe duties.

There are many treatise and conventions in relation to the so-called "right to property" (that such a right is *philosophically* assailable, see F. Cohen, *Dialogue on Private Property* (1954) 9 Rutgers Law Rev. 357). Perhaps the most astute and contemporary (post 1937) is Art. 1 of the First Protocol to the European Convention on Human Rights, which entitles a person to:

> " ... peaceful enjoyment of his possessions. No one shall be deprived of his possessions except in the public interest and subject to the conditions provided for by law and by the general principles of international law."

The provision goes on to qualify:

> "The preceding provisions shall not, however, in any way impair the right of the State to enforce such laws as it deems necessary to control the use of property in accordance with the general interest or to secure the payment of taxes or other contributions or penalties."

Nevertheless, and as indicated in this provision, this right is qualified in many ways by law. One obvious source of limitation of the right of the individual is what has been called the overwhelming authority of Parliament's sovereignty, which is legally able to sanction taxation and compulsory acquisition. This view must be taken in the English context who do not have the same constitutional position with respect to property.

The concept of property is generally the possession of things. Put more academically, the "[o]wnership, property and title all refer to intimate rights to a thing, after accounting for any limited rights in particular persons" (A.M. Honoré, 'Ownership', *Oxford Essays in*

Jurisprudence' ed. A.G. Guest (1961), p. 107). This refers to all sorts of "things" including intellectual property which extends to the proprietary interest in ideas as protected by patents, copyrights, trademarks and industrial designs. The so-called "franglais" concept of choses in action has perhaps sensibly been translated fully to *things in action* in the definition of property. Nevertheless, the concept retains its antiquity and remains a type of intangible property, which frequently is the subject of offences under this Act (see comments of Beldam L.J. in *Hallam* (1994) CA No. 92/4388). Despite the recommendation of the Law Reform Commission, "information" of itself is nowhere in the Act referred to as property (LRC 55/97, p. 181); *cf.* s. 92 of the Trade Marks Act 1996; see opening remarks of Hull, "Stealing Secrets: A Review of the Law Commission's Consultation Papers on the Misuse of Trade Secrets" [1998] Crim.L.R. 246). This is unfortunate as the removal of the requirement permanently to deprive the victim created an opportunity to make a viable inclusion to the host of things which can be stolen of intellectual property or of confidential or secret information of State, industry and commerce (see Charlton, p. 896).

The challenge in setting down the rules in relation to theft was that of keeping apace of the rapidly developing concept of property and what constitutes a "thing" which can be possessed. Indeed, one writer stated that "[o]nly a relatively small part of the total field of economic facility and human capacity is at present permitted to be the subject of private claims of 'property'. Amongst the challenges of the twenty-first century will be whether 'property' claims are to be allowed in relation to a wider group of assets and resources" (Gray [1991] 50 Camb.L.J. 298). One might say that the existing property law is unassailable and it was not for the legislature on theft to extend its remit. And yet, despite the wealth of accumulated experience, the draftsman had to be aware of future change (see A.T.H. Smith, para. 1–06). It is a truism that most *tangible* things can be the subject of these laws. Problems arise, however, at the limits not only of what is tangible but of tangible things not susceptible to alienation or valuation (the criterion of commercial commodity has not been a satisfactory delimitation upon what constitutes property; see *A.G. for Hong Kong n. Chan Nai-Keung* [1987] 1 W.L.R.; see also A.T.H. Smith, p.4, n.12). Living body parts are a case in point; long thought to be impossible to frame in terms of commercial value, even this limitation is subject to reassessment (see "Ownership of human tissue: Life after Moore n. Regents of the University of California" [1989] 75 Va. Law Rev. 1363). Certainly the body parts of the dead have been amenable to the law of theft (*Kelly* [1998] 3 All E.R. 741). Services, as the investment of a person's labour, have now become a protected entity within the law of theft (s. 7).

The Irish section situates much of the property definition in the list of exceptions to theft in subs. (5). The common understanding is that land cannot be stolen and yet this is not entirely true, quite apart from the inclusion of things severed from and fixtures to land. S. 5(2)(*a*) covers not only the "owner" but "agents" authorised to sell land. That authority may not be complete or specific to the disposition and thus consent is vitiated where the agent acts in breach of the confidence reposed in him or her. It is a condition for the purpose of the Act that the property must be capable of appropriation, *i.e.* it must be possible that the "rights" to that property may be usurped or adversely interfered with. Things in action and other tangible property include debts, shares, intellectual property and in theory any valuable entitlement that can be bought and sold (*Attorney General for Hong Kong v. Chan Nai-Keung* [1987] 1 W.L.R. 1339). Things in action consist also in such property as money lodged in a bank; this is a thing (or "chose") in action because there is in reality no money *in* the bank waiting to be taken out — in law it is the bank who owes the sum lodged to the account holder (*Foley v. Hill* (1848) 2 HL Cas 28; see also comments of Goddard L.C.J. in *Davenport* [1954] 1 All E.R. 602 at 603). This legal construct extends without much added complexity to debit accounts (*Kohn* (1979) 69 Cr. App. R. 395). Importantly, there is no *thing in action* to be stolen where the bank has not authorised the account holder to overdraw (*Navaabi* [1986] 3 All E.R. 102). The draftsman has not resolved difficulties in relation to cheques — which, strictly speaking, are not things in action but a means by which a thing in action may be created (*cf.* s. 7(3)). The thing in action, of itself only consists in a right to sue for the sum represented on the cheque; far from being worthless, the cheque is a valuable security which may be executed and which has special properties; Lord Lane C.J. stated in *Kohn* that "[I]t is not a mere piece of paper, any more than a key is just a piece of metal or a swipe card is a piece of plastic". And a valuable security *may* be stolen (*Arnold* [1997] 4 All E.R. 1), a position which found favour with the Australian High Court in *Parsons* 73 A.L.J.R. 27; *cf. Preddy* [1996] A.C. 815; see also comments of J.C. Smith (1998) Crim.L.R. 725). In any event, whilst the definition of property is vital for the founding of an offence in theft, it is not crucial to an offence of deception. Similarly, the difficult issues of electricity and phone calls used in the course of a burglary may be dealt with under the alternative kind of offence as not amenable to appropriation or theft (*Low v. Blease* [1975] Crim.L.R. 513; *Clinton v. Cahill* [1998] NI 200). Confidential information, before an exam *e.g.* is not property for the purpose of theft (*Oxford v. Moss* (1978) [1979] Crim. L.R. 119).

Dishonest operation of a computer to cause loss or make gain

Arlidge & Parry observe that information technology is so central to modern commerce that "any fraud of any complexity is likely to involve computers in one way or another" (11–001). How a provision such as this is to be policed and enforced remains to be seen; one draws both hope and concern from comments that: "[C]omparatively little technical skill is necessary for unauthorised users of any particular network to gain access to computer networks worldwide" (A.T.H. Smith, p. 356); one assumes that at least to some extent investigation might be easier than first appears. Interestingly, the use of the word "computer" only, which is undefined, is used and does not extend to "machine". The Criminal Damage Act 1991 made it an offence to unlawfully access data whether inside the State or not, and to add to, alter, corrupt, erase or move that data. Ironically, s. 9 of this Act will make it an offence to operate or cause a computer to be operated where damage (and therefore loss) results. S. 9 adds to the protections against computer crime. Couched in general, if terse, terms, it is to cater for the offence of theft committed with a computer or like device which until now had to be dealt with under laws conceived many years before the possibility of computer crime was even dreamt of. Thus, we are advancing slowly from what one judge called "procrustean attempts" to force the facts of this new breed of offences into laws which were not designed for them (Lane L.J. in *R v. Gold* [1987] 3 W.L.R. 803 at 809. See also Kelleher and Murray, *Information Technology Law in Ireland* (1997).

Money laundering

Money laundering is an offence where criminal conduct can convert unlawful gain into tangible financial gain. In other words it makes profit out of a crime. Far from being a recent phenomenon, money laundering has been around just as long as crime itself (Rider *Taking profit out of Crime*, in Rider and Ashe, *Money Laundering Control* (Roundhall Sweet & Maxwell, Dublin, 1996)). Money laundering is often large-scale and so clever and sophisticated that detection and prosecution become frequently impossible (see Ashe & Reid, p. 1). In 1988 the Basle Committee on Banking Regulation and Supervisory Practices stated:

> "[P]ublic confidence in banks and hence their stability, can be undermined by adverse publicity as a result of inadvertent association by banks with criminals. In addition, banks may lay themselves open to direct losses from fraud, either through negligence in screening undesirable customers or where the integrity of their own officers has been undermined through association with criminals" (Com (99) 352 final; 99/0152 (COD).

By virtue of Council Directive 91/308 the E.U. focused clearly on the prevention of the use of financial systems for the purpose of money laundering (see Art. 15). Art. 1 defines money laundering as any of the following conduct accompanied by the requisite intention:
– conversion or transfer of property, knowing that such property is derived from criminal activity or from an act of participation in such activity, for the purpose of concealing or disguising the illicit origin of the property or of assisting any person who is involved in the commission of such activity to evade the legal consequences of his action,
– the concealment or disguise of the true nature, source, location, disposition, movement, rights with respect to, or ownership of property, knowing that such property is derived from criminal activity or from an act of participation in such activity,

– the acquisition, possession or use of property, knowing at the time of receipt that such property was derived from criminal activity or from an act of participation in such activity,

– participation in, association to commit, attempts to commit and aiding or abetting or counselling the commission of any of the actions mentioned in the foregoing paragraphs.

Any problems with transposition can be seen from a comparison with Art. 1 and s. 31, as amended. It should be noted, finally, that the European Commission proposed a formal extension of the prohibition on money laundering beyond the proceeds of drug trafficking to cover the proceeds of all criminal conduct (COM (1999) 352 final 99/0152 (COD). This had been the view of the *Financial Action Task Force* (FATF) for some time and was arguably a consistent theme in the original Directive. The appearance of an amendment to the original section in this Act, then, is entirely consistent with this extension. It is unfortunate, given the opportunity taken to amend s. 31 of the 1994 Act, that its consequent deterrence measure in s. 32 was not amended in pursuance of the second part of the proposal of the Commission — the extension of the compliance provisions to certain non-financial institutions and profession was not undertaken. Perhaps it was with reservations such as those in relation to the reporting responsibilities of solicitors, that such a step was not taken (Ashe & Reid, 36).

In the present Act, the draftsman did not, as was done with forgery and counterfeiting, devote an entire Part to money laundering. This may be due to considerable attention already been given to the subject in the Criminal Justice Act 1994 — indeed Pt IV of that Act is devoted to it. It is chiefly an amendment of the provision in Pt IV of the 1994 Act with which ss. 21-23 of this Act are concerned. It does, however, make for an untidy ordering of sections to simply add these three sections onto Pt 3. The amendments of the 1994 Act remove reference to drug trafficking by instead referring to "the criminal conduct concerned". Thus, the drug trafficking context in which the money laundering provisions were set is no longer express and the scope of the offence may clearly be one of general application to "criminal conduct" (see Financial Action Task Force recommendation that the provision be broadened, as discussed in Ashe & Reid, p. 26). This is not to say that much of the problem associated with money laundering is in fact drug related (Ashe & Reid, p. 2). The 1994 Act was not, until now, concerned with the broader implication of international criminal activity — finding its impetus rather in the Vienna Convention on Illicit Drug Trafficking (December 20, 1988). Signatories of that instrument were required to have money laundering offences in their national legal orders to avail of mutual assistance which would become largely a theme of the present endeavour to build a European justice system (see Art. 7 of the Vienna Convention and Pt VII of the Criminal Justice Act 1994). Art. 3(1)(b)(i) of the Vienna Convention specifically in relation to money laundering required:

(i) the conversion or transfer of property, knowing that such property is derived from any offence(s) established in accordance with sub-paragraph (a) [a list of drugs offences] ... or from an act of participation in such offence(s), for the purpose of concealing or disguising the illicit origin of the property or of assisting any person who is involved in the commission of such offence or offences to evade the legal consequences of his actions;

(ii) The concealment or disguise of the true nature, source, location or disposition, movement, rights with respect to, or ownership of property, knowing that such property is derived from an offence or offences established in accordance with sub-paragraph (a) ... or from an act of participation in such offence(s).

Art. 3(3) permits the burden of proof to be discharged by inference from objective factual circumstances.

As to the concern that extradition limitations would limit the effect of these measures, Art. 3(10) "reduces the possibility" (Ashe & Reid, p. 20) of suspect activities being regarded as political or fiscal. It remains the position that the offence of money laundering may be committed in three different ways (see Ashe & Reid, p. 43, referring to the unamended section):

1. Primary money laundering (laundering the proceeds of one's own crime);
2. Secondary money laundering (laundering the proceeds of the crime(s) of another);
3. Incidental secondary money laundering (handling or using the proceeds of another crime).

Forgery and counterfeiting

The LRC set out an interesting brief history of the law of forgery beginning with the Roman Emperor Sulla's *lex Cornelia de falsis* (dated 81 B.C., referring to Turner). Earliest references to forgery concern not currency but the forgery of testamentary dispositions; only later did the law concern itself with coin counterfeits — and even then — issue was taken with false coins not because of the financial gain or loss but the treason of belittling the image (embossed upon the coin) of an emperor! But this is how, as *Turner* puts it, ". coinage offences, and forgery came to be intermingled. It seems to have been due to this situation that Early English law closely linked coinage offences, falsification of Royal Seals, and treason". Indeed, as we shall see, it is only really with the enactment of the current legislation that this confusion is resolved. A more direct antecedent to the present enactment was the statute 28 Eliz. 1, c. 3 which was construed over time (see Turner, pp. 943–944) to cover documents public *and* private in nature, and the horrendous punishments envisaged ensured literally "a perpetual note and mark of the convict's falsehood". Money tokens, however, carried a distinction even at an early stage (20 Edw. 1, c. 4). Two other statutes of that year concern the use of coins other than those of the Kingdom of England, Ireland and Scotland. In 1350, coinage offences were declared treasonable (Statute of Purveyors, 1350). By the reign of George III, customs stamps were being used and it was an offence (the penalty still being capital, though reduced to the gravity of felony) to counterfeit these custom marks (26 Geo. 3, c. 49). The persistent confusion between forgery and counterfeit can be seen by the offence under 32 Geo. 4, c. 56 of "counterfeiting" character reference for people "in service". As pointed out by Rowell, this would now be regarded as forgery, not counterfeiting. Gradually a distinction developed between the forgery of public documents, where the mere creation of a forgery was an offence, and private documents where an intent to use the document to defraud someone was required (Turner, p. 945). Then came the more recognisable Forgery Acts 1861-1913, which applied in this jurisdiction until the coming into force of this Act. Those acts draw a distinction between *counterfeiting* of seals and dies and *forgery* (or the making of false documents). Counterfeiting expanded as an activity during the Industrial Revolution "where the new technology and expansion of Empire provided a seed-bed for the inventive genius of the Victorian era" (Rowell, p. 3). Items or tokens of value are prime targets for those with the na'er-do-well and wherewithal to imitate them. It was considered at this stage that forgery is identifiable as distinct from replicating coins; "forged" banknotes fell somewhere in between. Because of the potential of multiple copies of banknotes, or perhaps because of the currency denomination, banknotes would ultimately be classified with coinage under the term "counterfeit". Forgery, on the other hand, was considered an offence of false "instruments" which "tells a lie about itself" (*Re Windsor* (1856) 10 Cox CC 118 at 123; this phenomenon is referred to as "automendacity" which is not strictly a requirement of the law of forgery (*R. v. Donnelly* [1984] 1 W.L.R. 1017). In other words, forgery was consigned to specific and generally single instances of documents which purported to be made by someone who did not make them. The English Law Commission's *Report on Forgery and Counterfeit Currency* (No. 55 July 17, 1973) finally drew a distinction between forgery:

> "In the vast majority of forgery cases the purpose of the forger is to lull the person to whom the document is presented into a false position in which he is unlikely, because of the apparent authenticity of the document, to make further enquiry into the correctness of the facts related" (*ibid*. at para. 14).

and counterfeiting:

> "The ease and rapidity with which forged banknotes pass as tokens of value make it very difficult to trace any false note to its source, and the fact that they are tokens of value means that once false notes are in circulation there is serious potential prejudice to a large number of innocent persons. These reasons justify special treatment for the forgery of banknotes" (*ibid*. at para. 18).

Stern magazine were induced to pay £2.3m some 25 years ago for diaries which falsely purported to be those of Adolf Hitler. In very simple terms, the offence of forgery is evidenced thus: the diaries (a) purported to have been made by someone who did not make them; (b) gave information which was a lie; and (c) were unique. This third step is a characteristic of nearly all forgeries and distinguishes the concept quite neatly from counterfeiting

(Rowell, p. 69).

Classic forgery is committed when the forger signs what purports to be the *victim's signature* on a cheque payable to the victim, in other words cashes another person's cheque and pockets the payment. It is curiously an offence of forgery only where he does so without the victim's authority (Smith & Hogan, (1st ed.), p. 474). This position is doubtful, however. Official documents very often contain warning clauses which indicate it is an offence to falsify the required information in any way. Whether authorised or not the signature purports to be signed by one person but is in fact the mark of another. Thus, it tells a lie about itself. It is difficult to see how one person can validly attempt to make another person's signature. He or she may alternatively alter the amount payable on a cheque made out to him or her without authority to do so or enter an amount exceeding the amount he or she was authorised to enter on the cheque.

Pt 5 of this Act now makes counterfeiting a separate compartment within the field of the law of theft and fraud. In 1992, the Law Reform Commission recommended that the offence of counterfeiting should apply to both bank notes *and* coins. It has long been considered an anachronism to confine the criminal law to the old concept of forgery of documents, dies and seals. In the U.K., the Forgery and Counterfeiting Act 1981 took steps to extend the definition of "document"; however there remained a separate law applicable to coins.

"Bank note" was delimited in the Central Bank Act 1942 to the meaning given to it in the Forgery Act 1913; s. 18 defined the concept to include "... any note or bill of exchange of the Bank of England or Bank of Ireland, or any other person, body corporate, or company carrying on the business of banking in any part of the world", and includes "bank bill", "bank post bill", "blank bank note", "blank bank bill of exchange" and "blank bank post bill". S. 55(1) of the 1942 Act provides that any "person who makes or causes to be made, or utters any document or uses for any purpose whatsoever, or utters a document purporting to be or in any way resembling or so nearly resembling as to be calculated to deceive, a bank note or part of a bank note, is guilty of an offence". Offences in relation to coins were probably the historical predecessor of the offence of forging bank notes; even in more recent times there has been more legislative provision for coins than for bank notes. The opening section of the Coinage Offences Act 1861, which is entirely repealed by this Act, referred to coins "lawfully current". S. 2 of that Act prohibited falsely making or counterfeiting coin resembling or passing for current gold or silver coin, as well as s. 3 which made it an offence for the gilding, silvering, washing, casing over or colouring of coins to make them pass for a silver or gold coin. The Act also contained various offences of uttering which is now an abolished term of art. The Decimal Currency Act 1969 updates changes effected by that Act as well as the Customs Consolidation Act 1876, the Revenue Act 1889 and the Currency Act 1927. S. 14 of Decimal Currency Act provides: "... no piece of metal or mixed metal of any value whatsoever shall be made or issued in the State as a coin or a token for money or as purporting that the holder thereof is entitled to demand any value denoted thereon ...".

After long and considered attention given both to the law of counterfeiting bank notes and coins, the Irish Law Reform Commission followed the view of the English Law Commission that no distinction was necessary, and Pts 4 and 5 of this Act thereby represent that view.

Convention on protection of European Communities' financial interest

Under Art. K.1 (as assigned) of the Treaty on European Union (of which Ireland is a signatory) it is proposed that a high level of safety for citizens of the Community will be achieved by preventing and combating crime, in particular crimes of corruption and fraud. Under Art. K.3, the Council recommended that Conventions drawn up be adopted by its members in accordance with their respective constitutional requirements. Art. 29 of the Irish Constitution enables the simple passing into law of such measures through an Act of Parliament, which in this case is the Theft Act. Though these are annotations to that Act, due to the still novel concept of semi-direct European legislative reform it is proposed here to give some explanation below of the genesis and origin of the Convention which now forms part of our criminal law.

The control of fraud against European Community financial interests is not a new concern but one which has ebbed and resurfaced from time to time over the past three decades. The current impetus is probably the result of the marked increase in the 1990s of problems relating to the fraud of Community financial interests and the work of the European Parliament, the Court of Auditors and the Directorate-General for Financial Control within the institutions of the European Union. Much of the initiative, however, also came from Member States themselves. In any event it is said that: "The controllability of the fraud problem is regarded as an essential condition for the further expansion of European economic and political integration. It is also seen (whether it be an opportunity or a burden) as an outstanding illustration of the need for harmonisation of Community legislation and enforcement practices (Vervaele, vii & ix).

– The meaning and subject-matter of fraud against the financial interests of the Community

Fraud against the Community can be defined as fraud against the flow of finances to and from the Community budget (Vervaele, 37). This is a wide brief for anyone who hopes to understand the nature of this field — it literally extends to all aspects of the E.U. budget. The gravest areas of concern are:
– the import and export of goods by evasion of import duties and abuse of export refunds, as well as fraud involving the quality, labelling and ingredients of commodities;
– VAT fraud and fraud affecting the GNP of Member States from which the Community derives a percentage of its revenue; and
– Community intervention fraud by manipulation of price support and intervention fraud at the expense of Community budget.

To understand the types of fraud which can be committed it is important to understand the subject-matter of that fraud. The European Community finances can for our purposes be divided into outflow and inflow. Sources of money coming into Community coffers are:
– VAT (Value Added Tax, which makes up over half of the inflow);
– Customs duties;
– Agriculture levies; and
– GNP (Gross national produce of which the Community receives a share).

Administrative expenditure and the grants and subsidies provided by the Community account for expenditure. These subsidies are vulnerable to fraud in many ways, not only in the payment of the largest category — agriculture subsidies — and the equally sizeable structural funding. There are particular problems, however, with fraud in relation to research and development, non-E.U. development funding and environmental and consumer protection (see, *e.g.* "General Budget" [1998] O.J. L44/119; see also U. Sieber, *Eurofraud-Study*, 1997).

– The nature and extent of Community fraud

As noted above, Community fraud is by no means a recent phenomenon — in its comparative youth, the Community was already victim to a well organised and developed modus of fraud. A very good illustration of this and the kind of activity with which we are concerned with is the "Como Butter" case where 327 lorry loads of butter of extra-Community origin were stored in custom warehouses and purchased from an intervention agency in Rotterdam. National customs services notified the Commission that checks carried out at the scene of a road traffic accident uncovered 248 Community transit documents (Form T1) which had been falsified through the fraudulent use of customs stamps. The duties and levies avoided were to the value of Lit. 10.3 billion in April 1976. It is known from the investigation that a 10-man team had been assembled to carry out the transit, with the coordination of three companies in different countries; perhaps most significantly, however, there was clearly an astute examination of Community transit legislation to identify the weakness which made it possible to falsify the requisite forms. Finally, there was also a necessary inference of community officials having been bribed. Thus, it is no surprise that a spokesman for the European Parliament in 1987 reported:

"The Community's finances have not remained unaffected by economic crime. The Community institutions have been aware of this since at least the beginning of the

1970s, and this awareness formed the basis of ideas about the organisation of budgetary controls. These institutions also quickly found that criminal activity had got the measure of Community structures and in particular the cross-frontier nature of rules, the fragmented and departmental mechanisms for detecting, prosecuting and preventing fraud. The complexity of legislation, the unsuitability and lack of preparation of national administrations in terms of implementing it and, finally, the huge sums which are sometimes at stake." (Guermeur Report at B, I, European Parliament Working Document A 2-251/86).

Fraud may exist where an importer commits a fraud by making a false declaration of origin thereby obtaining a false certificate of origin. The offender gains unlawful preference to other goods thereby evading customs and anti-dumping duties. Similarly, an offence may be committed in the so-called transit of goods; goods which do not qualify for import into the Community might unlawfully gain entry by a false declaration that they are goods in transit (goods in transit avoid duties and VAT). The goods are never intended to leave the Community through customs but instead find their way into free circulation within the Community (see Kuhl, p. 260). Fraud may also take advantage of the export refunds provided by the Community to compensate for higher prices within the Union. Sophisticated fraud may involve both revenue and expenditure in what are known as carousel operations; import duties are bypassed and then claimed as an unjustified export refund on the same goods (see Kuhl, p. 261). There may also be a fraudulent sale of cut-price intervention products to buyers outside the E.U. and fraudulent invitations to tender with respect to foreign trade markets. Structural funds may be defrauded by claiming contribution or payment for either work or services that were never actually rendered. Similarly, with the direct expenditure of Community funds — where a grant is awarded for the completion of a certain project the recipient may subcontract the work. There are reported cases of subcontractors who increased the actual cost and hence the claim (Annual Report 1994, Chapter V, s. 5.4 (Tourism) as cited by Kuhl, p.262).

– Respective duties of Member States and the Union

Fraud affects the Community by tapping into the Community budget; this is a budget supervised by the Court of Auditors and the European Parliament. Nevertheless, Member States are under a duty to ensure that any infringement of Community law is dealt with by measures similar to those of a domestic nature by ensuring that the measures taken are effective, proportionate and dissuasive. This is established Community law (stemming from the original Art. 5 of the Treaty of Rome, the accepted primacy of Community law over national law laid down in Case 26/62 *Van Gend en Loos* and Case 6/64 *Costa/ENEL*; on effective enforcement, see Case 14/83 *Von Colson and Kamann*). As far back as 1962 the Council of Ministers formed an ad hoc working group ("Cour de Justice et protection pénale") to find a better way of harmonising the criminal laws of Member States. Even within this group, however, a consensus could not be reached until 1972 when a published draft document proposed the amendment of Art. 5 of the Treaty of Rome to include a so-called *European Crimes Treaty* which would provide regulations for the protection of Community financial interests from fraud ([1976] O.J. C222/2). The proposal dealt with two key principles:
– the "assimilation principle" — assimilation of measures taken to protect against community fraud to those used against domestic fraud, and
– the "community territory principle" whereby a Member State initiating any investigation does so where it considers fraud to have occurred within its own territory.

Problems from the outset consisted of the immunity from extradition which is extended to offences of a fiscal nature and also the reluctance to consider extraterritorial competence for the transfer of prosecution. If it were not for the concerted efforts of the Court of Auditors (see Court of Auditors Report, 1986; [1987] O.J. C336, §§ 6.14–6.19), the working group may not have resumed its work to find out whether, in the framework of the increasing need for adequate regulation of the financial interests of the Community, the differences of opinion could be overcome amongst the Member States on:
– the question of fiscal exemption to the rule of extradition;
– the exemption from the duty to create an extraterritorial competence for the transfer of

prosecution; and
– the legal formalities. (see Vervaele, p. 89)

When it did resume work, consensus was difficult and it was left to Member States to take the initiative, notably with Italy as chair of the Political Committee on European Political Co-operation. In 1990 an ad hoc group was formed ("Droit Pénal – Droit Communautaire") which reported on the relationship between criminal and Community law. Para. 4.1 of their report states, *inter alia*, that:

> "Legal problems can be found both at EC level and in the national system of law, and strike at the very heart of the relationship between Community law and criminal law … It is recognised that the enforcement of Community law is partly determined by the quality of this law. Criticism has often been expressed in the past about the complex nature of Community law and of its susceptibility to fraud." (para. 4.3)

In late 1991, under the chairmanship of the Netherlands, the efforts of the *Cour de Justice et protection pénale* working group were once again resumed and finally, in November 1991, a report was presented to the Council of Ministers requesting the Commission to undertake a comparative assessment with a view to co-ordinating anti-fraud legislation through the Directorate-General of Financial Control and the Anti-Fraud Coordination Unit (UCLAF). This request took the form of a resolution which intended that "the Member States should not simply adopt for themselves the necessary general or specific measures to ensure the upholding of Community law and effective operation of the Communities themselves, but that it is likewise important to have in place an effectively functioning system of instruments for administrative and criminal co-operation for the purpose of preventing and combating infringements of community law and of other practices by which the interests of the Communities are damaged" (Resolution of Council, November 13, 1991, 91/C328/01, J.4). The next major advance was the inclusion of the relatively tame Art. 209A in the Treaty on European Union, referred to below.

– Harmonisation and the genesis of European legislative measures against fraud

The problems with which these measures are concerned are primarily administrative irregularities which require criminal enforcement. Arts. 9 and 18 of the Shengen Agreement (concerned with the free movement of goods and persons by the abolition of border checks) aimed to make possible direct mutual assistance in criminal matters between police and customs authorities of the Member States. Art. 50 commits signatories to mutual assistance regarding the infringement of their rules with respect to custom and excise duty and VAT. These early initiatives on mutual assistance were still very much confined to administrative control where the activities which cause concern were distinctively criminal in nature. The move towards political union brought with Art. K.1(9) stipulates that "Member States shall regard, as a matter of common interest, police co-operation for the purposes of preventing and combating … serious forms of international crime including if necessary certain aspects of customs co-operation …". Interestingly, Parliament has swung quite radically from the view that, irrespective of such co-operation, harmonisation could not be achieved.

An overview of reports commissioned by the European Parliament from the period 1977–1991 provides an interesting evolution of attitudes towards the measures taken against Community fraud. Vervaele comments that the Parliament has not only fulfilled the role of public conscience but has also made constructive proposals to make the problem manageable. The reports of the rapporteurs show continuity and uniformity and the evolution of ideas concerning fraud against the Community can clearly be followed. (Vervaele, p. 83)

The *De Keersmaeker Report*, 1977 stated that:

> "[t]he main problem here is the variation among Member States in the manner in which protection under criminal law has been developed and put into practice. These differences are even more evident in the protection of commerce under criminal law … A second problem is that the national criminal law provisions are not geared to protection of the specific financial interests of the EEC and effective controls of fraud against the European Community. Penalisation and sanctions are often lacking in that domain …" (Vervaele, p. 76, commenting on European Parliament Working Documents 1976–77, 431/76).

The *Gabert Report*, 1984 stated that:

"The complexity of Community regulations has led to a flood of national implementation legislation, which often differs from one country to another. Another factor, alongside the complexity and specificity of the rules, is the implementation of the legislation by national administrative bodies in national administrative structures which are not geared to the objectives of EEC legislation and are inadequately prepared to carry out such a task. In short the differences in national administrative and legal structures lead to a highly divergent implementation of the Community's financial mechanisms" (Vervaele, p. 77, commenting on European Parliament Working Documents 1983–1984, Document 1–1346/83).

The *Guermeur Report*, 1986 contains recommendations for the simplification and codification of Community legislation with a view to more diligent and effective control with formalised views on detection and prosecution. Part of the Report states (report at B, I) that:

"The Community's finances have not remained unaffected by economic crime. The Community institutions have been aware of this since at least the beginning of the 1970s, and this awareness formed the basis of ideas about the organisation of budgetary controls. These institutions also quickly found that criminal activity had got the measure of Community structures and in particular the cross-frontier nature of rules, the fragmented and departmental mechanisms for detecting, prosecuting and preventing fraud. The complexity of legislation, the unsuitability and lack of preparation of national administrations in terms of implementing it and, finally, the huge sums which are sometimes at stake." (European Parliament Working Document A 2-251/86)

The *Dankert Report*. In 1987 the parliamentary reporting moved on in 1989 to consider definite consideration of prevention and prosecution calling for Community legislation which was more lucid, comprehensible, complete, simply designed and practical in its application. Requirements for such would include a good central exchange of information among Member States and the Anti-Fraud Co-ordination Unit, to include:
– an operational computerised fraud database;
– swift approval of draft protocols amending the treaty to combat fraud;
– greater co-operation in criminal law including extradition, transfer of criminal proceedings and enforcement; and
– Community competence in the imposition of penalties. (European Parliament Working Document A 2-20/89)

By 1990, the submissions to Parliament had become formulated demands that the Treaty itself be amended to include specific provision for anti-fraud measures.

The *Theato Report*, 1991 recommended that revision of the Treaties establishing EU should include amendments specifically providing for anti-fraud measures. These amendments were to be based on a number of principles, including the legislative power to generate regulations and directives; to harmonise, protect and sanction the area of criminal law; and mutual assistance to include extradition and on the spot investigation of fraud. The system regarding sanctions prior to European Union was criticised as incoherent and fragmentary. Nevertheless, the thinking in Parliament advanced considerably from the late 1970s where it seemed impossible that criminal law and Community affairs would ever even approach harmonisation. In her concluding paragraph Theato states that:

"Experience acquired since then and the profound changes brought about by the Community means that [this view] can now be refuted ... this kind of harmonisation and, more generally, the introduction of uniform and appropriate criminal law to protect the Community's financial interests, accompanied by a wide range of administrative penalties is an essential precondition for the smooth functioning of the Community and the single market which will be established in 1993" (European Parliament Working Document A3-0250/91).

By the time it came to ratify the Treaty on European Union, however, these demands were not implemented by the Heads of State. Thus, the Maastricht Treaty does not specifically provide for the harmonisation of either criminal law or sanctions within the administrative area. What was included was a rather tame version of the proposed Art. 209A, requiring Member States to deal with community fraud in the same manner it deals with domestic fraud, though it does require co-operation and co-ordination in its fight against fraud. The

Council provided itself the power to adopt joint measures, promote and take joint action, and draw up conventions.

– Article K of the Treaty on European Union

As things stood prior to the enactment of this Act, the Community had authority to create legislation but the Member States in many respects remained responsible for its enforcement. In criminal matters, in particular, the Community was dependent on national legislation and enforcement practices. This was unfortunate considering that the systems national and supranational often did not correspond; penalties differed, as did discretionary powers of judges — this in particular created major difficulties in what was known as trans-national fraud (Kuhl cites *Customs and Excise v. Ghiselli*, May 15, 1996. EP, Committee of Inquiry in to the Communty Transit System, Vol. III Written Contributions, No. 39, 220.895/ Vol.III, p. 334.) What can be seen from the *Ghiselli* case is primarily the difficulty in harmonising penalties: Firstly, what one country may deem satisfactory retribution may not apply in another; secondly, a national court is restricted as to the admissibility of evidence over which it has questionable jurisdiction. finally, it is far easier to establish who the actual victim is where Community financial interests is the subject of the law's protection. Thus, Member States were not given a free hand on how to enforce Community legislative initiatives in a manner compliant with Community notions of efficiency, effectiveness, proportionality and deterrence (see Vervaele, p. 183). Thus, national authorities would be bound to enforce the principles set out, for example, in Art. K of the Treaty on European Union:

> "… in keeping with the general principles of Community law and the fundamental laws which, through the jurisprudence of the European Court of justice, form an integral part of Community laws' general principles of justice. Equality before the law, legal security, proportionality, etc., play an important role in community law" (Vervaele, p. 193).

From a Community perspective it is interesting that the Commission, the ultimate machine from which these laws take solid form, has proved relatively ineffective in its control and sanctioning authority (Vervaele, p. 193). This is surprising given the success in the field of unfair competition. Nor is it likely — in this limited context — that any objection will be entertained for the Commission to act as the role of investigator, prosecutor and judge (*Pioneer case*, Case 100 136/80 Jur. 1983 (1825)). By limited context we mean verification, detection and sanction; this with the saver that there is an appeal to the European Court of Justice. It is crucial that legal — as opposed to administrative — protection be extended to any preliminary enquiry at Commission level (see *National Panasonic* Case 136/79 Jur. 1980 (2033)). We have seen the issues which arise from the powers of investigation and sanction of Community institutions in private business (see the powers of access to business premises and means of transport, audit, copying of documents and requesting on-the-spot verbal explanations, Art. 14 of Regulation 17/62; on which see *Hoechs* Case 46/87 and 227/88, Jur. 1989 (2859)). It goes almost without saying that the inviolability principle must apply and powers of investigation must bear the scrutiny of constitutional and internationally recognised principles pertaining to human rights; certainly the due process and privacy requirement must be adhered to; of particular relevance are Arts. 5 and 8 of the European Convention on Human Rights. Thus:

> "[t]he establishment of proper legal protection within the double legal order with respect to supervision, detection and punishment is a *sine qua non* for the success of the harmonisation process. There is therefore, a need for clarity on the Community principles of good administration (fairness – openness) in its substantive and procedural aspects. But the road to harmonisation is still bristling with pitfalls" (Vervaele, p. 195).

– Common standards of fraud protection throughout the E.U.

In 1994 the U.K. and the Commission proposed a joint action initiative on the criminal aspects of legal protection against fraud under Art. K.3(2) of the Treaty on European Union (Title VI). The Council, composed of E.U. Justice Ministers, issued a resolution in December 1994 identifying outstanding issues with precise focus on the need, in the interest of

Community financial interests, of improving co-operation between Member States on criminal matters ([1994] O.J. C355/2). On July 26, 1995, the Convention on the protection of the European Communities' financial interests was adopted. In addition, two Protocols have been adopted by the Council. The First Protocol deals with corruption involving officials and the Second Protocol concerns the criminal liability of legal entities, money laundering and co-operation in the prosecution of fraud. Finally, a Protocol on Interpretation is to be annexed to the Convention which is concerned with interpretation and the giving of jurisdiction for that purpose under the Convention to the European Court of Justice. The Convention is said to be the first tangible achievement under the so-called third pillar of the Treaty on European Union. Certainly, any failures of these laws to be properly implemented and applied may cause serious harm not only to Community finances but also to the credibility of the Union, and this, consequently could even challenge pre-existing Community law requirements arising out of Arts. 5 and 209a of the E.C. Treaty (Kuhl, p. 324). In any event, it is the Member State legislature which is now largely competent to ensure the protection of community financial interests. Thus, it is the Member State itself that must take all measures to guarantee the application and effectiveness of these laws. An effective execution of this duty will be crucial where there is no specific penalty provided by European law: "[m]ember States must ensure that infringements of Community law are penalised under conditions, both procedural and substantive, which, in any event, make the penalty effective, proportionate and dissuasive" (Kuhl, citing *Commission v. Greece Case* 68/88, September 21, 1989, Reports p. 2985 point 24).

Investigation of offences – Powers of search and mutual assistance

The Act provides for a broad power of search both of any place or persons found there, subject to the satisfaction of a District Court judge that there are reasonable grounds for suspecting that evidence relating to the commission of an offence is located there. It is an offence to obstruct the member named in a search warrant, and that member may be accompanied by such other persons as may be necessary. Forfeiture of stolen property or articles and items under the Act is provided for and an application can be made, somewhat akin to a police property application, for their return to the appropriate person. Concealment of any document is an offence and extends to falsification, destruction or disposal which any person suspects might be of relevance to an investigation undertaken by the gardai. We note, in this regard, the consideration of and ultimate opposition of the LRC to the establishment of a Serious Fraud Office (43/92, paras 38.14–15).

The investigation of offences is a wider issue in relation to the Theft Act and concerns:
– powers (including the duty to co-operate imposed) under the Acts such as:
  • the Criminal Justice Act 1994 in relation to money laundering;
  • the Convention on the protection of the European Communities' financial interests; and
  • the Europol Act 1999;
– the so-called "improved effectiveness and co-operation of the competent authorities in the Member States in preventing serious forms of international crime" (money laundering and property offences are included by annex to the Convention);
– the undertaking to facilitate international co-operation with the investigation, search, seizure and confiscation of the proceeds of all types of criminal activity under the Strasbourg Convention (Council of Europe, September 12, 1990); and
– the Vienna Convention on Drug Abuse and Illicit Drug Trafficking which prescribes measures to be taken to enable the competent authorities to identify, freeze, trace and confiscate the proceeds derived from drug trafficking and drug-related money laundering (December 20, 1988).

On July 26, 1995, all Member States signed the Europol Convention, which was incorporated into Irish law by virtue of s. 2 of the Europol Act 1997. Under Art. 3 of the Convention, the principal tasks of Europol are:
– to facilitate the exchange of information between Member States;
– to obtain, collate and analyse information and intelligence;
– to notify the competent authorities of the Member States without delay (via the national units of information concerning them and of any connections identified in criminal

offences);
- to aid investigations in Member States by forwarding all relevant information to national units; and
- to maintain a computerised system of collected information containing data. The database, which will be the sum of contributions made by Member State national units in respect of crime and criminal profiling, is said to be one of the most significant developments under the Convention. The Convention aims to restrict access to this data in accordance with data protection (Arts. 9, 11, 14 and 19). Supposedly, an equivalent to the U.S. famed FBI the national units are to co-operate in forming a palpable European justice system. (See Karen Murray, "An Overview of the Europol Act 1997" [1998] I.L.T.R. 73).

Trial of offences

Interesting is the decision to provide a section containing the criteria by which an indictable offence may be considered a summarily triable minor offence (without a jury and certain of the formalities of trial on indictment) in the District Court. Many of the offence sections set out a penalty on indictment only, leaving it open to the District Court, once the accused, the DPP and the District Court itself are happy to proceed summarily, to decide the matter within its own jurisdiction (s. 53).

The Act is determined to ensure that persons whose trial may not ultimately secure a conviction for theft may alternatively result in conviction for a "theft offence", such as handling or possession of stolen property or vice versa (s. 55). Where possible, orders of restitution of the property the subject of wrongful appropriation under the Act may be made to its rightful owner (s. 56).

This also contains the innovative measure for the provision of information to juries in fraud cases (s. 57). This is considered necessary because fraud cases present greater problems in terms of complex evidence than would be the case in offences, for example, of physical aggression. It is not merely a question of witness or forensic evidence which can be bewildering to a judge and juror alike. Fraud can take on the dimensions of a full scale financial investigation which few lay persons can come to grips with in the course of orally communicated evidence (and in this we include judges unversed in the fields of accountancy, book-keeping, underwriting and so on). The section may prove difficult and unwieldy; certainly teething problems are indicated by the fact that the section at the time of writing remained the only one not yet brought into effect by Ministerial order.

Corporate liability and the duty to report offences

The Act aims to bring companies and financial institutions as well as their controlling officers within the remit of the fraud provisions. The Act specifies certain duties of persons working in the commercial sector. Reporting is now a duty and any obstructing of investigations will, as we have seen, attract prosecution under the Act.

It has long been accepted that a company has legal personality and can be liable in civil law to pay debts (*Solomon v. Solomon* [1897] A.C. 22). In certain circumstances this potential liability has been extended to criminal law (*DPP v. Mutual Enterprises Ltd* unreported, High Court, Lynch J., November 29, 1985. This was not always the case (*Anon* (1701) 12 Mod Rep 560). However, the criminal liability of a company is somewhat empty where there is an immunity or "veil" which protects its members from any responsibility. It is true that the veil can be lifted — s. 4 of the Companies Act 1963 provides that where a person dealing with a company is aware that the dealing is outside the powers of the company, that dealing is void. Nevertheless, the idea of attaching any *criminal* responsibility to a company has been difficult (*Wells*). A company, a legal entity capable of purchasing, borrowing incurring debt and contracting, is by no means a moral entity, nor can it be attributed with any conscience, intention or recklessness (*Tesco Supermarkets Ltd v. Nattrass* [1972] A.C. 153). Thus, it may be "blamed" for causing or procuring certain wrongs — even criminal wrongs — but is not in any real sense "blameworthy". It remains paramount, however, that an intention to commit any crime must be identified, *i.e.* a servant or agent of the company must be accessible, in terms of liability, in order to find the will or intention behind any criminal "act" imputed to the company; after all, it is through its servants and agents that a company acts. Indeed the writers in Charlton point to the fact that it is often difficult because to pinpoint who such actors are may have helped the acceptance of the doctrine of corporate criminal liability (para. 11.06). We must bear in mind, however, that we are referring here to the liability of bodies incorporated or unincorporated and not just individuals. In *ICR Haulage Ltd* [1994] K.B. 551, it was held that the acts of a company director were to be treated as acts of the company; thus, some 60 years ago, in one of the first findings of corporate criminal liability through a servant or agent, the fraud of the director was the fraud of the company.

From an early stage it was assumed that such liability could only attach through a servant or agent of a high-ranking level, *i.e.* it was only directors and managers who represented the directing mind and will of the company (*HL Bolton* [1957] 1 Q.B. 159 at 172). The *Tesco* case referred to above reserves the category of "controlling minds" to those entrusted with the exercise of the powers of the company. This provision prefers, however, to eschew such a restriction and follow the line of Lord Steyn in the *British Steel* case who stated: "... it would drive a juggernaut through the legislative scheme if corporate employers could avoid criminal liability where the potentially harmful event is committed by someone who is not the directing mind of the company" [1995] I.R.L.R. 310. Thus, where it is proved that an offence has been committed by a body corporate (as opposed to an offence committed by an individual on his own behalf), and where the offence is attributable (at the very least) to the neglect of either a manager, director, secretary or other officer, liability may rest against that individual. This test asks whether or not the company has committed an offence under this Act and only then does it go on to consider whether any individual was involved so as to attract criminal liability. It also makes clear that although this person does not have to be a manager or director, he does have to be an "officer" which indicates full responsibility within the organisation and connotes rank (*cf. Moore* [1944] 2 All E.R. 515). In addition, it covers someone purporting to act in the like capacity which raises the issue of persons not normally given such rank or position but who assume, to the knowledge of the organisation, such a position, *e.g.* apprentices, temporary replacements, liquidators, and examiners. The word "neglect" is likely to create problems; it is certainly not a notion sufficient to attach personal criminal liability as a principal. The reason, perhaps, why this word features in the provision is the impression made upon the LRC in a recommendation submitted by the current Attorney-General, Michael McDowell:

> "[W]e recommend that the legislation include a distinct offence consisting of controlling a company at a time when an offence of dishonesty is committed by a director, officer, servant or agent of the company in circumstances where the person in control had reasonable cause to believe that such an offence would be or was being committed, having regard to the nature and extent of the control thus exercised. It should be a defence to this offence that the defendant had *acted reasonably* in seeking to prevent the commission of the offence" [emphasis added].

By means of attributed liability s. 58 of the Act does not create a distinct offence but merely extends liability for other offences under the Act, nor does it provide a reasonable conduct defence mechanism. The implications for management are clear however: it is an individual in their ranks who may have to go to prison as the company cannot; indeed the only real punitive sanctions as against the company are monetary with the potential, possibly of damage to reputation and ultimately to the business itself. So it might have been the innocent shareholder who would have the only natural persons to suffer from the sanction were it not for this extension to management (the effect on shareholders, indeed is an unfortunate consequence, Charlton, para. 11.27). On the other hand, it would appear that sizeable fines are more appropriate punishments as against companies (see the Australian provision which sets fines for companies above those for individuals, Crimes Act 1914 (Cth) s 4B(3); though "sizeable" must of course at least hurt to some extent, see *Slapper*, as cited by Charlton 11.27). One outstanding issue is that of civil liability and the test applied to it; some feel it is inappropriate to ask simply whether the corporate body knew what was happening was dishonest (see Simon Gardner, "Property and Theft" Crim. LR (1998) 35). The very pertinent answer to this question is that the possible consequences in civil law are potentially of far greater import.

The debating of the Bill was relatively curt and almost disappointingly without much controversy; in any event the lawyer should be interested not in the polemic but in the construction of the language which in the recent case of *Crilly* has been limited as to its value before a court.

Though there was some criticism, the Act represents, in the main, the original draft submitted by the Minister. Such points of debate as occurred will be treated in the General Notes below.

Penalties:

S. 4(6) – A person guilty of **theft** is liable on conviction on indictment to a fine or imprisonment for a term not exceeding 10 years or both.

S. 6(2) – A person guilty of **making a gain or causing loss by deception** is liable on conviction on indictment to a fine or imprisonment for a term not exceeding five years or both.

S. 7(4) – A person guilty of **obtaining services by deception** is liable on conviction on indictment to a fine or imprisonment for a term not exceeding five years or both.

S. 8(7) – A person guilty of **making off without paying** is liable on conviction on indictment to a fine not exceeding £3,000 or imprisonment for a term not exceeding two years or both.

S. 9(2) – A person guilty of **unlawful use of a computer** is liable on conviction on indictment to a fine or imprisonment for a term not exceeding 10 years or both.

S. 10(3) – A person guilty of **false accounting** is liable on conviction on indictment to a fine or imprisonment for a term not exceeding 10 years or both.

S. 11(4) – A person guilty of **suppression of documents or valuable securities** is liable on conviction on indictment to a fine or imprisonment for a term not exceeding 10 years or both.

S. 12(3) – A person guilty of **burglary** is liable on conviction on indictment to a fine or imprisonment for a term not exceeding 14 years or both.

S. 13(3) – A person guilty of **aggravated burglary** is liable on conviction on indictment to imprisonment for life.

S. 14(2) – A person guilty of **robbery** is liable on conviction on indictment to imprisonment for life.

S. 15(5) – A person guilty of **possession of certain articles** is liable on conviction on indictment to a fine or imprisonment for a term not exceeding five years or both.

S. 17(4) – A person guilty of **handling stolen property** is liable on conviction on indictment to a fine or imprisonment for a term not exceeding 10 years or both, but is not liable to a higher fine or longer term of imprisonment than that which applies to the principal offence.

S. 18(4) – A person guilty of **possession of stolen property** is liable on conviction on indictment to a fine or imprisonment for a term not exceeding five years or both, but is not liable to a higher fine or longer term of imprisonment than that which applies to the principal offence.

S. 19(2) – If the person **withholds information regarding stolen property**, he or she is guilty of an offence and is liable on summary conviction to a fine not exceeding £1,500 or imprisonment for a term not exceeding 12 months or both.

S. 23 (6) – A person who fails to **report transactions connected with a designated state or territorial unit** (subs. (2)) or as supervisors fail to report suspicion of such a transaction (subs.(3)) comply with subs. (2) or (3) of this section is guilty of an offence and liable—

  (a) on summary conviction, to a fine not exceeding £1,000 or to imprisonment for a term not exceeding 12 months or both, or

  (b) on conviction on indictment, to a fine or to imprisonment for a term not exceeding five years or to both,

S. 25(2) – A person guilty of **forgery** is liable on conviction on indictment to a fine or imprisonment for a term not exceeding 10 years or both.

S. 26(2) – A person guilty of **using a false instrument** is liable on conviction on indictment to a fine or imprisonment for a term not exceeding 10 years or both.

S. 27(2) – A person guilty of **copying a false instrument** is liable on conviction on indictment to a fine or imprisonment for a term not exceeding 10 years or both.

S. 28(2) – A person guilty of **using a copy of a false instrument** is liable on conviction on indictment to a fine or imprisonment for a term not exceeding 10 years or both.

S. 29 (6) – A person guilty of **having custody or control of certain false instruments** is liable on conviction on indictment to a fine or imprisonment for a term not exceeding—

(a) in the case of an offence under subs. (2) or (4), five years,

(b) in the case of an offence under subs. (1) or (3), 10 years,

or both.

S. 33(2) – A person guilty of **counterfeiting a currency note or coin** is liable on conviction on indictment to a fine or imprisonment for a term not exceeding 10 years or both. (However, note s. 38 (1) listed below.)

S. 34(3) – A person guilty of **passing, tendering or delivering counterfeit a currency note or coin** is liable on conviction on indictment to a fine or imprisonment for a term not exceeding—

(a) in the case of an offence under subs. (1) [passing or tendering], 10 years, or

(b) in the case of an offence under subs. (2)[delivering], five years,

or both. (However, note s. 38 (1) listed below).

S. 35(3) – A person guilty of **having custody or control of a counterfeit currency note or coin** is liable on conviction on indictment to a fine or imprisonment for a term not exceeding—

(a) in the case of an offence under subs. (1) [custody or control with intent to pass, tender or deliver it], 10 years, or

(b) in the case of an offence under subs. (2) [simple control or possession], five years, or both. (However, note s. 38 (1) listed below.)

S. 36(3) – A person guilty of **having custody or control of materials and instruments for counterfeiting** is liable on conviction on indictment to a fine or imprisonment for a term not exceeding—

(a) in the case of an offence under subs. (1) [custody or control of anything intended to make a counterfeit], 10 years, or

(b) in the case of an offence under subs. (2) [custody or control of anything specially designed or adapted to make a counterfeit], five years,

or both.

(However, note s. 38 (1) listed below.)

S. 37(2) – A person guilty of **importing or exporting counterfeit currency note or coin** is liable on conviction on indictment to a fine or imprisonment for a term not exceeding 10 years or both. (However, note s. 38 (1) listed below).

S. 38(1) – A person who outside the State does **any act referred to, in ss. 33, 34, 35, 36 or 37** is guilty of an offence and liable on conviction on indictment to the penalty specified for such an act in the section concerned.

(2) S. 46 [Forfeiture of seized property] shall apply in relation to an offence under subs. (1) as it applies in relation to an offence under s. 45 [obstruction of a Garda acting on warrant].

S. 39 (5) – A designated body which **fails to withdraw counterfeit notes or coins from circulation** and transmit them with information of receipt to the Central Bank or which provides false or misleading information on matters referred to is liable, without prejudice to s. 58, to—

(a) on summary conviction, a fine not exceeding £1,500 or imprisonment for a term not exceeding 12 months or both, or

(b) on conviction on indictment, a fine or imprisonment for a term not exceeding five years or both.

S. 42 – A person who is guilty of **fraud affecting the European Communities' financial interests** is liable on conviction on indictment to a fine or imprisonment for a term not exceeding five years or both.

S. 43 – A person who is guilty of **active corruption** is liable on conviction on indictment to a fine or imprisonment for a term not exceeding five years or both.

S. 44 – An official who is guilty of **passive corruption** is liable on conviction on indictment to a fine or imprisonment for a term not exceeding five years or both.

S. 45 (3) – A person guilty of **extra-territorial fraud affecting the Communities' financial interests or extra-territorial money laundering** is liable on conviction on indictment to a fine or imprisonment for a term not exceeding five years or both.

S. 49(1) – A person who is guilty of **obstruction of a Garda acting on a warrant** under para. (*b*) or s. 48(5)(*b*) is liable on summary conviction to a fine not exceeding £500 or imprisonment for a term not exceeding six months or both.

S. 51(3) – A person guilty of **concealing facts disclosed by documents** is liable on conviction on indictment to a fine or imprisonment for a term not exceeding five years or both.

S. 52(8) – A person who without reasonable excuse **fails to comply with an order to produce evidential material,** is liable on summary conviction to a fine not exceeding £1,500 or imprisonment for a term not exceeding 12 months or both.

S. 59(4) – A **relevant person who without reasonable excuse fails to report an offence** is guilty of an offence and is liable on summary conviction to a fine not exceeding £1,500 or imprisonment for a term not exceeding 12 months or both.

Applicability of prior case law

Throughout the commentary to the sections below the reader may have materials to hand which refer to law prior to this enactment. The annotations, where appropriate, refer to "prior law" and the continuing relevance it might have. Caution must be exercised, however, in using prior law, especially prior case law. The Theft Act must be seen in this jurisdiction as a fresh start and the concepts used are in many respects divorced from the Larceny code. In respect of case law it might be worthy of note that Lord Wilberforce in his legislative role felt that it should not be permissible "to refer to any decision of any Courts prior to the passing of this Act, other than decision in general terms dealing with the interpretation of Statutes" (Parliamentary Debates, Official Report (HL) Vol. 290, Col. 897). These views were not, however, taken on board by the English legislature and thus we may take it that reference may be made to prior case-law where necessary and where prudent regard is made to developmental nuances and the differences intended by the new departure. J.C. Smith comments that "where terms with a well-settled meaning under the Larceny Acts have been used in similar context in the Theft Act, it would seem desirable – and certainly in accord with the intention of the framers of the [English] Act – that those concepts should be given their well-settled meaning" (para. 1–08). Indeed we must, of course, consider that cases decided under similar provisions in jurisdictions such as England where theft was introduced by an Act of 1968 are often of some relevance to our own Act.

Citation

Criminal Justice (Theft and Fraud Offences) Act, 2001.

Commencement

This Act (except s. 57) came into force at various dates between the passing of the Act and August 1, 2002. Ss. 23, 53, 58 and 60(1) and Pts 5 and 7 came into effect on the passing of the Act on December 19, 2001. It was for the Minister to appoint an operative date or dates for the remainder, which in the case of s. 23 (which inserts an new s. 57A into the Criminal Justice Act 1994) was April 2, 2002, and for the remainder (except for s. 57) August 1, 2002.

Statutory Instruments

Criminal Justice Act 1994 (Section 57A) Order 2002 (S.I. No. 101 of 2002).
Criminal Justice (Theft and Fraud Offences) Act 2001 (Commencement) Order (S.I. No. 252 of 2002).

Parliamentary Debates

527 *Dáil Debates* Cols. 246–290 (Second Stage).

Acts Referred to

ACC Bank Acts, 1978 to 2001	
Bail Act, 1997	1997, No. 16
Building Societies Act, 1989	1989, No. 17
Central Bank Act, 1971	1971, No. 24
Central Bank Act, 1997	1997, No. 8
Coinage Offences Act, 1861	24 & 25 Vict., c. 99
Continental Shelf Act, 1968	1968, No. 14
Credit Union Act, 1997	1997, No. 15
Criminal Evidence Act, 1992	1992, No. 12
Criminal Justice Act, 1951	1951, No. 2
Criminal Justice Act, 1984	1984, No. 22
Criminal Justice Act, 1994	1994, No. 15
Criminal Justice (Miscellaneous Provisions) Act, 1997	1997, No. 4
Criminal Justice (Public Order) Act, 1994	1994, No. 2
Criminal Law (Jurisdiction) Act, 1976	1976, No. 14
Criminal Procedure Act, 1967	1967, No. 12
Debtors (Ireland) Act, 1872	35 & 36 Vict., c. 57
Defence Act, 1954	1954, No. 18
Ethics in Public Office Act, 1995	1995, No. 22
European Communities Acts, 1972 to 1998	
Extradition Act, 1965	1965, No. 17
Falsification of Accounts Act, 1875	38 & 39 Vict., c. 24
Forgery Act, 1861	24 & 25 Vict., c. 96
Forgery Act, 1913	3 & 4 Geo. 5, c. 27
Gaming and Lotteries Act, 1956	1956, No. 2
Larceny Act, 1861	24 & 25 Vict., c. 96
Larceny Act, 1916	6 & 7 Geo. 5, c. 50
Larceny Act, 1990	1990, No. 9
Married Women's Status Act, 1957	1957, No. 5
Official Secrets Act, 1963	1963, No. 1
Police (Property) Act, 1897	Ch. 30
Road Traffic Act, 1961	1961, No. 24
Sale of Goods Act, 1893	56 & 57 Vict., c. 71
Summary Jurisdiction (Ireland) Act, 1862	24 & 25 Vict., c. 50
Taxes Consolidation Act, 1997	1997, No. 39
Trustee Savings Banks Acts, 1989 and 2001	

Be it enacted by the Oireachtas as follows:

PART 1

PRELIMINARY

Short title and commencement

1.—(1) This Act may be cited as the Criminal Justice (Theft and Fraud Offences) Act, 2001.

(2) Subject to *subsection (3)*, this Act shall come into operation on such day or days as may be appointed by order or orders made by the Minister, either generally or with reference to any particular purpose or provision, and different days may be so appointed for different purposes and different provisions of this Act.

(3) *Parts 5* and *7* and *sections 23, 53, 58* and *60(1)* shall come into operation

31

on the passing of this Act.

GENERAL NOTE

This section provides that only ss. 23, 53, 58 and 60(1) and Pts 5 and 7 came into effect on the passing of the Act on December 19, 2001. It was for the Minister to appoint an operative date or dates for the remaining sections. S. 23 (which inserts an new s. 57A into the Criminal Justice Act 1994) came into effect on April 2, 2002 and for the remainder (except for s. 57) August 1, 2002. Subs. (3) makes special provision for certain measures intended to implement commitments at E.U. level in relation to the protection of the euro against counterfeiting and measures to combat money laundering. The tight timeframe involved for the legislative process in the run-up to the introduction of the euro made it necessary to provide for commencement immediately upon enactment (see 546 *Dáil Debates* Col. 1150).

Interpretation (general)

2.—(1) In this Act—

"appropriates" has the meaning given to it by *section 4(5)*;

"deception" has the meaning given to it by *subsection (2)*;

"dishonestly" means without a claim of right made in good faith;

"document" includes—

> (*a*) a map, plan, graph, drawing, photograph or record, or
>
> (*b*) a reproduction in permanent legible form, by a computer or other means (including enlarging), of information in non-legible form;

"gain" and "loss" have the meanings given to them by *subsection (3)*;

"information in non-legible form" means information which is kept (by electronic means or otherwise) on microfilm, microfiche, magnetic tape or disk or in any other non-legible form;

"owner" and "ownership", in relation to property, have the meanings given to them by *subsection (4)*;

"premises" includes a vehicle, vessel, aircraft or hovercraft or an installation in the territorial seas or in a designated area (within the meaning of the Continental Shelf Act, 1968) or a tent, caravan or other temporary or movable structure;

"property" means money and all other property, real or personal, including things in action and other intangible property;

"record" includes any information in non-legible form which is capable of being reproduced in permanent legible form;

"stealing" means committing an offence under *section 4*, and cognate words shall be construed accordingly;

"stolen property" includes property which has been unlawfully obtained otherwise than by stealing, and cognate words shall be construed accordingly;

"theft" has the meaning given to it by *section 4(1)*; and

"unlawfully obtained" means obtained in circumstances constituting an offence, and cognate words shall be construed accordingly.

(2) For the purposes of this Act a person deceives if he or she—

> (*a*) creates or reinforces a false impression, including a false impression as to law, value or intention or other state of mind,
>
> (*b*) prevents another person from acquiring information which would affect that person's judgement of a transaction, or
>
> (*c*) fails to correct a false impression which the deceiver previously cre-

ated or reinforced or which the deceiver knows to be influencing another to whom he or she stands in a fiduciary or confidential relationship,

and references to deception shall be construed accordingly.

(3) For the purposes of this Act—

 (*a*) "gain" and "loss" are to be construed as extending only to gain or loss in money or other property, whether any such gain or loss is temporary or permanent,

 (*b*) "gain" includes a gain by keeping what one has, as well as a gain by getting what one has not, and

 (*c*) "loss" includes a loss by not getting what one might get, as well as a loss by parting with what one has.

(4) For the purposes of this Act—

 (*a*) a person shall be regarded as owning property if he or she has possession or control of it, or has in it any proprietary right or interest (not being an equitable interest arising only from an agreement to transfer or grant an interest);

 (*b*) where property is subject to a trust, the persons who own it shall be regarded as including any person having a right to enforce the trust, and an intention to defeat the trust shall be regarded accordingly as an intention to deprive of the property any person having that right;

 (*c*) where a person receives property from or on behalf of another, and is under an obligation to that other person to retain and deal with that property or its proceeds in a particular way, that other person shall be regarded (as against the first-mentioned person) as the owner of the property;

 (*d*) where a person gets property by another's mistake and is under an obligation to make restoration (in whole or in part) of the property or its proceeds or of the value thereof, then the person entitled to restoration shall to the extent of that obligation be regarded (as against the first-mentioned person) as the owner of the property or its proceeds or an amount equivalent to its value, and an intention not to make restoration shall be regarded accordingly as an intention to deprive that person of the property, proceeds or such amount;

 (*e*) property of a corporation sole shall be regarded as belonging to the corporation notwithstanding a vacancy in the corporation,

and references to "owner" and "ownership" shall be construed accordingly.

(5)(*a*) A reference in this Act to a Part, section or Schedule is a reference to a Part, section or Schedule of this Act unless it is indicated that a reference to some other Act is intended.

 (*b*) A reference in this Act to a subsection, paragraph or subparagraph is to the subsection, paragraph or subparagraph of the provision in which the reference occurs unless it is indicated that a reference to some other provision is intended.

 (*c*) A reference in this Act to any enactment shall be construed as a reference to that enactment as amended, adapted or extended, whether before or after the passing of this Act, by or under any subsequent enactment.

GENERAL NOTE

This is an extensive definition section where terms and phrases used in the Act are formally defined. The section provides that:

– any Part, section or Schedule referred to in this Act is a reference to such *within* the Act itself.

– any subsection, paragraph or subparagraph referred to in this Act is a reference to such within the phrase which refers to it.

– any enactment referred to is to be understood as the amended version of that enactment.

In *Baxter* [1971] 2 All E.R. 359 at 362, Sachs L.J. was of the learned view that the words of the English Theft Act should be interpreted in their natural meaning in order to produce sensible results. In *Treacy v. DPP*, Lord Diplock felt that:

> "[t]he [Theft] Act is expressed in simple language as used and understood by ordinary literate men and women. It avoids so far as possible those terms of art which have acquired a special meaning understood by lawyers in which many of the penal enactments which it supersedes were couched" ([1971] 1 All E.R. 110 at 124).

In this regard it must be remembered that in Ireland the Theft Act is a new departure in conceptual terms as well as in the terminology used, although it might not be accurate to say it uses simple language. It will be tempting to continue to use the terms developed and used under the law of larceny (indeed, in the case of "fraud", this writer's opinion is that it should be used). The Larceny Act, it must be remembered, simply codified the preceding common law; this Act, however, starts afresh (see J.C. Smith, 1–07). The courts should be aware (and reminded) that they should:

> "... shun the temptation which sometimes presses on the mind of the judiciary, to suppose that because a particular course of conduct ... was anti-social and undesirable, it can necessarily be fitted into some convenient pigeon-hole ... It does not follow that there is necessarily a convenient alternative criminal pigeon hole provided which fits the facts under the provisions of the [Theft] Act" (*Charles* [1976] 1 All E.R. 659 at 666, *per* Bridge L.J.).

The full reference is to be taken from context, where appropriate.

Subs. (1) contains a number of definitions including the following:

– "appropriates" means to usurp or adversely interfere with the proprietary rights of the owner, (see s. 4.(5));

– "deception" (see subs. (2));

– "dishonestly" means without a *claim of right* in good faith. "Good faith" imports an inevitable moral signature (though it should remain focused upon "*legal* right") to the offence (the LRC specifically recommended that the definition of theft be based upon a mental element which would itself be based on the absence of a claim of right, 43/92, 321). It precludes mistake and requires knowledge. The phrase "claim of right" originates for our purposes in the case of *Norman* where a "claim of right" was found to be a defence for the offence of embezzlement ((1842) C. & M. 501; see also the comments in the General Introductory Note above as well as in relation to s. 31 below when referring to the decision of *Grey* and of *O'Loughlin*). Arlidge and Parry advise caution not to allow the use of such an untechnical term as "dishonesty" obscure the fact that the concept is a highly complex one. They analyse "dishonesty" as embracing four requirements, failing which, the subject of the analysis will be found to have been dishonest (Arlidge & Parry, para. 1–003):

1. The generally accepted standards of honest conduct referring to:
   (a) an objective assessment of such standards;
   (b) the subjective assessment of what such standards the defendant believes.
2. The legal limits of a person's conduct:
   (a) objectively assessed, and (arguably)
   (b) subjectively assessed according to the defendant's conception of those limits.

In this enactment the concept of claim of right depends upon the mental element — it is relevant only in s. (4)(1) with respect to "*dishonestly* appropriates" and in s. 4(4) regarding the defendant's reasonable belief as to consent, absence of dishonesty, and absence of discoverable owner. The provision does not easily allow for the accepted "right" by virtue of civil law which authorises appropriation. Indeed, that is only half the dilemma, as it is possible that an accused might have had authority and not know it. J.C. Smith, when referring to the proposed defendant, "D", takes the view:

> "There are many cases where the civil law authorise or even requires ... appropriation ... Suppose, however, that D is unaware of the civil law which authorises or requires him to act as he does and he proceeds in a furtive manner evincing a dishonest intention. He now falls literally within the terms of the [English] Act unless "dishonestly" is interpreted to include the objective element at one time discerned by Arlidge and Parry. The court would, it is submitted, have to find some means of avoiding the conviction of D for doing no more than the civil law expressly authorised or required him to do" (p. 21).

The illusive concept of "current accepted standards" must inevitably reflect the judicial interpretation of such a notion — so we might more realistically refer to "current judicial attitudes" especially in the District Court. It is perhaps the changing form of such attitudes, which explains the lack of legal definition of "dishonesty". We have learnt from the much criticised failure to define the concept of dishonesty in England — where the draftsman chose rather to list what is not dishonest. This is also done in s. 4 regarding the three special cases of honesty which are differently worded versions of the three English special cases. The first is very different in its wording as it seems to indicate a bald *de facto* issue of whether or not there was honesty (whereas the English statute bases its first special case upon the concept of *belief* in one's honesty). The first case does not appear to be very special as it is *de facto* honesty. This must necessarily revert to the traditional general test, streamlined into a formula to be put to juries for honesty (on the reservation of this issue for the jury alone, see the decision in *Painter* [1983] Crim.L.R. 189), which according to subs. (4) will depend on reasonable grounds for the belief that one is acting honestly in conjunction with any other relevant matters (see s. 4(4)(*a*) below). Dishonesty, as a concept, should hopefully not create the problems that arose in England if we adopt the simplistic formula finally arrived at in the case of *Ghosh* ([1982] Q.B. 1053) that dishonesty arises according to the ordinary standards of reasonable and honest people and that the accused realised that.

Of particular concern is that dishonesty is not used to sweep broad swathes of conduct under the carpet of the offences under this Act. Of Arlidge & Parrys' four criteria above it is important to note that the last two are concerned with legal conduct. We note that *Ghosh* is premised upon "what is *done* and what the defendant was *doing*". As mentioned in the General Introductory Note above, placing dishonesty at the heart of any definition may cause confusion. Dishonesty is inherently internal as a concept. It is a *mens rea* criteria (J.C. Smith comments that the first part of the *Ghosh* test, *i.e.* asking what was done is really only a necessary first step to assessing the mind of the particular defendant (p. 18)). Where an offence shows sufficient dishonesty, however, it will be tempting for the courts to "fudge" the essential external element in order to secure conviction. *Actus reus* cannot merely be dispensed with because of an over-broad approach to the accused's state of mind (Shute comments that recent English cases have pared down the *actus reus* of theft to vanishing point: "as the *actus reus* of the crime shrinks, so the role played by the *mens rea* concept of dishonesty will necessarily increase; it will have to take much more of the strain of filtering out cases that ought not to be regarded as theft ..." (p. 452)). Terms, however, which intimate some externalisation of one's intention or objective are "deception" and "fraud". These also carry the weight of much judicial consideration. As things stand, however, the old formula "fraudulently and without claim of right" now replaced with "dishonesty". The "claim of right" element is retained but "fraudulently" is consigned to obsolescence and with it, unfortunately, the jurisprudence which it has inspired (it was said in England that the Theft Act, "intended to sweep away all the learning which over the centuries had gathered round the common law concepts of larceny," however, I cannot accept that either it or the Victorian legislature has such a destructive intention, *per* Fulager J. in *Salvo, infra*, p. 424). It was felt that juries would feel more comfortable with the term "dishonest" than with the term "fraudulent". The LRC itself, however, admits of "as many different potential definitions of dishonesty as there are differences in age, social status, nationality, moral outlook and nature" (LRC 43/92 143). The dangers associated with leaving the entire notion to the jury are identified by the appropriately named Supreme Court *Salvo* decision of Victoria ([1980] VR 401) in its attack on the "amateur" approach to dishonesty, *i.e.* the "ordinary decent folk" perspective (see *Feely* [1973] Q.B. 530). Fulager J. felt the judge should refrain from such vagueries and charge the jury within established legal principles:

"[I]t is contrary to the most fundamental tenets and traditions of the common law and of the English judicial system itself that the judges of the Courts of law should set themselves up or allow themselves to be set up as the judges of morals or of moral standards. The public respect for the Courts, upon which the Court's authority and existence ultimately is held *because* they decide cases according to known legal principles. It is equally important that the principles applied be legal principles and known principles. Feelings and intuitions as to what constitutes dishonesty and even as to what dishonesty means must vary greatly from jury to jury and from judge to judge and from magistrate to magistrate" (*Salvo* at 430).

Thus, we are back to where we started with the essential *legal nature* of a formulation now couched in layman's terms. Dishonesty may be amenable and familiar to juries but it must be fleshed out in legal terms by the judge. This gives pause for thought at comments that the word "dishonest" in this respect was referred to as a dispensable concept by Elliot, "Dishonesty in theft: A dispensable concept" [1982] Crim.L.R. 395). Without the notion of fraud the legalism must derive from the phrase "claim of right made in good faith". This must now become the somewhat uncomfortable bedfellow of dishonesty. We are left, then with the pertinent views of the LRC : " it was suggested that the parameters of dishonesty are not identical with those of legal right. ... We accept that dishonesty and the absence of a claim of legal right are not identical, but we nonetheless continue to see merit in the definitional strategy which we propose" (LRC 43/92, p. 145).

"Document" has two distinct functions in this Act, a general purpose for which is defined here and in the context of an instrument for the purpose of defining an instrument of forgery. The meaning of "document" was of particular relevance in the Forgery Acts 1861–1913 but was nowhere in those Acts defined. Even if it had been, technology has brought with it fundamental changes in what is to be regarded as a document. In the context of forgery and the definition "instrument", "document" is a much more expansive concept than the one referred to in the interpretation section. Here, the simple and brief list of possibilities is for use in:

(a) The limited context of investigation provisions, where documents must be produced to investigating gardai;
(b) Fraud against the European Communities' Finances;
(c) False Accounting, (s. 10);
(d) Suppression of documents, (s. 11).

Some helpful commentaries and cases discuss the traditional conception of what we would now refer to as "hard-copy" or "*tangible* documents" (see the analysis of the English Crown Court Cases Reserved in *Closs* Dears & B 460, 169 E.R. 1082 (1857) as cited and discussed by Charlton at p. 851; see further Williams, "What is a Document" 11 M.L.R. (1948) 150 at 160. Perhaps the necessarily vague definition of Russell is most instructive: *whether the purported document conveys a meaning by words from one person to another* (*Russell on Crime*, p. 1219)). Note, however, in the forgery analysis, the document as made or altered must, in some material particular, be false (Charlton, p. 169). The definition as contained within the Act is clearly updated. This new definition encapsulates maps, plans, graphs, drawings, photographs and records. This is only the "update" of the traditional analysis which of itself clearly goes beyond the "meaning by words" definition referred to above. Para. (*b*) tackles the binary conversion dilemma. A computer does not retain information in a form readily understandable to the human eye. Information is input from "legible" or cognisable form and converted into computer language. It may be retrieved for the purpose of human use (as opposed to being transferred to another computer host) by reconversion to "legible form". This process of transition to and from computer-understood formats presented the obvious problem of being "illegible" and therefore, practically speaking, a step removed from the purpose of theft or fraud. Para. (*b*) resolves this problem to some extent by including in the definition of the word "document", print-outs or other *tangible* manifestations of information from within the computerised format, to legible form. This is to include the conversion of visual images which are enlarged by the same translation to and from computer format as above.

- "Gain" and "loss" are given a specific definition in subs. (3);
- "Information in non-legible form" is probably defined here for the purposes of under-standing the scope of the meaning of "document" defined above. Reference to "information" will extend to information whether or not legible to the human eye, kept in the current (and currently conceptual) media which the draftsman attempts to encapsulate by the use of the words "microfilm, microfiche, magnetic tape or disk or in any other non-legible form";
- "Owner" and "ownership" have the meanings given to them by subs. (4) (see below);
- "Record" includes any information in non-legible form which is capable of being repro-duced in permanent legible form;
- "Property", see Introduction and General Note;
- "Stealing" means committing an offence under subs. (4). This is a very curt delimitation of the parameters of a term which is fundamental to the entire concept of theft. Theft is used as the verb form of the substantive concept of theft. Indeed, it is unfortunate there is no usable substantive form of the word "steal" (stealing being an unwieldy gerund) nor a usable verbal form of the word "theft" (thieving being somewhat archaic);
- "stolen property" goes somewhat further than the definition of "stealing" to include prop-erty which has been unlawfully obtained otherwise than by stealing. This reveals the unfortunate consequence of using two different words to refer to dishonest appropria-tion. It is incongruous to say on the one hand that stealing means theft and then to say that stolen property goes beyond property susceptible to the term theft. This difficulty arises, for example, under s. 17 where the prior statutory law which provided for the offence of handling stolen property specifically extended the scope of stolen property to property obtained by means of such other offences as embezzlement and extortion. This explicit extension of the term "stolen property" is conspicuously absent from the new provision in s. 17. Nor is there any provision which equates in terms to s. 24(4) of the English Theft Act 1968. This might be to rely too heavily upon this definition section which is far from being conclusive;
- "theft" has the meaning given to it by s. 4(1) which is to dishonestly appropriate without the owner's consent with the intention to deprive that owner;
- "unlawfully obtained" means obtained in circumstances constituting an offence; see com-ments in relation to "stolen property" above and General Note on s. 17 below.

Subs. (2) defines "deception" in the General Note on s. 6 below.

Subs. (3) defines "gain" and "loss" to refer to temporary or permanent gain or loss *in money or other property*. Moral or sentimental loss would presumably, then be excluded, at least for the purpose of the criminal law and therefore this Act. Interestingly, the first con-cept, *i.e.* "gain", is to include both *keeping* as well as getting; and the second concept, "loss", is to include both not getting as well as parting with (see further comment in General Note on s. 6 below on "making gain or causing loss by deception").

Subs. (4) defines "ownership" and attributable concepts. The subsection clarifies the crucial concept of ownership with five specific principles:

(a) the owner of property is the person having possession or control, or any proprietary right or interest (see Buckley J. in *Re London and Globe Finance Corporation Ltd.* [1903] 1 Ch. 728 at 732);

(b) property subject to trust shall be regarded as owned by any person having a right to enforce the trust (any intention to defeat the trust is therefore theft as it is an inten-tion to deprive of the property any person having that right);

(c) persons receiving property from another person (or on that person's behalf), to do something specific with it is *not* the owner. The owner is the person from whom or on whose behalf the property is received;

(d) where ownership is by mistake, the mistaken owner is generally obliged to restore it to its proper owner, whether by total restoration or by giving back the proceeds or value of the property. It is clearly the person to whom the property must be given back who is the rightful owner. Thus, an intention not to restore such property is an intention to deprive the rightful owner of the property, its proceeds or value;

(e) the property of a company whose rights are vested in an individual, *i.e.* a "corpora-tion sole", does not cease to be that company's property just because the individual in question vacates his or her status.

The concept of property is a complex one which is perhaps better explained in works specifically devoted to the subject of civil law and the law of property both personal and especially real. What we must know about the concept of "ownership", however, is generally the conceptualisation referred to above in the General Introductory Note. Furthermore, we may embark upon an analysis of the law of theft and fraudulent offence only when we understand at the very minimum that ownership extends beyond absolute ownership of a thing; there are many more intricate and sophisticated notions known to our law where property rights are referred to in terms of "qualified ownership". Property the subject of a trust in law belongs both to the trustee and the beneficiary of the trust. Thus, a proprietary right may be both legal and equitable. In *Clowes*, this position was reasoned on the basis of the civil law position that where a trustee mixes his or her own money with the funds the beneficiary automatically may enforce a charge on the trust; which in turn makes the fund amenable to the law of theft (*Clowes No. 2* [1994] 2 All E.R. 316). It is submitted that caution here, as elsewhere in criminal matters, should be used in reliance on the civil law (see concluding comments in General Note on s. 21 below; it is difficult, however, to disagree with the practical view taken by Arlidge & Parry, 3–017). Subs. (4)(*a*) is effectively identical to s. 5(1) of the English Theft Act. Gifts, trusts, equitable interests, all of which are well versed concepts in civil law, must also arise in the context of theft. In s. 62 of the Sale of Goods Act 1893 property in a thing is referred to as the full title; this does not preclude for instance, beneficial ownership. Critical is the moment when the property is said to have last changed hands; the civil law has it that ownership passes as soon as the contract for sale is completed; indeed it is the duty of both parties to the contract, in the proper course, to complete the sale. Thus, theft can only be an issue where a party sells an item which is not their own and where the buyer re-sells dishonestly or dishonestly refuses to complete the contract. A party to a contract may validly walk away where the contract can be said to be rescinded. Importantly, however, the equitable interest is not covered by the law of theft in two circumstances: where it arises out of an agreement to either grant or transfer an interest even though this might come about dishonestly.

To be the owner, a person need not have actual possession or control. Ownership may be precarious or short-lived; the essence of ownership seems to be the power to exclude others (Smith & Hogan (10th ed.), pp. 537-538). A thief may steal from a thief (*Meech* [1973] All E.R. 939, CA, discussed in Card Cross & Jones (15th ed.), 9.43). The owner may not necessarily be aware of the property over which he or she may claim title (*Woodman* [1974] 2 All E.R. 955, CA). The more tenuous the link, obviously the easier this link is to negate (*Edwards and Stacey* (1877) 13 Cox CC 384). Flowers on a grave were said to remain the property of the leaver (*Bustler v. State* 184 SE 2d 24 (1944); see also commentary to without out the consent of its owner in General Note on s. 4 below).

A particular purpose might be contemplated in the possession and control of property and a person might *legally* be entrusted with securing this purpose; such a person (the defendant) may steal from the person who so entrusted him or her (the victim). The bipartite relationship envisaged here is exclusive and should not involve third parties as was the unfortunate result in *Floyd v. DPP* [2000] Crim. L.R. 411. Indeed the case of *Reid* might be another example of taking the matter outside of its intended remit. In that case a bribe (from a third-party) was allowed by the Privy Council to figure in the equation, the defendant was seen as a trustee to pay over the bribe (which he did not) to the beneficiary (the victim). Within the defendant–victim relationship, it is not enough that the defendant owed the victim money and did not pay up vitally, he or she must "retain" property on the victim's behalf thus a debtor will have borrowed the money from the victim for some other reason than simply retaining it. Equally it is not enough that the defendant simply owed money, whether he or she obtained it from the victim or from another source to forward it to the victim (*Lewis v. Lethbridge* [1987] Crim. L.R. 59; *cf.* Wain [1995] 2 Cr.App.R. 660). For the position to be otherwise, there must be a requirement in the "deal" either:

– "*that* particular money" be paid over (it would be otherwise with identifiable property), *Huskinson* [1988] Crim. L.R. 620, or
– a separate fund or reserve be created with the subject-matter of the deal.

So the person entrusting property to another is well advised to specify the particulars of it (on how things can go wrong see the case of *Hall* [1972] 2 All E.R. 1009). The draftsman avoided difficulty in dropping the phrase "on account" in the English Model (s. 5(3)).

As to mistake, para. (*d*) is drawn in similar terms to para. (*c*) but was originally intended for a quite specific purpose. Where an employer overpays a worker the worker is morally obliged to bring this to the employers attention. The money was given properly in law and becomes the property of the worker and thus a specific criminal saver was required to render the furtive silence of the "lucky" worker an offence (the original case was *Moynes v. Cooper* [1956] 1 All E.R. 450). This is not the same as a debtor who determines not to pay up. A mistake has been made and no legal obligation is outstanding without the provision in this paragraph. It must be relevant also that the relationship is on-going. Where equity is brought into the equation as suggested by J.C. Smith the provision may be redundant. In any event, in the particular case of employment there is a claw-back provision in s. 5(5)(*a*) of the Payment of Wages Act 1991. The civil law has long provided for restitution in cases of unjust enrichment (*Norwich Uunion Fire v. William H Price Ltd.* [1934] A.C. 455); one wonders then whether criminal law is necessary here at all?

Subs. (5) explains reference to provisions both from this Act and to other instruments. References to provisions within the Act are presumed to be the immediate source (*i.e.* section, subsection, paragraph or subparagraph) and reference to other instruments are understood to be the current version of that instrument.

Repeals, etc.

3.—(1) Subject to *section 65*, the Acts specified in *Schedule 1* are repealed to the extent specified in the third column of that Schedule.

(2) Any offence at common law of larceny, burglary, robbery, cheating (except in relation to the public revenue), extortion under colour of office and forgery is abolished.

(3) The abolition of a common law offence mentioned in *subsection (2)* shall not affect proceedings for any such offence committed before its abolition.

GENERAL NOTE

This section simply introduces the opening Schedule to the Act and removes entirely or in part an extensive number of older statutes from the Statue Book. The extent of the repeal is indicated in column 3 of the Schedule. This is subject to the transitional measures set out in s. 65 below.

S. 3 removes several historic concepts from the recognition of the law. Henceforth there shall be no such offences, as set out, known to the law and any charge or indictment containing them will be void where the offence is committed before the Minister orders commencement of this section. The defunct offences are the common law offences of:
– larceny,
– burglary,
– robbery,
– extortion under colour of office,
– forgery,
– embezzlement,
– fraudulent conversion, and
– obtaining by false pretences.

Cheating is also abolished except in the sole context of cheating public revenue. The removal of these historic concepts will render a great deal of legal development obsolete in the strictest sense, however the wealth of experience gained from their treatment will no doubt serve to shed light upon the interpretation of the new offences defined to replace them. There is some concern in the survival of the "blunderbuss offence" of cheating the public revenue; this concern pertains to the unlimited penalty at common law, the breadth of the offence and the existence of specific statutory offences which render it superfluous (see Ormerod, "Cheating the Public Revenue" [1998] Crim.L.R. 627).

Like most of the Act's provisions, it came into effect on August 1, 2002. It is inevitable that persons charged with one of those common law offences and which is alleged to have occurred before August 1, but whose cases had not been heard before that date, will contemplate the possible argument that the offence with which they were charged is no longer known to the law. This would mean that the courts have no power to try such a person as was the case in *People (DPP) v. Kavanagh* unreported, Special Criminal Court, October 29, 1997. This scenario appears to be taken account of subs. (3).

As noted by Bacik (ICLSA 1997, p. 26-24), the abolition of offences normally takes effect prospectively, *i.e.* that persons are prosecuted under the law as it stood on the date the offence was committed. The relevant legislative provision is s. 1 of the Interpretation (Amendment) Act 1997 which provides that:

> "Where an Act of the Oireachtas abolishes, abrogates or otherwise repeals an offence which is an offence at common law, then unless the contrary intention appears, such abolition, abrogation or repeal shall not—
> (*a*) affect the previous operation of the law in relation to the offence so abolished, abrogated or repealed or any other offence or anything duly done or suffered thereunder,
> (*b*) affect any penalty, forfeiture or punishment incurred in respect of any such offence so abolished, abrogated or repealed or any other offence which was committed before such abolition, abrogation or repeal, or
> (*c*) prejudice or affect any proceedings pending at the time of such abolition, abrogation or repeal in respect of any such offence or any other offence."

S. (2) goes on to provide:

> "Where an Act of the Oireachtas abolishes, abrogates or otherwise repeals an offence which is an offence at common law, then unless the contrary intention appears, any proceedings in respect of any such offence or any other offence committed before such abolition, abrogation or repeal of any such offence at common law may be instituted, continued or enforced and any penalty, forfeiture or punishment in respect of any such offence at common law or any other offence may be imposed and carried out as if such offence at common law had not been abolished, abrogated or otherwise repealed."

This provision was passed as a direct response to the drafting flaw in the Non-Fatal Offences Against the Person Act 1997.

In *Quinlivan v.Governor of Portlaoise Prison* unreported, High Court, December 9, 1997, McGuinness J. referred to the Interpretation (Amendment) Act 1997, observing that it had been passed to remedy the Special Criminal Court's decision in *Kavanagh* (above). She expressed the view that it had been drafted rather hastily and found it necessary to provide a very detailed consideration of relevant case law on statutory interpretation. In conclusion she held that while the inclusion of an explicit saver in the 1997 Act would have been preferable legislative practice, the absence of such a provision was not the end of the matter. Instead, she asked the question whether it was the intention of the Oireachtas to apply the abolition to cases still pending before the courts. She followed the Supreme Court decisions in *Buckley v. A.G.* [1950] I.R. 67 and *Hamilton v. Hamilton* [1982] I.R. 466 in holding that the issue must be read in light of the constitutional requirement of non-interference with the judicial process and that where two constructions or interpretations of the relevant statutory provisions are open, the courts must adopt that which is not in conflict with the Constitution.

The clear intention of the Oireachtas here is to act prospectively, and not to interfere with prior prosecutions under common law which can continue in respect of a person whose cases were still pending prior to August 1, 2001 (as with *Mullins v. Harnett and A.G.*, unreported, High Court, O'Higgins J., April 1, 1998; see generally Bacik, "Striking a Blow for Reform" (1997) 7 I.C.L.J. 48).

PART 2

<small>THEFT AND RELATED OFFENCES</small>

Theft

4.—(1) Subject to *section 5*, a person is guilty of theft if he or she dishonestly appropriates property without the consent of its owner and with the intention of depriving its owner of it.

(2) For the purposes of this section a person does not appropriate property without the consent of its owner if—

    (*a*) the person believes that he or she has the owner's consent, or would have the owner's consent if the owner knew of the appropriation of the property and the circumstances in which it was appropriated, or

    (*b*) (except where the property came to the person as trustee or personal representative) he or she appropriates the property in the belief that the owner cannot be discovered by taking reasonable steps,

but consent obtained by deception or intimidation is not consent for those purposes.

(3)(*a*) This subsection applies to a person who in the course of business holds property in trust for, or on behalf of, more than one owner.

    (*b*) Where a person to whom this subsection applies appropriates some of the property so held to his or her own use or benefit, the person shall, for the purposes of *subsection (1)* but subject to *subsection (2)*, be deemed to have appropriated the property or, as the case may be, a sum representing it without the consent of its owner or owners.

    (*c*) If in any proceedings against a person to whom this subsection applies for theft of some or all of the property so held by him or her it is proved that—

        (i) there is a deficiency in the property or a sum representing it, and

        (ii) the person has failed to provide a satisfactory explanation for the whole or any part of the deficiency,

    it shall be presumed, until the contrary is proved, for the purposes of *subsection (1)* but subject to *subsection (2)*, that the person appropriated, without the consent of its owner or owners, the whole or that part of the deficiency.

(4) If at the trial of a person for theft the court or jury, as the case may be, has to consider whether the person believed—

    (*a*) that he or she had not acted dishonestly, or

    (*b*) that the owner of the property concerned had consented or would have consented to its appropriation, or

    (*c*) that the owner could not be discovered by taking reasonable steps,

the presence or absence of reasonable grounds for such a belief is a matter to which the court or jury shall have regard, in conjunction with any other relevant matters, in considering whether the person so believed.

(5) In this section—

"appropriates", in relation to property, means usurps or adversely interferes with the proprietary rights of the owner of the property;

"depriving" means temporarily or permanently depriving.

(6) A person guilty of theft is liable on conviction on indictment to a fine or imprisonment for a term not exceeding 10 years or both.

GENERAL NOTE

This section creates a new offence in Irish law, the offence of theft. The law — the offence of larceny — which generally consisted of stealing or fraud at common law, as well as those within the Larceny Acts, will be consigned to antiquity, the offence of theft encapsulating and replacing the offence of larceny, as well as embezzlement, fraudulent conversion and obtaining by false pretences. No confusion should be made between this, the new law, and incongruent and different prior law (on which see comments in relation to interpretation section above). Theft is the dishonest appropriation of property without the consent of the owner with the intention of depriving the owner of it. Unlike the deception offences there is no specific reference to making a gain or causing a loss (though the latter is implicit in "deprive"). Indeed, "deprive of it" confines the offence to the property stolen and not the loss caused (*cf.* s.3(*b*). Profit is not a necessary objective. No motive of profit is necessary under the English model either. Thus, it must be the express intention of the draftsperson and the legislature that there be no specific reference to the so-called *lucra causa* of an offence concerning property. Nor do we have a statute on criminal attempts which serves to bridge the "conditional intention" dilemma in England. On the one hand, *Easom* held that an intention must be specific and a rummage through a taken handbag finding nothing of interest to take is not enough ([1971] 2 All E.R. 945 at 947); on the other we have the prosecutorial tendency which advises specific forms of indictment to cover conditions and contingencies (*Re A-G's references (Nos. 1 and 2 of 1979)* [1979] 3 All E.R. 143). It is submitted that an endorsement of the wider "dishonesty" approach to stealing (undisciplined as exemplified by *Gomez*) will inevitably lead to the second approach.

Section 4(1)

S.4(1) contains a definition of theft which, considering its crucial significance, has been reduced to a relatively terse formula, "the dishonest appropriation of property with the intention of depriving its owner of it without the owner's consent". We are given a substantive formula for theft consisting of four essential elements:
1. dishonesty,
2. appropriation,
3. absence of consent, and
4. intention to deprive.
Dishonesty is defined in s.2; appropriation, which is the *actus reus* of the offence, is also defined in s. 2 (see General Note on s.2). Consent is dealt with in the context of s.4(4)(*b*) below.

– Intention to deprive owner

Fundamentally, the offence does *not* require the intention to deprive "permanently", as did its legislative predecessor (for a concise review of the argument against the element of permanently depriving in English law, see A.T.H. Smith, 6–06). The concept of depriving is also referred to in s.4(5) in the definition of "appropriation" and includes both permanent *and* temporary deprivation. The new formula may now cover situations of "user" where to take and use falls short of an intention permanently to deprive (common law larceny did not cater for the Roman Law concept of *furtum usus* — the theft of use). As to user, or the simple "taking possession," an example is the "taking possession" of a car, an offence which has attracted the unfortunate name of "joy-riding" did not contain the vital mental element of permanence; the intention was generally to take and use and then to abandon. Thus the legislature had to specifically cater for this scenario by making it an offence under s.112 of the Road Traffic Act as amended to "take possession without lawful authority." This longstanding theoretical dilemma will now hopefully be met with a disciplined use of the word "appropriate" tempered by a sensible use of the concept of "honesty". When suggesting an amendment which includes "taking possession of such property, exercising dominion over such property, usurping or otherwise adversely interfering with the property rights of the owners of such property", the response was a considered one:

> "The intention of the [Act] is that an appropriation will only arise where there is an assumption by the person of the rights of the owner. When taken with the requirement for dishonesty in s. 4 it corresponds to the idea of converting the property for one's own use or benefit" (Minister O'Donoghue, 527 *Dáil Debates* Col. 962).

It is not necessary for the prosecution to establish an intention to deprive *by* [or at the time of] *the act of appropriation (Morris* [1984] A.C. 320). A present intention to deprive only is required to show appropriation even in England where the *mens rea* of "deprive" requires permanence. We may assume that this authority represents the proposition that appropriation and depriving need not be simultaneous under our law. Thus a person could always come into possession without incurring liability. The offence of theft is concerned, however, with "property rights" which is larger than either the larceny definition or the English "assumption of the rights of the owner." Appropriation occurs when the intention coincides with interference with property rights. Thus the proposition in England that a thief never becomes the owner is not relevant here.

– Without the consent of its owner

Those anticipating the passing of this Act will breathe a sigh of relief that the formula chosen includes the saver "without the consent of the owner". Without revisiting the issue addressed above, the English experience has been to depend so heavily upon the meaning of dishonesty that legal claim of right takes second place. In the much cited decision in *Gomez* [1993] A.C. 442 we see the unusual step of a House of Lords decision reversing its position of barely ten years earlier in *Morris* [1984] A.C. 320 (which held that no appropriation could take place where there was express or implied authority of the owner). The effect of this remarkable jurisprudence is the extension of the law of theft beyond what had been intended, subsuming an offence of deception (Shute, p. 446). The Irish formula is express in its revision of the English provision. Hopefully the law of theft in this jurisdiction will be construed to deal with what it was intended to deal with and not, as in England, stray into a field reserved for other provisions within the same enactment. Where it is has been the intention of the legislature to designate the concept of theft a clear and separate role in the protection of property rights, it must be obvious that by the designation of other distinct offences to different forms of conduct, they are meant to deal separately and clearly with that conduct (see commentary entitled *offences not amenable to theft* in General Note on s.6 below). Thus, we should not invite the observation as in England following *Gomez* and *Hinks* [2000] 3 W.L.R. 1590 that "it was possible for the prosecution to bring a charge of theft where prior to *Gomez* the charge ought properly to have been one of obtaining property by deception under *s.15* [the equivalent to our s. 6] of the Theft Act ..." (Shute, p.446; see also Shute and Horder, "Thieving and Deceiving: What is the Difference?" (1993) M.L.R. 548; Heaton, "Deceiving without Thieving?" [2001] Crim. L.R. 712). It is submitted, nevertheless, that we should be mindful that the temptation will spill over into our law to prefer to prosecute under the law of theft because it does not require deception and that the deception made possible the causing of loss or the making of a gain (see comments in General Note on s.6 below). This might be an empty fear because of the lesser penalty involved in the deception offence. If it is not, then improper use of the offence with the higher penalty will give rise to objections of the most fundamental kind.

Consent "of the owner" makes it necessary for the property to actually have, or have had, an owner, where the owner is discoverable by the taking of reasonable steps (s.4(4)(*c*)). Even where the owner cannot be discovered, one anticipates the observation that "it must have been owned by someone"; thus the English provision's requirement that the relevant property belong to another (and case law upon it) is not irrelevant. Certainly no immunity lies where the owner is claimed not to be discoverable but no reasonable steps were taken to do so. The defendant need only be able to meet the case in as far as the prosecution can oblige, and the indictment may be framed in terms of stealing the property of a person unknown. Establishing the mental element, however, where there is a demonstrable belief that the property was abandoned, is another matter (see *Small* [1987] Crim. L.R. 777).

Early case law shows that abandonment is far from an automatic inference, even where the apparently abandoning owner has no further use for the goods. Even where the owner loses something and gives up hope of ever finding it, the property may not be assumed to have ceased to be owned (*Hibbert* [1948] 1 All E.R. 860).

The ownership nexus of property may be far from clear as can be seen from the case of *Marshall* who collected tickets which were still valid on the tube in London and resold them at the expense of the London Underground (hereafter referred to as "the L.U."). The court seemed willing to take on its face the reservation on the back of the ticket that it remained in the ownership of the L.U. even when in the possession of the passenger. If, as should properly have been the case, the L.U. had taken reasonable steps to bring the issue of retained ownership to the buyer's attention, the L.U. might have retained some rights in the ticket (Smith & Hogan (10th ed.), p.534, n.17); and a term printed on a ticket issued by a machine once the money has been paid is too late in terms of notice (*Thornton v. Shoe Lane Parking Ltd* [1971] 2 Q.B. 163 (CA)). However, the ticket could possibly belong to either the L.U., the buyer or the defendants who freely consented in giving the ticket to them. If the property is not owned by the L.U., it is not theft. A person may own a thing notwithstanding that he must return it (Kenny, *Outlines of Criminal Law* (1st ed.), p.244; J.C. Smith, "Stealing Tickets" (1998) Crim. L.R. 723, n.5, *cf.* Potter [1958] 2 All E.R. 51). Whatever contractual right the transporter might have, this does not (and this is important in the context of "property rights" in our provision) create a proprietary right in the chattel (J.C. Smith, *supra,* p.724). The *actus reus,* and thus the criminal liability, is removed from this particular instance of the "ingenuity of rogues".

Another difficult case is where the property is dishonestly appropriated but the true owner is, in fact, the defendant. In *Turner (No. 2)* [1971] 2 All E.R. 441, the defendant left his car in for repairs indicating he would pick it up and pay for it the next day. He came back a few hours later and dishonestly and without payment repossessed his car (which by that stage had been fully repaired). Though this is a clear case of s.7 deception, the issue presented is interesting. The defendant was convicted of stealing the car! J.C. Smith endorses the alternative approach in *Meredith* where the defendant's car was impounded by the police (Smith & Hogan, 10th ed.), pp. 535 *et seq.* The police are in such circumstances entitled to be paid an impounding charge. The defendant, however, managed to remove his car from the police compound without authority or paying any charge. He was charged with theft but acquitted (the *Meredith* case is reported at [1973] Crim L.R. 235 and cited in Smith & Hogan (10th ed.), p.535). The matter is arguably covered by s. 2(4)(*a*) of the Act. Finally, consent is not real where it is wrongfully procured whether by deception or intimidation.

Section 4(2)

S.4(2) sets out two particular circumstances (where there is no deception or intimidation) which the offence does not apply; they are:
1. appropriation is with the consent of the owner (s.4(2)(*a*));
2. the true owner cannot be found (s.4(2)(*b*))

Thus, in addition to the exceptions to theft in s.5, and the possible general defence of absence of dishonesty, this subsection sets out the further possible defence of "consent" whether express or implied (or by default) to appropriate. Dishonesty is repeated elsewhere in the section (note s. 4(4) in the context of belief). Discussions of dishonesty and its repitition in s. 4(4) is apposite to s. 4(2). The re-mention of deception seems a clear invitation to the dangers of over-emphasising the term and confusing fraud and theft as outlined above. It may be that the courts will find some relevance to the duplication, or that they will refer to s.4(4) as the secondary consideration in the restatement of concepts referred to in it. It is, after all, a provision for the consideration of the jury of a question of fact — whether the defendant had reasonable grounds to believe in the bona fides of his or her actions.

Section 4(3)

S.4(3) deals with dishonest appropriation by trustees. The ownership of the property, which is the subject of a trust, should include any person having the right to enforce the trust. A difficulty (and a limitation of the effect of this provision) arises in the requirement that the appropriation must be for the defendant's own benefit. This means that it is not true to say, as it is in the English Act, that any intention to defeat the trust is theft. This comparative limitation would not appear to be substantially affected by reference in s.5(2)(*a*) to breach of trust. The subsection applies to any person holding property in trust for two or more persons who appropriates the property of the trust for his or her own benefit. One concern has been the dilemma of "mixed" money which is dealt with by the concept of "general deficiency". Theft will be established where a deficiency is shown in the property entrusted and where no satisfactory explanation is forthcoming. It will no longer be an issue that the money had been intermingled, that the precise monies can no longer be separated or traced to source (*Tomlin* [1954] 2 Q.B. 274). This so-called deficiency offence was recommended by the Government Advisory Committee on Fraud and makes it an offence for a person holding funds in trust as agent for another where there is failure to maintain in the account sufficient funds to pay what is due to each person. Thus, a person in the responsible position of holding funds for a group (the phrase *en bloc* was used by the Minister (see 527 *Dáil Debates* Col. 961)) may not dip into the kitty for personal use at the expense of any member of the group. Though it is thus referred to in commentaries, there is no requirement here that the deficiency be "general", hence it must be assumed that deficiency means a short-fall of however small an amount. This provision literally places the responsibility on such a person to explain any deficiency, and where no satisfactory explanation is forthcoming, theft will be presumed. Defences available to rebut this presumption include honesty, consent and absence of intention to deprive. It is not, strictly speaking, a presumption of intention where the accused person is in a special and entrusted position to explain any deficit which may be discovered. Once there is failure to do so, s.4(3)(*c*) activates and places such a person upon proof. Indeed, a failure to bring a loss to the attention of the owner(s) is arguably an instance of "deception" under s.2(2)(*c*). The chosen procedure under s.4 will no doubt increase efficacy, but should not be construed so as to infringe upon inalienable rights of the accused.

Section 4(4)

S.4(4) concerns the trial of the offence of theft. The prosecution must clearly overcome the evidential burden of negativing any purported belief of the defendant that he or she acted honestly or with a claim of right made in good faith (though it appears to be up to the defence to provide reasonable grounds for such a belief). The criteria set out in s.4(2) as well as the general concept of dishonesty are set out in the alternative for the consideration of the jury (or judge, as the case may be). They may consider the defendant not to have been dishonest; alternatively, they may conclude that the defendant may have had reasonable grounds for believing he or she had such an entitlement or claim of right (that he or she was making in good faith) to appropriate the relevant property. Appropriation which is immune from liability under this section occurs in three special cases of "belief on reasonable grounds that the defendant acted with:
1.   *de facto* honesty, or
2.   the consent of owner, or
3.   where there was no discoverable owner.

There are three "special cases" of honesty also in the English Act (s.2 defining "dishonesty"). We may note, however, that the Irish provision differs significantly. Instead of, as in the English section, defining three circumstances where *belief* in a claim of right (express or implied) can defeat the *dishonest* requirement in dishonest appropriation, the Irish section considers belief of claim of right in three different circumstances, the first being, rather awkwardly, that it was not dishonest. The second and third concern consent and discoverability of the owner. The introduction of "reasonableness" into the mental element criteria of belief is a clear policy step and is in clear contrast to the traditional attitude to belief in England (see Smith & Hogan (10th ed.), p. 549).

"Claim of right" is not expressly contained in the wording of the subsection but is implicit in the use of the word dishonestly, which is defined as "a claim of right made in good faith". The subsection concludes with the phrase "in conjunction with any other relevant matters." It is submitted that these include the many permutations which such a claim might take. These are considered further in the commentary on the definition of "appropriates" in s.4(5) below.

Mention of dishonesty here is the second appearance of that term in the section. From a procedural perspective, one issue which might arise either by way of correction of strict application is the application of these "special cases" *independently* of the general question of dishonesty. Are these alternative or cumulative? In other words, does s.4 require two considerations of the word dishonest, or does one dispense with the necessity of the other? The requirement to prove dishonesty in one subsection in the context of appropriation and then to *consider* it in the context of belief is unfortunate and probably the result of an attempt to improvise upon an imperfect (but at least consistent) legislative import (see comments on s.4(2) above as to which element of the possible duplicity will take precedent).

The subsection, of itself, seems to indicate a bald *de facto* issue of whether or not there are reasonable grounds to support a defendant's belief of not acting dishonestly. This may be established by showing he or she had consent (express or implied) or the non-discoverability of the owner. If s.4(4) can defeat an inference of dishonesty in s.4(1), then an accused has a good defence in consent alone — whether or not the accused believed he or she acted dishonestly. To this extent, such an application may be workable. However, a difficulty arises where the discoverability of the owner is unclear — and yet the accused is clearly dishonest. Again, if s.4(4) can of itself defeat an inference of dishonesty in s.4(1), this brings us to the *Gomez* position in England. The lesson in *Gomez* might indicate how the issue is likely to play out; dishonesty as a concept is the order of the day, both in *Gomez* and the legislative intent which forms the basis of the Act.

Section 4(4)(a)

De facto honesty does not appear to be very "special" at all in that it is demonstrable "honesty" or belief thereof. The following are possible ways of looking at the role of s.4(4)(*a*) in the context of the section:

Interpretation I: A restatement of the general honesty requirement

This may then be simply a specific restatement of the traditional and general "dishonesty" test, streamlined into a formula for honesty to be put to juries. (On the reservation of this issue for the jury alone, see the decision in *Painter* [1983] Crim. L.R. 189.) Dishonesty in this formulation will depend on the existence of reasonable grounds for the belief that one is acting honestly, in conjunction with any other relevant matter. This leaves the greater part of the interpretation to the jury, who are arbiters of fact. Smith states:

> "The meaning of words may be controlled by the context in which they appear; and the jury are not a suitable body to study the general wording of the Act or the general legislative approach to the problem in hand. For this reason, the interpretation of words in a statute is traditionally regarded as a matter for the judge, while the jury consider only the application of the meaning to the facts" (A.T.H. Smith, p. 269).

The experience in England has been, first of all, to allow the jury to determine whether the accused was dishonest applying the "current standards of ordinary decent people" (*Feely* [1973] Q.B. 530). This was modified to the formula: "according to the ordinary standards of reasonable and honest people and that the accused realised what he or she was doing was dishonest by that standard" (*Ghosh* [1982] Q.B. 1053). Time will tell how the formulation is embraced by Irish juries and judiciary alike.

On the "restatement" interpretation, dishonesty need only be required once, either under subs. (1) or (4). We may note that the word dishonesty in the formula in s. 4(1) merely replaces "fraudulently" in the antecedent law of stealing, larceny. Many felt the word was superfluous (even the eminent J.W.C. Turner, see *Russell on Crime* (12th ed.), p.996). In short, then, dishonesty is a direct substitute for a superfluous term in the opening formula save in that it is supported by the restatement of the word in terms of belief in s.4(4). This would suggest that dishonesty is not required to be considered at all where one of the other "special cases" applies. This would mean that a person may act dishonestly but with a claim of right, and does not thereby commit theft (this would endorse the *Morris* view).

Interpretation II – A separate requirement of "honest belief"

An alternative (and, it is submitted, more likely) interpretation of the two, is that this particular "special case" tries in vain to distinguish itself from the English Act. The act defines dishonesty in s.2 so it is an independent criteria — though it relates directly to appropriation — in the opening formula of s.4. There is no particular need to restate the "dishonesty" criterion and therefore logically, we are left to conclude that s.4(4)(*a*) has a separate and distinct purpose in the Act as an "honest *belief*" provision. This would mean that dishonest appropriation in s.4(1) is the objective theoretical starting point of an assessment of liability but requires a more subjective assessment in the context of belief under s.4(4). Such an interpretation necessitates an analysis of the concept of "belief" in the context of theft. Again we are drawn by convenience and perhaps design to the case-law of our common law neighbour(s). We can presume that belief in one's honesty in the act of "depriving" a person of their property amounts to negating that person's ownership or entitlement to (continued) possession. This is founded in the common law recourse of "distress" or "self-help"; in effect a person considers that they are entitled to appropriate the property from another or from what might be a state of abandonment. Thus, a person can lawfully take property from another as security for a debt (see *Clay* (1909) 3 Cr. App. R. 92, as cited by J.C. Smith, *supra*). Though the taker may be mistaken as to their entitlement, this does not defeat the defence. What places us in difficulty in approaching the difficult concept of "belief" is that we step beyond what is objective and demonstrable. Belief cannot be subjected to objective analysis as it would perhaps be in civil law. The focus of belief is not whether or not it is reasonable but whether it is sincere (See *Bernhard* (1938) 2 K.B. 264; *Clayton* (1920) 15 Cr. App. R. 45; *Gilson and Cohen* (1944) 29 Cr. App.R.; *Hancock* [1963] Crim L.R. 572).

On this interpretation it might be that the section as a whole would require a defendant to first prove the appropriation was not dishonest under s.4(1) or, failing that, establish reasonable grounds for believing one of the three "special cases" in s.4(4). This would certainly avoid the unsatisfactory position in England where one might have a claim of right and yet be dishonest so as to be guilty of theft (*Gomez*). But even if the section were treated thus, it might unfortunately be wiser to be fatalistic and *expect* them to adopt the dilemma. A person might be successful in establishing a claim of right under s.4(4) but fail to persuade a jury of their honesty under s.4(1). The preferable view is that the difficulty in *Gomez* was to have been avoided at all costs. This, the draftsman would have been very much aware of. It might further be considered a consequence of this interpretation that consent in s.4(1) and s.4(4) are also to be assessed separately. As s.4(4) deals with special claims of right which by definition go to dishonesty, this would mean that consent in s.4(1) would be a separate consideration altogether. In turn, this would mean that appropriation could still be assigned the meaning attributed to this term under English case law, as the only thing preventing this from being so is the presence in s.4(1) of the consent criterion. This would bring the matter back within the reach of *Gomez*.

Preferred Interpretation – Alternative requirements to consider dishonesty

The sole purpose of s.4(4) is to provide a criteria for the consideration of whether or not the defendant had reasonable grounds to support his or her belief in a claim of right. Thus it is possible to establish a claim of right to rebut directly any inference of dishonesty by means of the three special cases. This means to embark upon a consideration of dishonesty in the first special case to rebut dishonest appropriation is just unhappy wording. It does not necessarily repeat the requirement to consider dishonesty because the two appearances of the word in s.4 coincide. This would mean, however, that dishonesty would become unnecessary where either of the second two special cases applied. They would rebut dishonesty automatically, and thus dishonesty would not have to be considered at all. If this were not the case, one wonders why the draftsman specifically chose not to replicate s.2 of the English Theft Act 1968. With this interpretation, *Morris* (in this context) is endorsed, *Gomez* is avoided and the section is subject only to the possible criticisms that dishonest appropriation should of itself be a stand-alone offence (an option expressly rejected both by the LRC and the legislature on this occasion). The ultimate concern of those who would seek an extended application of the law of theft is that a person who appropriates dishonestly should be convicted even where they have some claim of right (a view that apparently found favour with the House of Lords in *Gomez*). One view taken of this criticism is that a claim of right must be made in good faith which might possibly be interpreted to extend to such cases.

Section 4(4)(b): That there was consent of the owner of the property

This special case is significant in that it simply renders incomplete the formulation of theft; with an honest belief of consent there can be no dishonest appropriation. Perhaps the most significant element in this special case, however, is its inclusion of the conditional sense, "or would have consented". This defence is likely to be construed strictly, and even the openness suggested by the "or would have consented" formulation will probably be tempered, as it has been in the U.K., by a requirement for virtual certainty in one's belief that consent existed (A.T.H. Smith, 7–27). Nevertheless, the absence of consent must effectively be established by the prosecution (*Flynn* [1970] Crim. L.R. 118). A person may deal with another person's property on the understanding that they have or would have that person's consent. Presumably, to follow the common law, the criteria for this special case will be such matters as the amount of property taken, the likelihood of its return and the relationship between the owner and accused (A.T.H. Smith, *ibid.*). The taking of a thing whilst leaving money for its payment — in the absence of the owner — is one situation which has been deemed to be covered by this specific provision (119 New L.J. 561); so too would a person who purportedly "borrows" an item meaning to replace it (*See* case noted at [1956] Crim. L.R. 360). This is not to say that such arguments will find favour where the taker was fully aware that no consent would be forthcoming, for instance where the item was not for sale (even acting in what the accused believes to be the owner's interest will be unacceptable (see *Kinsella* [1961] (3) S.A. 519 (C))); nor is it likely to suffice to show that the taker was willing to pay (see the peculiar s.2(2) of the English Theft Act 1968).

Section 4(4)(c): That there was no discoverable owner

A second person may validly become the owner of a thing where the first person abandons it (*cf.* where gold or bullion is discovered there is a special law known as treasure trove which basically provides that where the trove is deliberately hidden and no successor to the title can be found, the find becomes the property of the State; where this is not the case, the finder keeps all; however, see the case of *Hancock* [1990] Crim. L.R. 125). This paragraph is a good example of double contingency for situations in the contemplation of the draftsman. It is surely not necessary to cater for situations where the owner is undiscoverable because the taker who can establish such, will also be establishing that they did not intend to "deprive". One argument might be that the incidental finding of an item apparently lost is that the finder will contribute to already obvious deprivation of the owner of their property. This might be inappropriate as "... the finder is not dishonest ... Ordinary decent people who find small sums of money in a crowded street have no qualms about pocketing their windfall", A.T.H. Smith, para. 7–35. Nevertheless, this provision does afford some measure of specific allowance to those who find property which is apparently lost or abandoned. It does not matter that the finder intends to keep the item found even if the owner eventually is ascertained (*Glyde* (1868) L.R. 1 C.C.R. 139; see A.T.H. Smith, para. 7–36). This rather secure position is vitiated, however, by any act of appropriation from the time the original owner is ascertained. Abandonment by the original owner is effective abandonment of property rights in the original owner; merely being lost is not necessarily so. A definite distinction must be drawn between civil liability and criminal liability here. Where one finds and uses and perhaps expends the use of the item found, the finder will not be criminally liable where the apparently undiscoverable owner eventually turns up and claims the item. They may, however, have incurred civil liability for the use and expenditure (see A.T.H. Smith, para. 7–35).

"Reasonable steps", has been interpreted in the U.K. as meaning the subjective belief of the finder as to what steps would be reasonable to ascertain the original owner of the item found (*Small* (1987) 86 Cr. App. R. 170). This does seem to be something of a contradiction, as the very nature of "reasonableness" is itself an objective concept. The issue, however, has become whether the court or jury believe the belief of the finder was so unreasonable that the finder could not possibly have so believed (*Knight* (1871) 12 Cox 102). In considering this question, the court or jury look to the value of the item found, the circumstances of discovery and the action (or inaction) of the accused (*MacDonald* (1983) 8 Aus. Crim. L.R. 248). As to the issue of whether reference in the theft provision to the "consent of the owner" requires proof of ownership, see comments in section entitled "Section 4(4)(b): That there was consent of the owner of the property" above.

Section 4(5)

S.4(5) defines the concepts of "appropriates" and "depriving". It is fortunate that the draftsman had regard to the problem with respect to the former concept which arose after the passing of the English Act of 1968 (on which, see A.T.H. Smith, para. 1–17). It was not clear, and remains unclear in the English Act, whether or not "appropriation" requires an unauthorised act. S.4 may avoid this problem in its first subsection by making it clear that we speak of *dishonest* appropriation *without the consent of the owner.* It would perhaps have been advisable to include the requirement of "authorisation" in the definition of "appropriates". S.4(5) demonstrates a rare independence from the English model with the dropping from both our prior law and the English Theft Act's definition of the word "permanently" as a requirement. Like the over-simplicity which was found to exist in the idea of "permanently depriving", there is also a very real limitation to the idea that to commit theft is simply to take and carry away. A theft may also occur where the wrongdoer is already in possession of the property or where, quite simply there is no need or possibility of removal or carrying away. The term chosen to denote the larger concept was "appropriation", defined as "the making of a thing private property, whether another's or (where owned in common) one's own; taking as one's own or to one's own use" (Oxford English Dictionary, see further below). We are most fortunate to have such an expansive yet delineated item in our lexicon; it is an appropriate and effective word for the purpose of this Act. It means to take possession without taking "ownership". In more complex terms, it suggests a unilateral acquisition rather than a consensual transfer (see A.T.H. Smith, para. 5–01).

Where property is owned in common, in a partnership for instance, where one common owner makes off with it, he or she steals it (*Bonner* [1970] 2 All E.R. 97). Spouses also may steal from each other. The meaning of "deprive" as contained in the Act will have to be thrashed out as a concept by the Irish courts, as it does not contain the "permanent" component which features in other common law jurisdictions. It is important to note that theft is not necessarily an isolated and independent act, but may be composed of a series of acts which need not be made distinct one from the other to constitute separate acts of theft; instead they may be combined to form one act of theft over time, for example, by establishing a general deficiency in the property said to be appropriated in some way. The LRC stated:

> "[t]he law requires there to be a distinct charge for each act of theft. But an employee can steal small sums of money from his or her employer over a protracted period. This usually comes to light for the first time as a deficiency in the accounts. In the absence of an admission by the employee, these cases are very difficult to prove. Every other possible thief has to be eliminated from the case, beyond a reasonable doubt. It is usually impossible to prove each specific taking. Even where a statement of admission is obtained, the admission is usually couched in general terms. It takes a very contrite thief with a good memory and a painstaking and thorough investigator to secure an admission which would sustain charges for distinct takings."

When distinct takings cannot be proved, the law permits a charge to be laid for a general deficiency arising between dates (*R. v. Balls* (1871), L.R. 1 C.C.R. 328). Appropriating property means to usurp it, or to interfere in some adverse manner with the owner's rights in the property. Usurp means "to seize or assume wrongfully" (Oxford English Dictionary). The definition contrasts in its simplicity to the English provision, which provides further that:

> "any assumption by a person of the rights of an owner amounts to an appropriation, and this includes, where he has come by the property (innocently or otherwise) with-

out stealing it, any later assumption of a right to it by keeping or dealing with it as owner" (Theft Act 1968, s.3(1)).

There does appear to be some prospect of this concept avoiding the difficulty its English counterpart has experienced (see the difficult case of *Lawrence* [1972] A.C. 626, which, despite its imprecision, was affirmed in *Gomez* [1993] A.C. 442). Indeed, we might take advantage of the very resource of accumulated experience of which English law has currently deprived itself. It appears, according to the decision in *Gallasso* [1993] Crim. L.R. 495, that there remains an element of "taking" in the meaning to be given to "appropriates". In that case, a nurse undertook to lodge cheques for a mentally handicapped patient. She opened a building society trust account and lodged the cheque. This was suspicious because the patient already held at least one such account, and she specifically sought a cash-card account. She claimed she sought to make unauthorised withdrawals easier (*i.e.* dispense with the need for written consent each time). The court considered whether the lodgement of this cheque was theft and if it had been done dishonestly with the intent to deprive. The court held, however, that there had been no appropriation irrespective of the issue of consent and that there still had to be taking. Lord Lloyd stated that: "[t]his is not to reintroduce the concept of carrying away [*i.e.* a larceny criteria] in to the definition of appropriation. It is to do no more than to give appropriation its ordinary meaning ...". The concern has been expressed above that it might be tempting to engage in the resurrection of terms abolished by this Act simply because we might be familiar with them. Indeed, J.C. Smith suggests this dicta would be to set the law back 200 years! Furthermore, that commentator strongly disagreed with the merits of the dicta, before arguing that once the nurse had exercised the rights of the owner (*i.e.* by taking possession of the cheque and paying it in), with the necessary intent there was appropriation (p.17). For one thing, the right of the patient as against the source of the cheque expired once it was paid in. This might easily be said to be usurping or adversely interfering with the owner's rights under s.4(5). Indeed in another cheque case we note that it is not necessary for any actual loss to be caused to the owner; a person who draws a forged cheque against the owner may never be at a loss, because even where the cheque is honoured by the bank, the transaction is not valid and may be reversed. The English courts, however, took the view that it was sufficient appropriation to assume the rights of the owner over the credit balance (*Chan Man-sin v. A-G of Hong Kong* [1988] All E.R. 1).

We might take from the decision in *Gomez* the untainted remarks of Lord Browne-Wilkinson that: "For myself ... I regard the word 'appropriation' in isolation as being an objective description of the act done irrespective of the mental state of either the owner or the accused" (p. 39).

J.C. Smith would demur, commenting:

> "no meaning can sensibly be given to the word 'in isolation.' One has only to compare the phrase 'appropriates goods to the contract' in the [English] Sale of Goods Act 1979 to see that its meaning depends entirely on the context in which it is used" (p.14).

Appropriation is distinct from obtaining, and it is not concerned with the presence or absence of deception. We must note this to avoid confusion with theft and an offence under s.6 below. It is helpful to remember *why* the word appropriate was chosen — it was chosen because it is one step removed from the idea of "taking"; it does not require actual taking; "appropriate" focuses on either:

1. assuming/usurping the rights of the owner (*Gomez*), or
2. interfering with the rights of the owner (*Morris*; C.L.R.C.).

In fact, it was the English C.L.R.C. who preferred the choice of appropriation as a cognate of conversion because is would be more a layman's term (para. 34). The formula chosen in s.(4)(1) will have a knock-on effect on the precedent value of English case law, a favoured recourse, it must be said, for the Irish criminal law practitioner. Thus cases which turned upon the issue of consent may now be authority for the contrary view under s.4. In the case of Morris, which took the view that absence of consent is a necessary component in appropriation, precedential value is arguably retained. Taking goods from a supermarket shelf or clothes rack will *not* be appropriation, because the customer normally has consent to do so. Consent will not, of course, extend to placing the item in a bag (*Mc Pherson*

[1973] Crim. L.R. 191). It might be a defence, however, that the taking was merely absent minded and not considered (*Ingram* [1975] Crim. L.R. 457). Even if the customer does so with the intention to deprive, it is not theft until that consent expires, which will normally be at the point of egress. A customer is equally given consent to fill his or her petrol tank with petrol from a filling station; intention to deprive should be irrelevant until that consent expires (see *McHugh*, which turns on the issue of consent (1976) 64 Cr. App. Rep. 92). A dishonest sale by a buyer on sale or return would not appear to be appropriation (Smith & Hogan (7th ed.), pp.525-526). Where a person undertakes to deliver property, he obtains consent so to do irrespective of whether it is always his intention to dispose of the property to his own benefit; therefore, it is not appropriation (*Fritschy* [1985] Crim. L.R. 745 *cf. Gallasso* [1993] Crim. L.R. 495). One consequence of this *post-possession* appropriation, which is possible by the absence-of-consent requirement, is that separate instances of taking possession, with consent, may later form the subject of a single count of theft as the intention to deprive does not occur at the time of taking possession, but at a later stage (*Skipp* [1975] Crim. L.R. 114). Where an offence of deception is committed to obtain possession of property, again with implicit consent, it will be difficult to argue that it is theft to dispose of it (*Hircock* [1979] Crim. L.R. 184). To obtain a car under a hire-purchase scheme is one such scenario where it is clear that upon signing the agreement the deceiver acknowledges he or she is not the owner of the car. Where two prices are exhibited for the same item on sale, it is not theft to dispose the item with the lower price tag and purchase it at that price (*Dip Kaur v. Chief Constable for Hampshire* [1981] 2 All E.R. 430). There does not need to be any overt dealing which demonstrates active appropriation (*A.G.'s Reference (No. 1) of 1983* [1985] Q.B. 182), but to assume the rights of another requires some conduct demonstrating such an assumption (Smith & Hogan (10th ed.), p.522). Conduct might be by deliberate omission, however, in refusing to return an item received. But the intention, as we have seen, does not have to be simultaneous, and thus it may not be to usurp or adversely interfere to allow time to pass, whatever the intention. Nonetheless, the untainted comment of Ward J. in *Gomez* was:

"(1) Theft can occur in an instant by a single appropriation but it can also involve a course of dealing with property lasting longer and involving several appropriations before the transaction is complete; (2) theft is a finite act – it has a beginning and it has an end; (3) at what point the transaction is complete is a matter for the jury to decide upon the facts of each case; (4) though there may be several appropriations in the course of a single theft or several appropriations of different goods each constituting a separate theft as in *R. v. Skipp*, no case suggests that there can be successive thefts of the same property" [1993] 4 All E.R. 215 at 223.

It was submitted above that there are many permutations which a claim of right to property might take. For instance, it might be that property passes by a contract which may ultimately be voidable. In such a case, the defendant may claim that the victim can only seek to prosecute a claim in civil law. Alternatively, Shute suggests that a prosecution may proceed under the deception offence (s.6 in this Act; see Shute, p. 447 quoting the Criminal Law Revision Commission's Eighth Report, Cmnd. 2977 (1966), para. 38). That provision, however, is also couched in terms of honesty which are susceptible to the claim of right defence. The transfer of the property might equally have been a gift; in *Mazo* [1997] 2 Cr. App. R. 518, it was held that where a valid gift is made, there could be no theft. That court volte-faced once again, however, in the case of *Hinks*, falling back upon the *Gomez* line. It is now the position in England that there is nothing in the concept of appropriation that requires a jury to consider whether a gift has been validly made, and that the position of the House in *Gomez*, which they still maintained, was incompatible with a claim that an indefeasible gift of property could not amount to an appropriation (Shute, pp. 449–450). We know that the Irish provision includes a saver as to consent of the owner, so *Gomez* would not appear to apply.

To "deprive" the owner of his or her property means either to temporarily or permanently deprive them of it. This would seem to cover the long-excluded circumstances of borrowing a thing intending to return it. However, a realistic appreciation of the wealth of jurisprudence on the more innocuous "borrowing"-type scenarios must surely survive this new development. In any case, intention has never really been a great problem to the working of the criminal law protecting property, certainly not to the extent that it has become complex in the context of offences against the person (A.T.H. Smith, para. 6–01). A useful starting point in the mental element to "depriving" is to consider:

1. the taker who realises he or she is depriving the owner at the time of taking — but has a change of mind; and
2. the taker who only realises later that the owner may not get back his property.

The former is theft (*Eggington* (1801) 126 E.R. 1410); the latter is not (*Addis* (1844) 1 Cox. 78). Despite the clear distinction between *mens rea* and *actus reus* it would appear that the depriving need not be completed to amount to theft. In England, the intention to deprive at some time in the future suffices. Fingering a purse in someone's pocket is an appropriation and can be theft, though there is no deprivation at that point (A.T.H. Smith, p.3; see also comments on intention above). Intention in property offences is specific, and recklessness is difficult to establish as amounting to intention. The offence of so-called "joy-riding" is again illustrative. The taker, under the former law, would have had to have been almost certain that the car would be written off to be convicted of theft (*cf. State v. Davis* (1875) 38 N.J.L. 176). Nevertheless, the notion of recklessness is consistently endorsed by this Act. The concept of recklessness is derived in the main from the Model Penal Code of the American Law Institute and, importantly, was approved of by the Supreme Court in *People (DPP) v. Murray* [1977] I.R. 360. Recklessness will be established where the prosecution show more than negligence, but culpable disregard of circumstance which ought to have alerted the accused to wrongdoing. Yet if it is found to be difficult to apply to or to prove, this is not to say that other terminology and other offences (*e.g.* reckless abandonment and conspiracy to defraud) would not cover such behaviour (A.T.H. Smith, para. 6–04).

Section 4(6)

S.4(6). A person guilty of theft is liable on conviction on indictment to a fine or imprisonment for a term not exceeding 10 years or both. The subsection leaves summary matters to be considered under s. 53 below.

Exceptions to theft

5.—(1) Where property or a right or interest in property is or purports to be transferred for value to a person acting in good faith, no later assumption by that person of rights which that person believes himself or herself to be acquiring shall, by reason of any defect in the transferor's title, amount to theft of the property.

(2) A person cannot steal land, or things forming part of land and severed from it by or under his or her directions, except where the person—

(*a*) being a trustee, personal representative or other person authorised by power of attorney or as liquidator of a company or otherwise to sell or dispose of land owned by another, appropriates the land or anything forming part of it by dealing with it in breach of the confidence reposed in him or her, or

(*b*) not being in possession of the land, appropriates anything forming part of the land by severing it or causing it to be severed, or after it has been severed, or

(*c*) being in possession of the land under a tenancy or licence, appropriates the whole or part of any fixture or structure let or licensed to be used with the land.

(3) For the purposes of *subsection (2)*—

(*a*) "land" does not include incorporeal hereditaments,

"tenancy" means a tenancy for years or any less period and includes an agreement for such a tenancy,

"licence" includes an agreement for a licence,

and

(*b*) a person who after the expiration of a tenancy or licence remains in possession of land shall be treated as having possession under the tenancy or licence, and "let" and "licensed" shall be construed accordingly.

(4) A person who picks mushrooms or any other fungus growing wild on any land, or who picks flowers, fruit or foliage from a plant (including any shrub or tree) growing wild on any land, does not (although not in possession of the land) steal what is picked, unless he or she does it for reward or for sale or other commercial purpose.

(5) Wild creatures, tamed or untamed, shall be regarded as property; but a person cannot steal a wild creature not tamed or ordinarily kept in captivity, or the carcase of any such creature, unless it has been reduced into possession by or on behalf of another person and possession of it has not since been lost or abandoned, or another person is in course of reducing it into possession.

GENERAL NOTE

S.5 relates generally to land and so-called "real property". The once vital component of larceny, "trespassory taking", made theft of real property impossible. Though this concept as an obstacle to liability has been removed in favour of the concept of "appropriation", nevertheless, the idea that real property cannot be stolen remains (see comments in relation to property in the General Introductory Note above). Nowadays, the wrongful appropriation of property is more a matter for disputes of title in civil law. J.C. Smith comments that certain rights are regulated by the civil law and "... in an advanced society, their structure is inevitably complicated. This is something of which the reformer of the criminal law must take account in the legislation which he proposes, but which he cannot alter" (para. 1–04). Nevertheless, he goes on to say that the concepts of the civil law must be utilised in the definition of crime. Land, in the sense of real property, has long been distinguished from personal property, the latter being amenable to theft as it could literally be carried away. We know from a simple jurisdictional division that a District Court did not ordinarily have jurisdiction to deal with title to land. Where title is in issue, then the matter would not generally enter the realm of the criminal law. Indeed, even with the exceptions contained in the this section, the immunity of land appropriation from the law of theft persists; the courts generally favour the civil law option of dealing with such appropriations as ordinary business transactions, however improper, rather than criminal offences (*see Daniels v. Daniels* [1978] Ch. 406, approved in *Eastman Co. v. G.L.C.* [1982] 1 W.L.R. 2). But this complication notwithstanding, rights over land are, in theory, just as susceptible to appropriation as rights in goods. However, the inherently civil nature of boundary disputes and the sufficiency of that law were felt by the C.L.R.C. to be reason enough to leave such cases outside the law of theft (paras. 40–44; *cf.* the claim of right asserted after 12 years' acquiescence).

S.5 is a general list of exceptions to the exception of land from the law of theft. Unlike the English model, it takes the purchaser for value exception out of the definition of appropriates and places it at the head of the list.

Section 5(1)

S.5(1) is a replication of s.3(2) of the English Theft Act 1968. The C.L.R.C., recommending it, stated:

"A person may buy something in good faith, but may find out afterwards that the seller had no title to it, perhaps because the seller or somebody else stole it. If the buyer nevertheless keeps the thing or otherwise deals with it as owner, he could ... be guilty of theft. It is arguable that this would be right; but on the whole it seems to us that, whatever view is taken of the buyer's moral duty, the law would be too strict if it made him guilty of theft" (para. 37).

The exception is premised upon the buyer acting in good faith but this is at the time of transfer. It might come to his or her attention at a later stage that the property was illicit and decide to continue to hold it — this is an assumption of property rights which, but for this exception, would be theft. Where the buyer can be attributed with this kind of "wilful blindness", however, such conduct may be seen as acquiring property knowing that it represents the proceeds of crime under s.31 of the Criminal Justice Act 1994 as amended by this Act — in other words, money laundering.

Section 5(2)

Section 5(2)(a)

S.5(2)(a) deals generally with the responsibilities under the criminal law of fiduciaries (first see reference to this paragraph in the General Introductory Note above). It is practically identical to the equivalent section of the English Theft Act 1965 (s4(2)(a); the only difference is the use of the phrase "belonging to another" instead of "owned by another"). Subs. 2(a) is included to take account of the criminal offence of fraudulent conversion in as far as any breach of fiduciary responsibility, where the component elements of theft are present, will amount to the final element of theft, that of "appropriation". Thus, a breach of fiduciary responsibility may amount to theft. The elements required may specifically be those as set out in *Daniels v. Daniels. i.e.* the accused must generally have a power of sale; the accused must be of such a position in relation to the land to fall within one of the roles as set out in the section (*i.e.* trustee, personal representative or other person authorised to dispose of assets); there must be dishonesty and no other reasonable explanation for the misdealings ([1978] Ch. 406, approved in *Eastman Co. v. G.L.C.* [1982] 1 W.L.R. 2; see comments in relation to appropriation and to property above; on trustees, see, Brazier "Criminal Trustees?" (1975) 39 Conv. (England) New Series 29).

Section 5(2)(b)

S.5(2)(b) sits awkwardly with the initial wording of the subsection in relation to the concept of "severing". We know that the general rule is that one cannot steal real property; we know also that occupation of property — even some casual occupation such as squatting — may mean that such occupiers who ever do not steal. It would appear then, that severing (or property severed) would form part of the immunity of real property from the law of theft; yet here we have an exception to that immunity. This exception is by no means a recent anomaly and serves to show the theoretical weaknesses that can arise from the persistence of the immunity. Read literally, the provision seeks to make liable a person taking severed property. A person, however, who commits the apparently more serious offence of wrongfully seizing the land itself may sever what he or she pleases and only be liable under civil law (Hobbes, in *Dialogue Between a Lawyer and a Philosopher*, had the following to say about just such a scenario:

> "How unconscionable a thing it is, that he that steals a shilling's worth of wood which the wind hath blown down, or which lieth rotten on the ground, should be hanged for it, and he that takes a tree worth twenty or forty shillings should answer only for the damages".

Occupation, of course, comes in various degrees. The trespasser will not avail of the immunity, nor indeed will a squatter who has not attained adverse possession (*Edwards* [1978] Crim. L.R. 49). The point, however, remains that it should not be for the criminal courts to have to determine questions of title to real property. (This was a view of C.L.R.C. above before the enactment of the equivalent English provision.) Severance brings property within the remit of theft; removing soil, garden fixtures and even growing grass may be theft. It is theft of pasture to have cattle graze it (*McGill v. Shepherd*, referred to in Williams & Weinberg, *The Australian Law of Theft* (3rd ed.), p. 116 as cited by Smith & Hogan (10th ed.), p.531, n.10). The size of the severed property seems not to matter, an actual railway station (Cleckheaton Station, which was dismantled and removed) having been deemed to be stealable (Smith & Hogan, *ibid.*). Happily, however, the defendant who went to such trouble was found to have a claim of right (*ibid.*).

Section 5(2)(c)

S.5(2)(c) stands or falls upon the concept of a "fixture", which may be stolen, as opposed to real property which may not. This paragraph differs from s.5(2)(*b*) in that it concerns tenants and licensees and the item need not be severed, nor is it express in the provision that it form part of the land — though this might be difficult to distinguish. Megarry and Wade define a fixture as a chattel which has been affixed to the real property becoming part of the real property depending on (a) the degree of joining or annexation, and (b) the purpose of the real property (*The Law of Real Property* (5th ed., 1984), p.731). Though the matter is doubtless more complex than this, the essence is the substantial connection with the land to which the item in question is fixed. One distinction to be noted is that a fixture remains a chattel where it is attached merely for the purpose of the use or enjoyment of that item — that is to say, the item remains the property of the person who attached it (A.T.H. Smith, 3–41). Generally speaking, the fixture falls within the phrase "whole or part of any fixture or structure let or licensed to be used with the land" where the landlord, and not the tenant, has attached the item.

Section 5(3)

S.5(3) places vital importance in paragraph (*b*) on the concept of possession which may remain once a licence or lease has expired and the occupier under that instrument has not vacated. Interestingly, there is the same insistence as that found in s.4(2) of the English Theft Act 1968 that incorporeal hereditaments do not constitute land. Thus, what is in theory an "interest in land" does fall within the ambit of the law of theft. This effectively means that easement rights, profits and rents may be appropriated and therefore may be stolen.

Section 5(4)

S.5(4) is a sensible preclusion from the law of theft of, for example, taking blackberries from the roadside. The C.L.R.C. felt that "a provision could reasonably be criticised which made it even technically theft in all cases to pick wild flowers against the will of the landowner" (para. 47). With the exception of fungus and mushroom, the taker may not take the whole plant. The word "pick" is specific and would suggest the use of an instrument such as a scythe to be theft (A.T.H. Smith suggests that "picking" such flowers as roses is normally done by scissor-like instruments and thus such an instrument would constitute "picking", 3–49). "Or other commercial purpose" would seem to extend wider than mere sale, and isolated opportunism may well be covered — though it is difficult to see how a schoolboy selling mushrooms on a once-off basis would be sufficient; a plant is wild if it is not planted for food, ornament, commerce or some such purpose, or it it has been cultivated by such means as pruning, spraying, watering or weeding (*ibid.* at 3–50).

Section 5(5)

S.5(5) is a replication of s.4(4) of the English Theft Act. "Creatures" is a wide term including such fauna as fish, birds, insects and reptiles as well as the more typical objects of theft such as deer and rabbits. Tame animals, whether originally wild or domestic, are property and therefore may be stolen. This is not the case of wild animals neither tamed nor ordinarily kept in activity. We may assume that we refer here to individual creatures, and not to the species (the C.L.R.C.'s draft provided that "it will be theft to take a particular creature which has been taken, or is ordinarily kept in captivity ..." (p.126)). The reason for this is that a wild animal will naturally cross boundaries and real property limitations of any purported owner. This position changes where such an animal is killed or "reduced into possession". The question then is, where did this occur? Where it occurs on a landowner's property, the creature, in ordinary course, becomes the possession of the landowner (*Swans*

Case (1592) 7 Co. Rep. 15b, 17b; *Blades v. Higgs* (1865) 11 H.L.C. 621). The position becomes more complicated depending on who has killed or rendered the creature and/or on whose behalf. The English C.L.R.C. recommended that poaching should be theft if done "for reward or for sale or other commercial purpose" (para. 52) but this was not accepted and it has even been suggested that poaching — though unlawful — is an accepted country pastime! (Smith & Hogan (10th ed.), p.533.) An important distinction here is that the killing or rendering itself cannot be theft; it is the appropriation which makes for the act of stealing. The meaning of wild creature, however, depends largely on the notion of captivity:

– whether or not the creature need ordinarily to be kept in captivity.
– where captivity is not strictly necessary we refer to a very old concept known as *animus revertendi, i.e.* whether the creature will revert to, or intends to return to, the purported owner.
– where captivity fails or comes to an end, we must consider whether the creature takes flight and whether the purported owner pursues it — if there is no pursuit, another may capture and take the creature.

(A.T.H. Smith cites Halsburys *Laws of England* (4th ed.), Vol. 2, para. 205. *See also Hamps v. Derby* [1948] 2 K.B. 311 at 321).

Interestingly, the law deals with the act of rendering or reducing a creature into one's possession. Thus, it is theft to take a creature which has been rendered by another; equally it is theft to take a creature which is in the process of being rendered by another. Whether or not such an offence will require the necessary intention may often depend on how the accused person has acted in respect of the animals (see for example *Howlett v. Howlett* [1968] Crim. L.R. 222; see A.T.H. Smith, para. 3–53).

Making gain or causing loss by deception

6.—(1) A person who dishonestly, with the intention of making a gain for himself or herself or another, or of causing loss to another, by any deception induces another to do or refrain from doing an act is guilty of an offence.

(2) A person guilty of an offence under this section is liable on conviction on indictment to a fine or imprisonment for a term not exceeding 5 years or both.

GENERAL NOTE

The essence of fraud is that the victim parts with his or her property voluntarily but does so under a misconception which is the result of the offender's deception. Thus the ingredients formerly ascribed to the offence of obtaining by false pretences as set out in *People (AG) v. Bristow (No. 2)* unreported, Court of Criminal Appeal, March 27, 1962) may yet (with slight modification) be of service to an understanding of "making gain/causing loss by deception". Certainly:

(a) must the accused actually make gain or cause loss?;
(b) he or she must do so by "any act of deception" by which the injured party was induced (induced);
(c) that the deception was to an existing fact or situation (deception);
(d) that the accused had knowledge and [dishonest] intention of the deception (dishonestly, with the intention of).

Gain or Loss

The draftsman has certainly succeeded in providing legislative scope for consequences of deception in as wide a manner conceivable. Whether or not it may adequately deal with the scope we shall have to wait to see. If it does prove unproblematic, it is a remarkable simplification on the English approach. There is no offence of obtaining pecuniary advantage by deception in the Irish provision (see s.16 of the English Theft Act 1968). The assumption must be that s.6 incorporates such an offence. Both gain and loss are to be considered in monetary terms or in terms of property only. It does not matter that the loss or gain is temporary (*e.g.* where an underwriter agrees finance for a car purchase and the car is subsequently repossessed when the falsity is discovered).

The term gain contemplates keeping what one has (where a further falsity is procured to prevent the car from being repossessed.) Loss is not confined to loss of money or property held at the time of the offence but includes property one "might" get (an unfortunate word), which refers to items or sums not acquired because of the deception. Gain to the defendant (or someone else) and loss to the victim is what is contemplated. A taxi driver gains extra fare by telling his or her passenger that the shorter route is blocked (*Levene* [1976] Crim. L.R. 63). Securing a bet on a horse by a falsity which turns out to be a winner, however, is not deception as the courts have chosen to view the matter as contingent; the money gained was because a winning horse was chosen, not directly because the bet was placed, which was the deceptive act (*Clucas* [1949] 2 K.B. 226). Another case cited by J.C. Smith is a teacher who obtains a job by falsity. It was held that though he gained the means of earning a salary by deception, the salary itself was gained by having worked for it (*Lewis* (1922) Somerset Assizes, taken from Russell, 1186n). We must be careful with this particular position as it illustrates a judicial preparedness to separate an opportunity or employment unrelated to the deception and the deception as a mere device to secure it. Under the Irish formula, it is open to the court to treat them both as gain or loss, however "by deception" is somewhat strained. In *King and Stockwell* [1987] Q.B. 547, the defendant duped the victim by telling him that his trees were dangerous and needed cutting. Needless to say the work was inherently less meritorious than in *Lewis* but the comparison is clear. This payment was held to be deception. It might be that a competitor who tenders for a job suffers loss by such a deception which would, in fact, be more straightforward.

Any Act of Deception

Deception as defined in s.2 must contemplate the giving of a false impression, or failing to correct such an impression (which is at least partly attributable to the defendant) on matters ranging from law, value or state of mind. Alternatively, it might deny the full facts or fail to warn the victim so that he or she makes an uninformed decision. Finally, deception will be operative where the defendant is bound by fiduciary or confidential relationship to correct a false impression acting on the victim's mind and fails to do so.

The extent to which there must be an "act" is illustrated by the much-cited case of *Barnard* which held that the mere clothing worn by the defendant was enough to create a deception that he was entitled to a discount ((1837) 7 C&P 784). J.C. Smith cites an Australian case which found that the wearing of a badge of authority was sufficient (Smith & Hogan (10th ed.), p.592, citing *Robinson* (1884) 10 V.L.R. 131). The act of deception thus may be implied where, for example, a person books into a hotel on the understanding that he will pay on leaving (*Harris* (1975) 62 Cr. App. Rep. 28; see also *Waterfall* [1969] 3 All E.R. 1048, that a taxi fare will be paid on arrival). J.C. Smith suggests that the facts in *Morris* would be more satisfactorily dealt with by imputing a deception to a customer who changes price tags on goods and proffers them at the cash register at the lower price (para. 4–19). More strenuous efforts to create a false impression can be the active concealment of property (even property as large a ship which was taken from dry dock and put afloat to conceal the state of her keel (*Schneider v. Heath* (1813) 3 Camp 506, as cited in Smith & Hogan (10th ed.), p.592)). That case raises the issue of whether a house should be viewed in the daylight, and if it is not, does an estate agent have to highlight anything hidden. Buyers may be prevented from acquiring information which would affect their judgement of a very important transaction. However, without some active duty to make problems known, or some active steps to prevent the full facts becoming known it is still true to say that "[t]he passive acquiescence of the seller in the self-deception of the buyer does not entitle the buyer to avoid the contract" (*Smith v. Hughes* (1871) L.R. 6 Q.B. 597, as cited by Smith & Hogan (10th ed.), p.592; see also *Firth* [1990] Crim. L.R. 326).

The strongly worded *actus reus* of the provision "by any deception induces another to do or refrain from *doing an act*" [emphasis added] is not part of the English section. This is perhaps to allow for the formula "making gain or causing loss" which may be misconstrued as passive. This active element may be relevant in the giving over of money or goods for the purported consideration of a "dud" cheque (see below). Under the new section it is essential that the deception intended is the means by which the impugned result is achieved. It is not deception where the plan does not work out but the result occurs by some other eventuality. Thus, it would not matter that the defendant relies upon a statement he or she knows to be false (*Ady* (1835) 7 C & P; *Light* (1915) 11 Cr. App. Rep. 111). A statement might be correct but the result achieved by it might be false, or a false statement intended to be relied on may be unnecessary to achieve a false result; but again it is not deception because it is necessary that the defendant achieve such a result by deception (*Miller* [1992] Crim. L.R. 744). The representation made by the defendant may turn out to be true — but it is for the defendant to show it is (*Mandry and Wooster* [1973] 3 All E.R. 996). Evidence of deception will almost inevitably involve direct evidence of the victim; nevertheless it is important to note that statements and representations are issues of fact — which, even if evidenced by documentation, must be decided by a jury (*Adams* [1993] Crim. L.R. 525; see also s.57 below).

The obtaining of pecuniary advantage through deception — which seems to be encapsulated in the Irish formula — would make it an offence for a person to dishonestly and by deception become engaged to perform a service and to thereby fraudulently make a gain or cause loss. The implications of this for the employment sector are potentially far-reaching. (See the case of *Jeff and Bassett* (1966) 51 Cr. App. R. 28, where two roofing contractors who convinced an old lady that her roof was in need of repair were found guilty of acquiring the contract by false pretences because the work they carried out was inherently less valuable to the old lady than the money they charged; see also the similar case of *King and Stockwell* [1987] Q.B. 547, where the old lady this time had not paid for the service, and the dishonest contractors were found guilty of attempted deception.) This is distinct from inducing a person to perform a service (which is dealt with by s.7). Thus a person professing to be qualified in a certain capacity who is paid to do work on that basis, but who subsequently does not do the work, has made a gain and caused loss by deception (see *Callender* [1992] 3 W.L.R. 501). The Irish provision avoids the difficulties of the English section on obtaining pecuniary advantage by deception which specifically uses the word "employment" which is difficult to delimit. The Irish approach is preferred as A.T.H. Smith has argued that if the English provision were understood incorrectly "there would be a yawning gap in the protection afforded for the public ...". Nor is it a defence simply to say that the money was earned by virtue of an intervening contract rather than by the original deception (as it was in *Lewis* (1922), Russell (12th ed.), p.1186). Smith adds that "[i]f Parliament had meant to say that a person was guilty of an offence when by deception he managed to secure for himself the opportunity to earn money, it would have said so; but did not" (A.T.H. Smith, para. 18.61). Our Parliament has chosen not to be specific, and from an Irish perspective it remains true that such scenarios in England have been taken to be theft, and the Irish provision was without doubt drafted with the English provision in mind (*cf.* the case of mere puffery and dishonesty of a limited and excusable kind, A.T.H. Smith, paras. 18-63 *et seq.*, p. 563).

A phrase often used is that the deception must have operated on the mind of the victim; in other words the victim must be taken in by the deceptive act. This is not an automatic inference, nor should it easily be inferred. Nevertheless, the prosecutorial tendency will inevitably be prompted to infer it where there is evidence of dishonesty. In *Ray* [1974] A.C. 370, the court found sufficient inference of "inducement" in a defendant's lingering at the restaurant table despite his intention to depart without paying (which ultimately he did). This the court felt induced the waiter (without hearing him on the matter) into believing he would pay.

Evidence should be heard to establish that the result achieved originated with the defendant, played upon the mind of the victim and was for this reason a result of the deception. In *Etim*, however, the court could see no conceivable *alternative* reason for the making of gain than a false document supplied (the only evidence) by the defendant ([1975] Crim. L.R. 234, D.C.); in contrast, the evidence in *Lavery*, where the defendant changed the chassis number and registration plates of his car and sold it, did not play on the victim's mind to the satisfaction of the court ([1970] 3 All E.R. 432; see comments of J.C. Smith in Smith & Hogan (10th ed.), p.586).

Deception

In *People (DPP) v. Ryan* (3 Frewen 107 (1986)) the Irish Court of Criminal Appeal adopted the following English definition:

"To deceive is … to believe that a thing is true which is false, and which the person practising the deceit knows or believes to be false. To defraud is to deprive by deceit: it is by deceit to induce a man to act to his injury. More tersely it may be put, that to deceive is by falsehood to induce a state of mind; to defraud is by deceit to induce a course of action" *per* Buckley J. in *Re London and Globe Finance Corporation Ltd* [1903] 1 Ch 728 at 732.

It is interesting that the draftsman chose to define deception in a separate subsection, whereas the more centrally-used concept of dishonesty shares the previous subsection. The concept of deception, which is particularly endorsed by this writer, is discussed in the General Introductory Note.

S.6 has taken the Law Reform Commission at its word and replaced the notion of *false pretences* with that of *deception* (L.R.C. 43/92, 195). Interestingly, it was only at Report and Final Stages that the inclusion of the word "deception" here was even considered (see 527 *Dáil Debates* Col. 963). Deception has the meaning given to it in s.2(2) above. We may assume that the adoption in *Ryan* of an English interpretation gives relevance also to s.15(4) of the English Theft Act 1968, which includes "deception (whether deliberate or reckless) by words or conduct as to fact or as to law, including a deception as to the present intentions of the person using the deception or any other person". This consists of elements both mental and physical. The need for a positive physical act of deception harks back to the attitude discussed in the context of this section above which suffered fools badly. It is not a crime to simply permit *näiveté* to run its course to one's advantage, nor is it an offence under this section to escape the notice of the victim, for example a ticket controller, as no false belief has been constructed. As to the mental element, it seems necessary that the deception take effect on the mind of another person, *i.e.* create a false belief, so that interference with a machine alone does not constitute deception (see A.T.H. Smith, p.539; a thorough analysis of the meaning to be given at pp.466 *et seq.*). A machine too might possibly be "deceived" (A.T.H. Smith, para. 11–02; Arlidge & Parry, para. 4–054). It can, however, certainly be interfered with in contravention of the Criminal Damage Act 1991 or used for the purpose of forgery. See also reference to the Lebanese-loop offence under s.15 below. This will not give rise in any case to lacunae by virtue of the technological implications implicit in "induce" and in s.9, the advent of the offence of unlawful use of a computer below and the broad scope of theft. In any event, it was likely that the old common law line of thinking with regard to "fooling" a vending machine by foreign coins or discs will be extended to one of these provisions (*Goodwin* [1996] Crim. L.R. 262).

Knowledge and Intention of the Deception

Ignorance of the falsity or belief in the truth of one's statement is an obvious defence, and this belief may be careless or negligent without incurring criminal liability (*Staines* (1974) 60 Cr. App. Rep. 160). Neither "knowledge" or "belief" are mentioned in the section but are relevant to that extent. The Irish definition does not extend to reckless as it does in England. Knowledge and intention might be inferred, however, from the stronger recklessness cases (see *Dip Kaur* [1981] 2 All E.R. 430). *Caldwell* ([1981] 1 All E.R. 961) recklessness will clearly be inappropriate here as it is not appropriate even in England (*Large v. Mainprize* [1989] Crim. L.R. 213 as cited by Smith & Hogan (10th ed.), p.591). Belief in the truth of one's statement then may show that there was no dishonesty. Where there is no dishonesty, there can be no criminal intention. However, dishonesty is to be considered separately from deception. Crucially (with regard to theft above), a person may employ deception to make a gain to which he or she honestly believes he or she is entitled. The C.L.R.C. stated in the run-up to the English enactment that "a person who uses deception in order to obtain property to which he believes himself entitled will not be guilty; for though the deception may be dishonest, the obtaining is not" (para. 88). "Dishonestly" means without claim of right made in good faith and carries considerable weight in the Act. Claim of right is a defence to dishonesty and remembering the criterion of good faith it should apply equally to this section. Finally, there must be an intention to make a gain or cause loss by deception. The gain can be for anyone, the loss must be to someone other than the defendant (see generally the Australian case of *Balcombe v. Desimoni* [2001] A.L.R. 513).

Cheques, Cheque Cards and Credit Cards

Though also susceptible to charge under Pt 4, if a person knows that a cheque by which he or she obtains money or goods is a forgery, he or she is guilty of making a gain by deception. Arguably also, the giving of a cheque knowing that it will not be honoured, whether because the person knows there are insufficient funds or that no account is held where indicated, a deception is perpetrated (*Page* [1972] 2 Q.B. 330n; *Maytum-White* (1957) 42 Cr. App. R 165; *Locker* [1971] 2 Q.B. 321), similarly where the cheque is post-dated and the giver knows there will be insufficient funds on that date (*Parker* (1837) 169 E.R. 1). But some levity is required to accommodate the person who feels confident that there will be sufficient funds in the account, for instance where the date of purchase or post-date is the last Friday of the month when he or she expects salaries to be lodged. We might accept, then the words of Pollock B. that the person tendering the cheque represents that "the existing state of facts is such that in the ordinary course the cheque will be met" (*Hazelton* (1874) L.R. 2 C.C.R. 134).

It is the issuer of the cheque who has agreed to provide the service. This has long been a tricky point. If the person who tenders the cheque fully intends that the transaction be carried out, then arguably he or she has not deceived anyone; Lord Reid's is the classic position: "If nothing is said to the contrary, the law implies that the giver of a cheque represents that it will be honoured" (*DPP v. Turner* [1974] A.C. 357 at 367E). It will not be a defence that the defendant intended to pay monies into the account which he or she knew to be insufficient to cover the cheque where those monies come from the victim (*Greenstein* [1975] 1 W.L.R. 1353). What is unclear, as yet, is whether the particular attention in s.7 to the service of "loans" will cover the various facilities provided by financial institutions which if abused, may arguably fall within this section.

Often the inducement may be said to have been contributed to by the eagerness with which the victim or third party seeks to entertain the defendant's proposition. It might simply be a case of welcoming the opportunity to do business. One particular method of facilitating business is to take on its face the bona fides of a credit card or cheque card. The seller is not particularly concerned with the relationship customers maintain with their banks; the whole point of these cards is to avoid this issue. The terms of credit agreed with the bank by the customer will often have a cut-off point, and the card holder is not authorised to exceed that point. But again, the seller is not immediately concerned with this and will not necessarily have notice that the card-holder is not good for the amount represented. But the dishonesty will be clear in purchasing in such circumstances, and the inference will be made that the seller was induced (*Charles* [1977] A.C. 177; *Lambie* [1982] A.C. 449). This means that the entire institution of credit cards and cheque cards is an automatic inducement; the point in any case seems to be covered in s.7 of this Act.

Offences not Amenable to Theft

Much has been said about the possibility of introducing a general fraud offence or a general dishonesty offence, the merit of deception as a concept in property offences and the possibility both of overlap and leaving gaps which can be exploited by the "ingenuity of rogues". We might note that the offence in the troublesome *Gomez* [1993] A.C. 442 was one which should have been prosecuted under the deception offence, but for reasons unknown proceeded under a theft charge and went on to cause all sorts of problems. But what remains the most convincing reason for a separate fraud based upon deception is that some breaches of rights to property are simply not amenable to the law of theft. S.5 sets out the various exceptions to theft. In particular, certain categories of land are not protected if the rightful owner is dishonestly dispossessed. Another issue which arises is that, under certain transactions, a claim of right may be made in respect of voidable contracts, thus denying the victim recourse to the law of theft to secure the conviction of the dishonest dispossessor. It is unclear whether this vitiates the consent in civil law, but would appear to be valid consent (while it may subsequently cease to be) for the purposes of the criminal law.

The section is broad and in some respects novel. This may mean that it will take time before the prosecutor feels confident enough to use it to its full and intended effect. Certainly there might be a temptation to use the offence of theft under s.4 where prosecutions should properly be brought under this provision. We have discussed how the breadth of scope of concepts such as dishonesty can be interpreted to over-extend the intended use of such provisions. Ironically, it might be the use of the word "dishonest" which will make this provision, and not s.4 easily amenable to the prosecution of fraud offences. The draftsman has taken measures to ensure that theft will not be contaminated by the concept of deception — consent is now a palpable defence to theft. But dishonesty instead has seeped into an offence primarily guided by the concept of deception. How this will play itself out is yet to be seen. In any case, we may not repeat the experience in England following *Gomez* where it was possible for the prosecution to bring a charge of theft where prior to *Gomez* the charge ought properly to have been one of obtaining property by deception under s.15 (the equivalent to our s.6) of the Theft Act." (See Shute, p.446; see also Shute and Horder, "Thieving and Deceiving: What is the Difference?" (1993) M.L.R. 548; Heaton, "Deceiving without Thieving?" [2001] Crim. L.R. 712). It has been suggested above, however, that this will not prevent a possible tendency to prefer to prosecute under the law of theft because it does not require the prosecution to establish deception nor that the deception made possible the causing of loss or the making of a gain. The implications, however, of the differing penalties have been discussed above.

Obtaining services by deception

7.—(1) A person who dishonestly, with the intention of making a gain for himself or herself or another, or of causing loss to another, by any deception obtains services from another is guilty of an offence.

(2) For the purposes of this section a person obtains services from another where the other is induced to confer a benefit on some person by doing some act, or causing or permitting some act to be done, on the understanding that the benefit has been or will be paid for.

(3) Without prejudice to the generality of *subsection (2)*, a person obtains services where the other is induced to make a loan, or to cause or permit a loan to be made, on the understanding that any payment (whether by way of interest or otherwise) will be or has been made in respect of the loan.

(4) A person guilty of an offence under this section is liable on conviction on indictment to a fine or imprisonment for a term not exceeding 5 years or both.

GENERAL NOTE

The Law Reform Commission favoured the introduction of a provision such as this (43/92, p.222) which was to be along the lines of the relatively recent English enactment. The 1978 Theft Act in England created two offences apposite here: obtaining services by deception *and* evasion of liability by deception. The Irish provision proposes to cover the first one, certainly, but in s.7(3) by the term "loan" also to cover liability (it is possible that it intends to cover also the English Theft (Amendment) Act 1996 in relation to credit transfers obtained by deception). Unfortunately "loan" is undefined and does not refer to situations referred to in the so-called three cases under the English statute (Smith & Hogan (10th ed.), p.610). The Irish draftsmen would have been very careful to avoid the difficult English experience where they were forced to abandon the notion of "fraudulent obtaining of service" in favour of the provision: "A person who by deception dishonestly obtains services from another shall be guilty of an offence" (s.1(1), Theft Act 1978). The English experience has also encountered case law anomalies. In *Turner (No. 2)* [1971] 2 All E.R. 441, the defendant left his car in for repairs indicating that he would pick it up and pay for the repairs the next day. He came back a few hours later and dishonestly and without payment repossessed his car (which by that time had been fully repaired). Though this is a clear case for this provision, in England it was sought and succeeded in convicting the defendant of theft.

Being notably broader, the Irish provision expresses a required intention to make a gain or cause loss with, again, the need for deception (which is defined at s.2(2) and discussed in relation to s.6 above). Dishonesty is defined in its adverbial form at s.2(1). The positive physical element is very strongly stated in the wording of the provision "by doing some *act* or causing or permitting some *act* to be done" which would be paid for [emphasis added]. The offence is broad enough to cover loss intended by disruption to an event or service by a person who buys a ticket but intends to make trouble. The deception here is that he or she pretends to be an ordinary ticket-holder but intends to disrupt and obstruct the service (A.T.H. Smith, 18–05). Purely gratuitous services are excluded by the requirement that the service be for payment, but the concept of services is otherwise impressively wide. Nevertheless, a mortgage was considered by the English Court of Appeal to be property and not a service though it is arguable that this was a service for payment (*Halai* [1983] Crim. L.R. 624; see arguments against, A.T.H. Smith, para. 18–10 and Griew, *Theft Acts 1968 and 1978* (7th ed., 1995), p.171)). Hire purchase schemes would appear to be services (*Widdowson* (1986) 82 Cr. App. R. 314). In any event, s.7(3) will be invoked where bank credit or overdraft services are obtained. Tendering of cheques or credit cards must be within the assurances given by the issuer to the supplier of the services. We have commented on the area in s.6 above that the particular attention given to loan facilities suggests that the legislature intended this section to be used to charge offenders with deceptions of financial institutions in the various services which they provide. An overdraft, technically speaking, is "money lent", and therefore within this section (see Hapgood, *Pagets Law of Banking* (10th ed., 1989), p.82, as cited by A.T.H. Smith). A.T.H. Smith gives the Oxford English Dictionary definition of an overdraft which is, "the amount by which a draft exceeds the balance against which it is drawn". Happily, the Irish provision has chosen the word "loan" to cover the oddly chosen word "overdraft" in the English legislation.

Insurance policies had always been the subject of some ambiguity, premised as they are upon contingency. It is important to distinguish between misleading statements to obtain such a service and the *civil* law duty to disclose material details to secure coverage. The *uberrimae fidei* duty on all parties to an insurance policy, however, does indicate the potential for deception under this section. It is now a statutory criminal offence to make misleading, false or deceptive statements, promises, forecasts or assurances or to conceal material facts so as to induce another to enter into an insurance contract (*Mackinnon* [1959] 1 Q.B. 150 followed in *Clegg* (1977) C.L.Y. 619).

Services suggested by J.C. Smith are the provision of board and lodging, social or sporting amenities or entertainment, repairing and decorating and the letting of goods on hire (pp. 607–608). This section seems eminently capable of covering situations of employment and services rendered for consideration. The C.L.R.C.'s view that the offence should concern employment only was rejected in 1966 (Working paper, paras 26–29 and 31–34). It must be remembered that this section is not specifically intended to protect against deceptive obtaining of pecuniary advantage — it is intended to protect against deceptive inducement to perform services. The former would be a protection from the rogue employee or independent contractor visiting some fraud through their service (See *Jeff and Bassett* (1966) 51 Cr. App. R. 28). This, if indeed considered theft, would be more suited to a charge under s.6. S.7 would cover the latter scenario; it protects the person performing the service. Thus, employees or independent contractors induced by dishonest deception to perform a service are victims of a criminal offence, theoretically whether they are paid or insufficiently paid, but certainly if they are not paid at all. Payment under the section is almost certainly in terms of money (J.C. Smith, p.609).

Making off without payment

8.—(1) Subject to *subsection (2)*, a person who, knowing that payment on the spot for any goods obtained or any service done is required or expected, dishonestly makes off without having paid as required or expected and with the intention of avoiding payment on the spot is guilty of an offence.

(2) *Subsection (1)* shall not apply where the supply of the goods or the doing of the service is contrary to law or where the service done is such that payment is not legally enforceable.

(3) Subject to *subsections (5)* and *(6)*, any person may arrest without warrant anyone who is or whom he or she, with reasonable cause, suspects to be in the act of committing an offence under this section.

(4) Where a member of the Garda Síochána, with reasonable cause, suspects that an offence under this section has been committed, he or she may arrest without warrant any person whom the member, with reasonable cause, suspects to be guilty of the offence.

(5) An arrest other than by a member of the Garda Síochána may be effected by a person under *subsection (3)* only where the person, with reasonable cause, suspects that the person to be arrested by him or her would otherwise attempt to avoid, or is avoiding, arrest by a member of the Garda Síochána.

(6) A person who is arrested pursuant to this section by a person other than a member of the Garda Síochána shall be transferred by that person into the custody of the Garda Síochána as soon as practicable.

(7) A person guilty of an offence under this section is liable on conviction on indictment to a fine not exceeding £3,000 or imprisonment for a term not exceeding 2 years or both.

GENERAL NOTE

This provision, recommended by the L.R.C. (43/92, p.321), is taken from s.3 of the English Theft Act 1978. The only changes are the dropping of the inconsequential qualification of "on the spot" (s. 3 of the English Theft Act 1978 provides "payment on the spot" includes payment at the time of collecting goods on which work has been done or in respect of which service has been provided), and an extended provision for the arrest of persons engaging in this misconduct. Like a contract, the transaction must be legal for a right or entitlement arising from it to be enforceable (s.2). The offence is intended to protect legitimate and lawful commercial activity only (see C.L.R.C., para. 19). The offence (s.8(1)) will consist of:
1.   knowledge that payment is to be immediate,
2.   that such immediate payment is either a requirement *or* is expected,
3.   dishonesty in making off,
4.   intention *not* to pay "on the spot", and
5.   making off, without so doing.
The offence by-passes substantially the issues faced in relation to the offences of theft and deception. With the enactment of this provision, there is no issue that a person filling the tank of his car at a petrol station has consent to do so before moonlighting, nor that a meal may be consumed before payment.

S.8 is not without difficulty, however, and should not be exclusive of theft or deception offences. In particular, the use of s.7, a new offence to our law, should not be neglected in favour of this offence, nor vice versa. It is suggested, however, that offences concerning problematic cheques and credit card fraud be reserved to deception (see *Charge Card Services Ltd* [1988] 3 All E.R. 702 and the implications of *Vincent* [2001] Crim. L.R. 488).

The offence appears to resolve the issue of the spatial and temporal remit within which the customer may wander without being expected to pay, and most importantly the suggestion that it was intended by the customer, having taken possession of the goods, to pay in his own time and after his own fashion. The intention not to pay, however, must be couched in terms of permanent default, as held by the House of Lords in *Allen* [1985 All E.R. 641. A customer being chaperoned to the exit and facilitated in his departure would not suggest making off (*cf. Hammond* [1982] Crim. L.R. 611). The victim is entitled to have been paid "as required *or* expected". The element of requirement suggests that an unenforceable position in civil law would be a defence in criminal law (*Troughton v. Metropolitan Police* [1987] Crim. L.R. 138). A person who refuses to accept a meal different to the one he or she ordered may presumably refuse to pay for it. It is necessary that the goods be *obtained* or the service be *done*. A hasty mid-meal departure is, therefore, problematic (see *Ray* [1974] A.C. 370, brought under a different section).

We note that asportation is now no longer a focus of the law of stealing. Making off may be overt or discreet (on which see *Brooks and Books* (1982) 76 Cr. App. Rep. 66). However, in either case it must be evasive to the extent that the defendant would not be traceable were he or she to succeed in leaving without arrest. Nevertheless, it should not be necessary to engage in an analysis of the defendant's subjective assessment of his chances of escape.

It is perhaps unfortunate that the words "on the spot" — a rather informal phrase in any case — was used a second time in s.8(1) as it ensures that persons with a *bona fide* intention of paying as soon as possible thereafter will be given no benefit of the doubt; neither does the English reference to the phrase, omitted from the Irish section, help in this regard. It is clear that payment may often be required or contemplated on more than one occasion or in more than one place (*Moberly v. Allsop* [1992] COD 190, 156 JP 514). What is certain is that the true owner of the goods cannot be said to have given implied consent to take possession of the goods so long as the taker remains on the owner's premises (*People (DPP) v. Keating* [1989] I.L.R.M. 561).

There is a power of arrest which extends to citizens — a power which has recently been endorsed by the legislature in s.4 of the Criminal Law Act 1997. The arresting citizen may only exercise such a power where he or she, with reasonable cause, suspects that the offender would otherwise avoid arrest by the gardai and must, with due expedition, hand over responsibility to the gardai. Similarly the gardai have power to arrest persons suspected, with reasonable cause, of *having* made off; this suggests that intention to make off does not so empower an arrest. The prior law would have asked in relation to the intention required whether the accused had "the true consent of the true owner at any stage of his taking and carrying away the [good]" (*People (DPP) v. Morissey* [1982] I.L.R.M. 487).

Unlawful use of computer

9.—(1) A person who dishonestly, whether within or outside the State, operates or causes to be operated a computer within the State with the intention of making a gain for himself or herself or another, or of causing loss to another, is guilty of an offence.

(2) A person guilty of an offence under this section is liable on conviction on indictment to a fine or imprisonment for a term not exceeding 10 years or both.

GENERAL NOTE

The Law Reform Commission had felt this a necessary addition to the protection of property to attempt to keep apace with technology (it recommended the provision of a new offence of "dishonest use of computers" L.R.C. 43–92, Chap. 29). It is not a deception offence, as the word deception is absent; thus comment by Arlidge & Parry (para. 11–003) that computers, "being inanimate ... probably cannot be subjected to 'deception' within the meaning of the Theft Acts", seems accounted for (see also Report of the Government Advisory Committee on Fraud 1992, para. 3.25).

The section itself employs the open-book definition once more. We must wait and see how it will be received. Interestingly, the provision does not make it an offence to access information, despite the concern expressed in some quarters that compromising any system undermines confidence in the integrity of the system which one assumes may cause loss (Law Commission (U.K.), whose recommendations are thoroughly analysed by A.T.H. Smith, Chap. 11).

Among the limited cases decided, there is confusion with data protection offences (*Bignell* [1998] 1 Cr. App. Rep. 1). Despite the C.L.R.C. concern that J.C. Smith alludes to that the hacker be apprehended before he or she gets to the point where the law of theft [or fraud] is required, hacking is not an offence under this Act. It is submitted, however, that the introduction of a virus, a worm, a so-called trojan horse or logic-bomb — though clearly not theft *per se* — can cause devastation to computer systems and thus cause loss to the victim, and, likely as not, gain to the originator, assuming a considered motive. (See also commentary in General Introductory Note above.)

False accounting

10.—(1) A person is guilty of an offence if he or she dishonestly, with the intention of making a gain for himself or herself or another, or of causing loss to another—

> (*a*) destroys, defaces, conceals or falsifies any account or any document made or required for any accounting purpose,
> (*b*) fails to make or complete any account or any such document, or
> (*c*) in furnishing information for any purpose produces or makes use of any account, or any such document, which to his or her knowledge is or may be misleading, false or deceptive in a material particular.

(2) For the purposes of this section a person shall be treated as falsifying an account or other document if he or she—

> (*a*) makes or concurs in making therein an entry which is or may be misleading, false or deceptive in a material particular, or
> (*b*) omits or concurs in omitting a material particular therefrom.

(3) A person guilty of an offence under this section is liable on conviction on indictment to a fine or imprisonment for a term not exceeding 10 years or both.

GENERAL NOTE

A conviction may result only where the following are proven of the circumstances of falsification; that the accused had knowledge of falsification, which, in the absence of clear intention, infers that he or she :
– intended a resulting gain or loss (the former being personal, the latter to another),
– effected the falsification or omitted to perform a duty so as to effect falsification,
– did so dishonestly, and
– did so by:
  • the destruction, defacement, concealment or falsification of an accounting document, or
  • failing to make an account of such document, or
  • giving misleading information with such document which he or she knows to be deceptive in a material particular.

S.10 repeats part the wording of s.17 of the English Theft Act 1968. It omits the destruction of records from s.10(1)(*a*), as well as use of a record which is misleading in a material particular (we note, however, that it is already a revenue offence to fail to retain records for a statutory period). S.10(1)(*b*) is entirely new. This was an offence which arose where there is a responsibility to keep records of financial transactions. It is odd, therefore, that the draftsman should take the radical step of removing the word "record" from the statutory offence. The provision as set out is more in the nature of "falsification of accounts", formerly provided for in an Act of the Falsification of Accounts Act 1875, which is repealed in its entirety by this Act. Thus, the law in relation to that offence will now be relevant to this new provision, having been described as "one of the most generally used and serviceable weapons against fraud" (L.R.C. 43/92, p. 247). We note then, that the old section referred to clerks, officers or servants or any person employed or acting in that capacity, and not to independent contractors. It was argued that this should be changed to include such contracts for services (Charlton, pp. 864–865) and indeed this appears to be the effect of the new section, silent as it is in relation to function.

The nature of the intent necessary to secure conviction depended on the nature of the defendant's position and function and the circumstances in which the discharge of that function misled or did not reflect the true nature of a transaction. This cannot now be of the same significance, as the offence extends beyond employment. An important distinction to make is that diversion of monies through one's function would formerly have been embezzlement, which now falls to be considered as theft under s.4; falsification of accounts is concerned only with the falsification of an account (*Williams* (1898) 19 Cox CC 239). False entries on accounts had always been capable of being effected through an innocent agent (*Butt* (1884) 15 Cox 564; see *Oliphant* [1905] 2 K.B. 67). The meaning of intention in this context may draw from the older formula of "intention to defraud" which could be inferred from *knowledge* of falsity, that "the mere falsity of entries was not sufficient to constitute the crime but that they must be satisfied that there was an intent to defraud" (*People (A.G)* *v. Foley* unreported, Court of Criminal Appeal, May 17, 1950) which was palpable in circumstances where the accused made false entries in a book "over which he had complete control and for the accuracy of which he was responsible". Interestingly, the new formula which requires an intention to make a gain or create a loss would not appear to cover situations where falsification of accounts are intended to maintain the status quo (which was the case in *Wine* [1954] 1 W.L.R. 64; [1953] 2 All E.R. 1497; 37 Cr. App. R. 197; see *Charlton*, para. 10.204); nor is awareness of the purpose of the falsity specifically relevant to the *mens rea* (Smith & Hogan (10th ed.), p.619, citing *Graham* [1997] 1 Cr. App. Rep. 302 at 314). Though dishonesty is a requirement in the section, it is difficult here to see how a claim of right may be made in good faith (*Wood* [1999] Crim. L.R. 416).

An "account or document made or required for an accounting purpose" does not apply to documents of all kinds, though the distinction may have little limiting effect (see *Holt* (1983) 12 A Crim. R. 1 (Victorial Court of Criminal Appeal)). A borderline case in England which did not fall foul of the limitation was *Att.-Gen.'s Reference (No. 1 of 1980)* ([1981] 1 W.L.R. 34). What is interesting and argued strongly by A.T.H. Smith is that in that case no *mens rea* was required though an offence of such severe a penalty should never attract strict liability (A.T.H. Smith, p.774). It is submitted that the commercial adage that a businessman should know his business will no doubt carry the day. As A.T.H. Smith puts it, the retailer must ordinarily be aware of the general use for which the document is required. Nevertheless, there should be at least some consideration of whether the document was contemplated to be for some accounting (and therefore inherently either commercial or personal financial purpose. The notion of "material particular" broadens the offence beyond the accounting purpose of the document so long as the document is required for the purpose of accounting. This was the position in *Mallet* [1978]1 W.L.R. 820, which established the meaning of "material particular" to the satisfaction of the English Court of Appeal as "an important matter, a thing that mattered."

It does not matter that the falsified document is ever actually acted upon; the document is relevant upon being made. Such a document need only be "required" for accounting, not devoted to that purpose (*A.G.'s Reference (No. 1 of 1991)*). It is the fact that it is required which is to be inferred from the circumstances (*Osinuga* [1998] Crim. L.R. 216). The unconvincing cases available on this point include *Manning* [1999] Crim. L.R. 151 and *Okanta* [1997] Crim. L.R. 451. Prosecutorial licence seems to have been employed in the judge's interpretation of a Report on Title as a document required (*Cummings- John* [1997] Crim. L.R. 660). The jury should be charged with care, and unfortunately it appears they *will* be required to consider accounting practice in deciding whether insurer's notes or claim forms are such documents (*cf. Sundhers* [1998] Crim. L.R. 660).

Suppression, etc., of documents

11.—(1) A person is guilty of an offence if he or she dishonestly, with the intention of making a gain for himself or herself or another, or of causing loss to another, destroys, defaces or conceals any valuable security, any will or other testamentary document or any original document of or belonging to, or filed or deposited in, any court or any government department or office.

    (2)(*a*) A person who dishonestly, with the intention of making a gain for himself or herself or another, or of causing loss to another, by any deception procures the execution of a valuable security is guilty of an offence.

    (*b*) *Paragraph* (*a*) shall apply in relation to—

        (i) the making, acceptance, endorsement, alteration, cancellation or destruction in whole or in part of a valuable security, and

        (ii) the signing or sealing of any paper or other material in order that it may be made or converted into, or used or dealt with as, a valuable security,

as if that were the execution of a valuable security.

    (3) In this section, "valuable security" means any document—

    (*a*) creating, transferring, surrendering or releasing any right to, in or over property,

    (*b*) authorising the payment of money or delivery of any property, or

    (*c*) evidencing the creation, transfer, surrender or release of any such right, the payment of money or delivery of any property or the satisfaction of any obligation.

    (4) A person guilty of an offence under this section is liable on conviction on indictment to a fine or imprisonment for a term not exceeding 10 years or both.

GENERAL NOTE

This is in part a substantial reform of s.83 of the Larceny Act 1861, which is now repealed (L.R.C. 43/92, pp. 247–250). The prior law, under that provision, made the odd distinction between management and other staff of bodies corporate and public companies. The necessity of retaining such an offence, even an improved one, was questioned in England (C.L.R.C., para. 106); nevertheless, the Irish provision is almost identical to s.20 of the English Theft Act 1968. The question of its relevance arises in Ireland by virtue of the criminal damage nature of the offence which has been legislated for with the Criminal Damage Act 1991. Though it is true that such offences may be committed as a preliminary step to the commission of fraud, it is equally true that attempted gain by deception could cover such an offence. It might be that the offence indicates the seriousness of defacing or destroying public documents.

Burglary

    12.—(1) A person is guilty of burglary if he or she—

    (*a*) enters any building or part of a building as a trespasser and with intent to commit an arrestable offence, or

    (*b*) having entered any building or part of a building as a trespasser, commits or attempts to commit any such offence therein.

    (2) References in *subsection* (*1*) to a building shall apply also to an inhabited vehicle or vessel and to any other inhabited temporary or movable structure, and shall apply to any such vehicle, vessel or structure at times when the person having a habitation in it is not there as well as at times when the person is there.

(3) A person guilty of burglary is liable on conviction on indictment to a fine or imprisonment for a term not exceeding 14 years or both.

(4) In this section, "arrestable offence" means an offence for which a person of full age and not previously convicted may be punished by imprisonment for a term of five years or by a more severe penalty.

GENERAL NOTE

The offence of burglary is not altered as significantly as the foregoing. The two changes to the prior law consist of:
1. the expansion of what constitutes a "building" now including not only inhabited vehicles and vessels but also "any other inhabited temporary or movable structure", and
2. the replacing of the specific offences accompanying trespass to property with the generic "arrestable offence", which means an offence punishable by a term of imprisonment of five years or more.

Point 1. renders obsolete the requirement of some degree of permanence in the meaning of the word "building", and thus the relevance of cases such as *B & S Leathley* [1979] Crim. L.R. 314. It may still be relevant that the construction of a building need not be completed (see *Manning* (1871) LR 1 CCR 338).

As to point 2, this formula was introduced by s.4 of the Criminal Law Act 1997.

Burglary is not simply breaking and entering (though ironically it might be entering and breaking). It is also a common misconception that burglary is singularly an unlawful trespass to property *for the purpose of stealing*. Burglary is an unlawful trespass to property either :
1. with the intention to commit one of a variety of "arrestable offences" (s.12(1)(*a*)), or
2. once inside the premises, to then form the said intention (s.12(1)(*b*)).

An important distinction, therefore, which remains in the new section is the trespass and the accompanying offence. There are thus *two* intentions involved: the intention to enter a premises without lawful authority, and the intention to commit an arrestable offence (*Collins* [1973] Q.B. 100; an anomaly may arise from the view that entry must be effective for the purpose intended (*Brown* [1985] Crim. L.R. 212)). The accused need only be reckless as to the circumstances which make him or her a trespasser (*Jones and Smith* [1976] 3 All E.R. 54). We may assume that the substance of trespass is, as it was since 1976, effective and substantial entry. Thus it is an offence merely to extend a hand into or upon the premises (or part thereof) without authority to do so (*Brown* [1985] Crim. L.R. 212). Minimal entry is required also of cases where the intending burglar does not succeed in entering. In *Ryan* (1995) 160 JP 610, [1996] Crim. L.R. 320 CA, the defendant became trapped in a window, with his head and arm inside. He claimed unsuccessfully that he was not capable of any taking from that position and so it could not be an entry. The authority given to enter may be for a given purpose and thus might be abused or exceeded. This will render the *entry* unlawful just as if no authority were given (*People (DPP) v. McMahon* [1987] I.L.R.M. 87). The extent of the permission to enter given must therefore be scrutinised; entry through permission obtained by fraud is trespass (A.T.H. Smith, para. 28–19). "General permission" to enter is not "unlimited permission" so as to permit a neighbour to pillage a house he has been asked to look after while its owner is away on holidays (*Baker,* decision of the High Court of Australia (1983) 57 A.L.J.R. 426). There has been no case law under the law of theft for the proposition that an innocent agent or instrument may effect entry on the defendant's behalf; a little more independence and initiative on the part of the draftsman could have ensured that remote-controlled entry and the sending of a child into a premises would be covered by the section.

Aggravated burglary

13.—(1) A person is guilty of aggravated burglary if he or she commits any burglary and at the time has with him or her any firearm or imitation firearm, any weapon of offence or any explosive.

(2) In *subsection (1)*—

"explosive" means any article manufactured for the purpose of producing a practical effect by explosion, or intended by the person having it with him or her for that purpose;

"firearm" means:

> (*a*) a lethal firearm or other lethal weapon of any description from which any shot, bullet or other missile can be discharged,
>
> (*b*) an air gun (which expression includes an air rifle and an air pistol) or any other weapon incorporating a barrel from which metal or other slugs can be discharged,
>
> (*c*) a crossbow,
>
> (*d*) any type of stun gun or other weapon for causing any shock or other disablement to a person by means of electricity or any other kind of energy emission;

"imitation firearm" means anything which is not a firearm but has the appearance of being one;

"weapon of offence" means:

> (*a*) any article which has a blade or sharp point,
>
> (*b*) any other article made or adapted for use for causing injury to or incapacitating a person, or intended by the person having it with him or her for such use or for threatening such use,
>
> (*c*) any weapon of whatever description designed for the discharge of any noxious liquid, noxious gas or other noxious thing.

(3) A person guilty of aggravated burglary is liable on conviction on indictment to imprisonment for life.

GENERAL NOTE

The difference between s.13 and s.12 is, firstly, that burglary carries a penalty of 14 years imprisonment whereas aggravation increases this to life imprisonment. This difference depends on the vital element that the defendant "has with him or her" one of four items, *i.e.* any:

1. firearm,
2. imitation firearm,
3. weapon of offence, or
4. explosive.

"[H]as with him or her" means, generally speaking, "with" the offender — including where he or she may put the prohibited item down for a moment (*Moir v. Williams* [1892] 1 K.B. 246), a concept which Charlton, McDermott and Bolger describe as "proximate possession" (Charlton, 10.162). In contrast to possession of certain articles under s.15 below, the formula "has with him" infers the necessity of proximity to a prohibited item. Thus a trespasser who may have left a weapon outside, in a car for example, commits no aggravation (A.T.H. Smith, 28–55; see also *Webley and Webley* [1967] Crim. L.R. 300, as cited by Smith). Controversially, and perhaps harshly, to forget one may have such an instrument or device on one's person qualifies to aggravate the burglary (*McCalla* (1988) 87 Cr. App. R. 372). The harshness comes of the fact that it was always a requirement that the *entry* must be effective for the purpose of the intended burglary — which goes to specific design; thus it is arguable that the possession must be effective for the purpose of doing harm or causing fear; this surely cannot be said of a tradesperson who forgets he or she is in possession of an otherwise useless instrument that qualifies as a weapon under the new provision (see Charlton, 10.162). The classic excuse is that the item was for self-protection — as in *Stones* [1989] 1

W.L.R. 156, who said he was afraid of being attacked by a gang. In that case a conditional intent was inferred that if challenged during the course of the burglary, he would be tempted to use it. To take up a weapon once inside the house, however, is aggravated burglary (*O'Leary* (1986) 82 Crim. App. R. 341). An obvious issue is where a weapon is carried by one person accompanied by an unarmed accomplice. The accomplice, according to the law of complicity, must have knowledge of the weapon (Charlton, para. 10.162; A.T.H. Smith, para. 28–55); Alternatively, the companion to the armed burglar may be a principal in his own right if he has knowledge of the weapon on the person of the companion (see *Jones* [1979] C.L.Y. 411). Thus, a burglary may be a joint enterprise without an *aggravated* burglary being such.

A substantial change is effected by the draftsman to the meaning of "firearm" which extends the definition to a "lethal firearm or other lethal weapon," the qualifying characteristic would appear to be that such a device is capable of discharging any shot, bullet or missile. We see the addition of "air *rifle*" to the arsenal, but more significantly we see the inclusion of improvised or specifically designed or modified devices, which will be covered by the formula "any other weapon incorporating a barrel from which metal or other slugs can be discharged". It is interesting that the rather Hollywood-inspired term "slug" does have an appropriate definition according to the Oxford English Dictionary: "2 *a* a bullet esp. of irregular shape. *b* a missile for an airgun". The meaning of "weapon of offence" is substantially wider than under prior law with the inclusion of "any article which has a blade or sharp point" and devices designed for the discharge of noxious gas or things. We see immediately that so-called "mace" canisters, screw-drivers, carpet knives and possibly corkscrews are more safely within the definition. The significance in the change here is that there is no requirement that objects or devices with blades or sharp points be "made or adapted for use for causing injury", which was formerly the case.

Prior law is applicable for the most part to the remainder of this provision with only subtle changes to the meaning of imitation firearm to mean anything which is not a firearm but which has the appearance of one — this excludes from this specific meaning an imitation firearm which may discharge a missile of some description (which presumably will now be included within the meaning of firearm).

Robbery

14.—(1) A person is guilty of robbery if he or she steals, and immediately before or at the time of doing so, and in order to do so, uses force on any person or puts or seeks to put any person in fear of being then and there subjected to force.

(2) A person guilty of robbery is liable on conviction on indictment to imprisonment for life.

GENERAL NOTE

There is no change to the wording of the section which is replaced by s.14, which is of itself testimony to the fact that the wording has been deemed workable and satisfactory. Furthermore, the section is a replication of s.8 of the English Theft Act 1968; and that Act, with the possible exception of the timing of the force and degree of force necessary, has not thrown up too many problems of interpretation. Robbery is theft, aggravated by the threat or use of force. Ashworth synopsises the offence as follows: "... there are three ways of committing robbery – using force, putting someone in fear, or seeking to put someone in fear" (Andrew Ashworth, "Robbery re-assessed" [2002] Crim. L.R. 885), Thus, the threat may be implied — for example, where it is indicated that failure to co-operate in the theft will result in the use of force. Neither is there any doubt about the use of imitation weapons to commit this offence (*ibid.*). The gravity of the threat is not decisive, and it does not matter that the threat would not amount to an assault. Importantly, the threat of force upon such a person may have been made at an earlier time and understood by both parties to be an ongoing proposition; conceivably a victim might exist in a state of intimidation — without actual manifestation of any force — until such time as he or she openly hands a thing over and a robbery is committed (see *Donaghy and Marshall* [1981] Crim. L.R. 644). Similarly, the victim may not notice the effects of any application of force until a later time — this is generally unimportant for the offence of robbery (*Tennant* [1976] Crim. L.R. 133).

The theft must arguably be complete for the robbery charge to stand. The theft may subsequently be foiled but where there is an adverse interference with property rights, theft occurs, so circumstances may still infer robbery (*Anderton* (1980) 71 Cr. App. R. 104). Appropriation will be in the form of taking (*cf.* Andrews *Robbery* [1966] Crim. L.R. 524). Robbery must be distinguished, though doubtless with some caution in practice, with re-possessing a thing which is the rightful possession of the aggressor – this is merely assault and not robbery (*Skivington* [1968] 1 All E.R. 483; however, see *Robinson* [1977] Crim. L.R. 173). This introduces the claim of right, which may be a defence against the essential element here of theft. A defendant may feel that he or she has a right of distress for a debt owing to him or her; separate provision is made for demands which cause distress or alarm in the Non-Fatal Offences Against the Person Act considered below. A person will clearly only commit robbery by something *at the time* which consists of more than mere "unwarranted menaces" or "demands causing alarm", for such would be:

1. (for debts) an offence under s.11 of the Fatal Offences Against the Person Act 1997 of making any demand for payment of a debt so frequently as to subject the debtor or a member of the family of the debtor to alarm, distress or humiliation (demands for payment are also an offence under that section where they falsely create apprehension of impending criminal proceedings or enforcement of an official nature), or

2. (to make gain or cause loss) blackmail under the Criminal Justice (Public Order) Act 1994, which provides in s.17(2)(*a*) that a demand with menaces shall be unwarranted unless the person making it does so in the belief that he or she has reasonable grounds for making the demand, and that the use of the menaces is a proper means of reinforcing the demand. The demand being "unwarranted" depends on the objective virtue of the defendant's claim as to the propriety of the use of a menace to secure it; thus

    "no assistance is given to any defendant, even a fanatic or a deranged idealist, who knows or suspects that his threat, or the act threatened, is criminal, but believes it to be justified by his end or his peculiar circumstances .... And where, as here, the threats were to do acts which any sane man knows to be against the laws of every civilised country no jury would hesitate long before dismissing the contention that the defendant genuinely believed the threats to be a proper means of reinforcing even a legitimate demand" (*R. v. Harvey, Ulyelt and Plummer* (1980) 72 Cr. App. R. 139).

We might note that the former is a summary offence and one not particularly central to the criminal law, as suggested by the L.R.C.'s lacklustre regard for it (L.R.C. 45/94, p.258). The second offence, whilst appearing to concern "menaces", intends that word to fall well short of the apprehension of fear under this section. This is despite, perhaps, the proper meaning of the term which seems primarily threats of violence and only *including* threats of any action detrimental to or unpleasant to the person addressed (*Thorne* [1937] A.C. 797; see dictum of Lord Wright at 817). It is submitted that the legislature in s.17 intended the latter import only.

The force must be real and noticed and must linger for a time, however short, in order for deliberate intimidation to produce the fear necessary to qualify as robbery and not simply theft (however, see A.T.H. Smith, p. 407; the C.L.R.C. did not "regard mere snatching of property, such as a handbag, from an unresisting owner as using force for the purpose of the definition", C.L.R.C. Report, para. 65). Thus, shoplifting and in some circumstances even bag snatching do not qualify as robbery where the contact between defendant and victim is fleeting. The courts in England do not appear to have taken up this view (*Clouden* [1987] Crim. L.R. 56). Interestingly, however, the word "force" is used and not "violence" as it was under the original Larceny Act. This would suggest that something less than brute or even directed force was required. It is submitted, however, that the force contemplated is *directed*, and not incidental, force. Thus "jostling" or inadvertently bumping into someone so that he or she loses balance would not suffice as "force" within the meaning in the provision (see, however, the opposite position held in *Dawson and James* (1976) 64 Cr. App. Rep. 170). The conspicuous absence of any attempt to makes distinctions in the gravity of the various means by which the definition is satisfied makes for clear inequity and disparity. *Ashworth* argues that "[t]he single offence is extraordinarily broad. The maximum penalty for theft is 7 years' [in our statute it is ten years] imprisonment; but, where force or the threat of force is used in order to steal, the category of robbery covers everything from a push or a raised hand in order to snatch a bag, to the most violent robbery of a security vehicle with guns fired and so forth. The single maximum penalty, life imprisonment, covers the whole range" (Andrew Ashworth, "Robbery Re-assessed" [2002] Crim. L.R. 855). Furthermore, we should remember that the genesis of robbery is stealing, which is made possible by the use of force — incidental force used to convert and enlarge the offence is prosecutorial overkill (see early development of the law in *Harman's Case* (1620) 2 Roll Rep. 154). The current provision retains the requirement of "in order to do so."

The target of the force may be property or "any" person, and it is for the jury to decide whether or not it was sought, by the force, to put the victim in fear. Reference to "any person" means that the person the subject of the threat does not have to care one way or another if the property is stolen. It is necessary only that the owner knows about the threat — it does not matter against whom the threat is made (however, see the case of *Reane* (1794) 2 Leach 616).

Though it is true that "[t]he essence of the offence is a stealing with the intentional accompaniment of the use or threat of force against any *person*" (Charlton, 10.155), it is established law that the distinction between property and force against a person should be determined by the jury (as recommended by the Law Reform Commission (L.R.C. 43/92) as cited by the Court of Criminal Appeal in *People (DPP) v. Joseph Mangan* unreported, January 20, 1995; see also *Dawson and James* (1976) 64 Cr. App. Rep. 170). Similarly, the ultimate effect of the force is relatively unimportant — it is the use of force and the intent with which it is used that is the requirement for the offence which, from a reading of the section, may not even be successful in putting the victim in fear.

The temporal aspect is specific — the force must be applied "immediately before, or at the time of" stealing to be robbery. Thus there should be no confusion with offences formerly known as blackmail (see above). The term "immediately before or at the time" of the stealing seems to solve the dilemma of a threat procuring theft which is made over the phone. The sniper rifle and mobile phone scenario suggested by Charlton, however, may well be robbery (para. 10.151). A criticism which arises from the temporal restriction is that force used *after* the taking cannot form part of the robbery. This would appear to even cover situations where it can be shown that the thief had the prior intention to apply the force (see L.R.C. 43/92, p.123). Charlton takes the view that courts will treat acts of force purported to be done in the course of the theft, for instance in the premises of a bank, as part of a robbery (para. 10.151). It is submitted that the temporal issue is quite strict ("then and there"), and a purposive interpretation may at most include force applied within the purpose and design of the theft as a whole and thus be "at the time" of stealing. This may be the net effect of the discussion in Charlton but those learned authors cite the case of *Hale* ((1978) 68 Cr. App. R. 415), which does not illustrate an instance of force which is arguably *post delictum*. It is common sense that, as in *Hale*, the tying-up downstairs of the owner by one robber while a second robber in concert takes the jewellery from upstairs should not be separated by a strict temporal view of the definition, and result in acquittal. But using force *outside* against a person who is trying to apprehend the robber is separate both in time and, arguably, context (*Harman's* case). A.T.H. Smith makes the valid point that "the inclusion of the reference to 'immediately before' coupled with the omission of any reference to 'immediately after' makes it impossible to introduce the latter phrase as a matter of genuine implication" (see paras. 14–30 to 14–33 at p.414). Interestingly, while the Irish legislature chose not to include it, the Canadian provision provides for force applied immediately *after* the stealing (Canadian Criminal Code, s.343).

Possession of certain articles

15.—(1) A person who is, when not at his or her place of residence, in possession of any article with the intention that it be used in the course of or in connection with—

  (*a*) theft or burglary,

  (*b*) an offence under *section 6* or *7*,

  (*c*) an offence under *section 17* (blackmail, extortion, demanding money with menaces) of the Criminal Justice (Public Order) Act, 1994, or

  (*d*) an offence under section 112 (taking a vehicle without lawful authority) of the Road Traffic Act, 1961,

is guilty of an offence.

(2) A person who, without lawful authority or reasonable excuse, is in possession of any article made or adapted for use in the course of or in connection with the commission of an offence referred to in *paragraphs* (*a*) to (*d*) of *subsection* (*1*) is guilty of an offence.

(3) Where a person is convicted of an offence under this section, the court may order that any article for the possession of which he or she was so convicted shall be forfeited and either destroyed or disposed of in such manner as the court may determine.

(4) An order under *subsection* (*3*) shall not take effect until the ordinary time for instituting an appeal against the conviction or order concerned has expired or, where such an appeal is instituted, until it or any further appeal is finally decided or abandoned or the ordinary time for instituting any further appeal has expired.

(5) A person guilty of an offence under this section is liable on conviction on indictment to a fine or imprisonment for a term not exceeding 5 years or both.

General Note

This is an offence traditionally associated with house-breaking implements such as a jemmy, key, picklock, crow, jack or bit found on the person of someone suspiciously watching or approaching a house at night. However, it was never an offence merely to "case the joint" (Charlton, 10.168). The items listed come from the provisions of s.28 of the Larceny Act 1916, which were amended by the Larceny Act 1990 and have now been repealed and replaced by the current section. In fact, this offence is used for the prosecution of offences as different and sophisticated as A.T.M. card theft by use of the so-called "Lebanese loop", a device which retains an A.T.M. card after it is introduced into a cash machine and to be retrieved by the offender later for theft from the account. A person may be guilty of an offence under this section regardless of the circumstances of its discovery, if it can be attributed to the possession of a person. The new section uses the phrase "residence" instead of the antiquated "abode". The English courts have interpreted this to include places where the accused intended to abide with emphasis on some degree of permanency at a "site" (which infers a residence as both *in situ* and *in stasis*; see *Bundy* [1977] 2 All E.R. 382). The abolished term "larceny" is replaced with "theft", and the offence for which the article is to be used, once applied only to burglary, is now applied to:

1. theft,
2. burglary,
3. making a gain or causing loss by deception,
4. obtaining services by deception,
5. blackmail, extortion, and demanding money with menaces, and
6. taking a vehicle without lawful authority.

The long gestation period of this much anticipated revision of the criminal law in relation to property offences must be seen to favour the view that the wording is careful in its extent and scope. It cannot easily be said, then, that the list of offences, theft, burglary, etc. can be added to. It was said of the prior law, for example, that robbery could be included because robbery was a form of larceny aggravated by force. It is curious then, that the robbery section in this Act uses the word "steals" rather than the new equivalent to larceny, "theft" in s.4. Can it be said that robbery is a form of theft aggravated by force? The answer is probably yes, but then why did not the legislature choose to use the word steal, or simply add robbery to the list? S.15 consists of two offences which overlap. The first, in s.15(1), is simple possession whilst outside one's place of residence of "any article" with the intention to use it in one of the above incursions to property. S.15(2) is an offence, again of simple possession, anywhere, of a relevantly adapted article.

Possession

Possession has long been a difficult concept to fully define (See comments of Parker L.C.J. in *Towers & Co. v. Gray* [1961] 2 Q.B. 351). Possession is understood as control over and knowledge of the suspect items, whether or not the accused has actual custody of them (*People (A.G.) v. Lawless* (1968) 1 Frewen 338 at 342). Indeed, the actual manual possession or touch of the goods is not necessary; it is sufficient if the accused has such control over the items that they would be forthcoming if he or she ordered it (Archbold (36th ed.), para. 2096). The removal from the original Larceny Act of the words "found in possession", is to be replaced simply by "possession" and puts paid to any suggestion that proximity is required. Nor is there any requirement that the accused be in possession at any particular stage or time. But then, constructive possession may also be found; an accused "cannot be said to have constructive possession of it unless it is in the actual possession of some other person over whom he has control so that it would be available to him if he wanted it" (*Minister for Posts and Telegraphs v. Campbell* [1966] I.R. 69 at 73). This latter case goes on to establish that: "[n]ormally speaking, a person can properly be said to be in possession of the contents of his own dwelling house, but only if he is aware of what it contains" (*per* Davitt P., *ibid.*). Awareness here refers to the *actus reus* element of the offence and means knowledge of its existence only without specific knowledge of its qualities (*Warner v. Metropolitan Police Commissioner* [1969] 1 A.C. 256).

This is not to say that a custodian is necessarily in possession, nor is he or she in "sole" possession (see also *People (A.G.) v. Kelly and Robinson* (1953) 1 Frewen 147 at 149–50). The custodian may well be innocently entrusted with keeping articles (*Sullivan v. Earl of Caithness* [1976] Q.B. 966 at 969 *et seq.*). He or she might keep them in the course of his or her employment where the true possessor for the purpose of this Act is the person who entrusted them to him or her (McCutcheon, ICLSA 90/9–05, 9–04). See further in the context of possession of a firearm, *People (AG) v. Foley* [1995] 1 I.R. 262.

The Mental Element

A mental element is a requirement under both s.15(1) and (2); this must be so in the absence of any indication that strict liability should apply (McCutcheon ICLSA 90/9–05). Thus, an intention is required in s.15(1), and knowledge is required in s.15(2). The requirement of knowledge relates to whether an item was made or made for relevant use. Absence of this knowledge under s.15(2) deprives the prosecution of the necessary proofs. Intention will be inferred from the circumstances of the case and we know from the above that the prohibited article does not need to be in the personal possession of the accused. Equally, the intent may extend to use by another of the article. It is implicit in s.15(2) — even though it appears not to require intent — that reasonable excuse will infer the absence of intention. The apparent onus of "reasonable excuse" placed upon the defendant must be understood in the light of the express withdrawal of such an onus in the original provision: s.28(2) of the Larceny Act 1916 contained the words "having in his possession without lawful excuse (*the proof whereof shall lie on such person*) any key, picklock, crow, [..., etc.]" (emphasis added). The "proof whereof" must therefore lie elsewhere. It is submitted that it lies with the prosecution who must disprove whatever lawful authority or excuse is offered in defence. The standard of this proof is not defined nor has it reached any accepted judicial parameters; see *R v. Patterson* [1962] 2 Q.B. 429 at 435:

> "the prosecution must prove the defendant was found in possession of ... either an implement ... capable in fact of being used as a housebreaking implement from its common, though not exclusive, use for that purpose, or from the particular circumstances of the case in question. Once possession of such an implement has been shown, the burden shifts to the defence to prove on the balance of probabilities that there was a lawful excuse for his possession of the implements at the item and place in question."

In that case, although the accused gave the excuse that he was carrying a hammer and screw driver in order to do work on the exhaust of his car, he was in fact found at night 150 yards away from the car in a florist's shop that had been broken into with the items on his person and his hand on the till. Needless to say, given the then emphasis on "night time" under the old provision, he was convicted; see also *R. v. Ward* [1915] 3 K.B. 696 at 698:

> "... he was a bricklayer. That being so, and the tools being admittedly bricklayer's tools, the appellant had established *prima facie* that he had a lawful excuse for being in the possession of the tools, and the onus was shifted on to the prosecution to prove to the satisfaction of the jury, if they could, from the other circumstances of the case that the appellant was not in the possession of the tools for an innocent purpose but for the purpose of housebreaking", *per* Reading L.C.J.).

One must assume that the time of day the accused is found with implements is no longer to be considered, as the express requirement of "night time" in the original offence under the Larceny Act 1916 was removed. It might not be irrelevant, however, that the accused person is not only equipped but is dressed in a manner suggesting intention to commit a theft. We might remember the old provision contained reference to having one's face blackened which also was expressly removed from the 1916 statute.

S.15(1) retains the defence that the accused is at his place of residence, but it is nevertheless a wider offence than its predecessor, linked as it is to the intention of the accused who is associated with the article in question. S.15(2), as with the prior law, applies irrespective of being at or in one's place of abode and focuses not on the intention the accused may have, but the use for which the article has been adapted or designed. It does not matter that the article may be put to, or retains, its innocent purpose (*Simpson* [1982] 1 W.L.R. 1494). For the very reason that the offence in s.15(2) tends not to focus on intent, there is a residual defence of reasonable excuse or lawful authority. It is not, however, an excuse that the implement was to be used by someone else (*Ellames* [1974] 1 W.L.R. 1391; note the English provision requires the accused to "have with him or her" such articles — rather than the more specialised Irish formula to possess them). No specific "job" (meaning proposed place and/or victim) is required for the possession to be an offence. Conditional intention, where the opportunity arises will suffice to use the article (*Buckingham* (1976) 63 Cr. App. R. 159, a case concerning the slightly different provision of going equipped to steal, cheat, etc.). A distinction, however, must be drawn from the purpose of s.15(1) from situations where the accused person would use the implement if he got the chance (*Hargreaves* [1985] Crim L.R. 243, CA).

Intended Use

The formula "any articles intended, made or adapted for use" in s.15(2) is retained from the prior statute. The corresponding requirement in s.15(1) is "with the intention that it be used in the course of or connection with". Thus we have two avenues of prosecuting intended use — one specific as to place (residence) and prohibited activity but unlimited as to "article", and a second which is unlimited as to place but specific as to the quality of the article and prohibited activity (burglary, theft, etc.). Experience gained in case-law dealing with similar statutory provisions may assist in understanding intended use. It is not necessary, for example, for there to be an actual opportunity to use the item — merely that the possession be established and the use be contemplated in the event that such opportunity might arise (*Ohlson v. Hylton* [1975] 1 W.R.R. 724, a case concerned with s.1 of the Prevention of Crime Act 1953 and the carriage of offensive weapons; Lord Widgery at page 728 states that such an offence is not limited to instant use of the prohibited item but, "is concerned only with a man, who possessed of an [article], forms the necessary intent before an occasion to use the actual [burglary] has arisen" ("weapon" and "violence" substituted for context).

The express use of the words "made" and "adapted" go some way to explain the intended use; in *R. v. Simpson (Calvin)* [1983] 1 W.L.R. 1494 at 1497, Lord Lane C.J. certainly lays emphasis on the word "made" when he stated: "... the mere fact that a particular [article] can be, and perhaps often is, used for an innocent purpose does not necessarily take it out of the [relevant] category. That is the reason why we emphasise 'made' in the definition ..." ("weapon" and "offensive" substituted for context).

The list of articles to which this section may be interpreted to refer is potentially limitless. No attempt will be made to embark on a listing of them here. McCutcheon makes some helpful observations at ICLSA 90/9–05, 9–06 but more helpful is the test he endorses, that given by J.C. Smith, para. 371; that is to say the "but for" test — that a person would not be in possession of an article "but for" the imputed objective of burglary, or theft and so on. Finally, it is expressed in the section that forfeiture of the prohibited article is not mandatory. Thus the article may be returned to its owner to be put to its rightful and proper use.

PART 3

HANDLING, ETC. STOLEN PROPERTY AND OTHER PROCEEDS OF CRIME

Interpretation *(Part 3)*

16.—(1) In this Part "principal offender", for the purposes of *sections 17* and *18*, means the person who has stolen or otherwise unlawfully obtained the property alleged to have been handled or possessed, and cognate words shall be construed accordingly.

(2) For the purposes of this Part, a person is reckless if he or she disregards a substantial risk that the property handled is stolen, and for those purposes "substantial risk" means a risk of such a nature and degree that, having regard to the circumstances in which the person acquired the property and the extent of the information then available to him or her, its disregard involves culpability of a high degree.

(3) This Part is without prejudice to section 31 (as substituted by *section 21* of this Act) of the Criminal Justice Act, 1994.

GENERAL NOTE

Far from taking the Law Reform Commission at their word and making a single offence of theft and handling (L.R.C. 23/87, para. 136), the end product in fact devotes (at least in title) an entire Part to handling instead of the single section in previous enactments (s.33 of the Larceny Acts 1916–1990). S.16 is the interpretation section for Pt 3 of the Act, which contains provision for offences of handling, possession of and withholding information regarding stolen property. The formulas include the controversial ideas of the accused being "without reasonable excuse" and it being "reasonable to conclude" that the accused had knowledge that property was stolen. In other words, it seems the accused is to be put on proof almost at the outset in regard to certain matters. It might be noted that the old offence of possession of articles under s.28 of the Larceny Act contained the formula "without lawful authority or reasonable excuse". The old s.33 of the Larceny Act contained the formula "in such circumstance that it is reasonable to conclude that he knew or believed the property to be stolen". The wording in s.21 of this Act, however, goes as far as to say that the proof of reasonable excuse lies with the accused.

Much was said at the debate stage about the apparent shifting of the onus of proof onto the accused. Any apparent encroachment upon the right of the accused to the presumption of innocence should ordinarily be subject to close scrutiny, and should, strictly speaking, never be construed to infringe upon the inalienable rights of the accused. Nevertheless, such a step is not unprecedented and indeed would appear to feature elsewhere in this Act (See ss.21 and 4(3)(*c*); other instances of statutory presumptions against accused persons are s.24 of the Offences Against the State Act 1939, s.3(2) of the Offences Against the State (Amendment) Act 1972), s.4(1) of the Explosive Substances Act 1883, s.4 of the Criminal Justice Act 1964, ss.15 and 29 of the Misuse of Drugs Act 1977, ss.18 and 19 of the Criminal Justice Act 1984 and more recently, though in civil jurisdiction, the Proceeds of Crime Act 1996, which was specifically cited by the Minister in support of this Act (*see* 527 *Dáil Debates* Col. 967). It is now judicially accepted that presumptions can exist and inferences can be drawn which may put the accused on proof. It is difficult (however healthy it is to raise the issue) to see this measure being struck down for unconstitutionality given the position of the Irish courts in this regard, and most recently the dictum of McGuinness J. in *Gilligan v. Criminal Assets Bureau* [1998] 3 I.R. 185 that "the State in certain circumstances is entitled to require a defendant to rebut an inference of criminal conduct."

The concepts of principal offender, reckless and substantial risk are defined here for the purposes of this Part. For the application of recklessness, see comments in General Note on s.17. As to the scope of the "property alleged to have been handled" see s.17 below. Finally, the offences of handling stolen property under s.17 or being in possession of stolen property may in practice often rest squarely on the accepted doctrine of "recent possession". It is important to sufficiently appreciate the true parameters of this so-called doctrine; it proposes no more than an *entitlement* to infer guilty knowledge from the fact of possession of property which has been recently stolen (see *People (A.G.) v. Oglesby* [1966] I.R. 163).

Handling stolen property

17.—(1) A person is guilty of handling stolen property if (otherwise than in the course of the stealing) he or she, knowing that the property was stolen or being reckless as to whether it was stolen, dishonestly—

    (*a*) receives or arranges to receive it, or

    (*b*) undertakes, or assists in, its retention, removal, disposal or realisation by or for the benefit of another person, or arranges to do so.

    (2) Where a person—

    (*a*) receives or arranges to receive property, or

    (*b*) undertakes, or assists in, its retention, removal, disposal or realisation by or for the benefit of another person, or arranges to do so,

in such circumstances that it is reasonable to conclude that the person either knew that the property was stolen or was reckless as to whether it was stolen, he or she shall be taken for the purposes of this section to have so known or to have been so reckless, unless the court or the jury, as the case may be, is satisfied having regard to all the evidence that there is a reasonable doubt as to whether he or she so knew or was so reckless.

    (3) A person to whom this section applies may be tried and convicted whether the principal offender has or has not been previously convicted or is or is not amenable to justice.

    (4) A person guilty of handling stolen property is liable on conviction on indictment to a fine or imprisonment for a term not exceeding 10 years or both, but is not liable to a higher fine or longer term of imprisonment than that which applies to the principal offence.

GENERAL NOTE

Commercial theft is largely an activity dependent on those who assist in the offence by various means such as receiving, concealing or passing along the stolen effects. The offence now known as handling stolen goods is a widening of the original concept of receiving stolen goods. Theft is often motivated by the prospect of sale or reward. The section itself resolves the obscurity of word "believing" the property to be stolen by introducing the well-recognised "recklessness" formula, defined in s.16.

The notion of "dishonesty" is not new to this offence, nor is the exclusion of persons actually stealing (as it would be absurd to make it an offence to steal something and also to be guilty of handling it). There is a distinction drawn immediately between goods handled which are stolen and the obvious handling which will occur in the course of stealing. Thus, handling stolen property is an alternative charge to that of theft, which was the position under the prior statutory provisions and means a person cannot be convicted of both theft and handling on the same facts. Where the accused is clearly not the actual thief, this should not present a problem. However, the sentencing provisions express that the punishment for handling should not be greater than that for theft. This suggests that the offence of theft remains the "principal offence". Thus it might be significant that the provision retains the phrase "otherwise than in the course of stealing", which is a concept inferring duration. It is only where the stealing, then, has ceased or has been completed, that the offence of handling becomes relevant. The formula becomes a question, then, of whether the accused either *received/arranged to receive* or whether he or she at least assisted in *retaining/removing/disposing of or realising* stolen property for the benefit of someone else.

Receiving is imputed, or constructive, possession at some stage in the process through which the accused can be said to have participated in dealing with the stolen property. Arranging the "reception" is an extension of the original offence of receiving. A person arranges by some act of conspiring or agreeing to arrange the "deal" by which the theft becomes profitable. It opens up the possibility — which is the intention of the offence as a whole — to catch those who make it possible for thieves to realise the monetary value of their ill-gotten items. The essence of the offence is intimated also by the requirement in both paragraphs s.17(1)(*b*) and s.17(2)(*b*) that culpable participation in dishonest dealing must be undertaken for the benefit of another person. This is crucial if the indictment or charge consists of *retaining/removing/disposing of or realising* stolen property. It effectively means assisting another, whether by assisting in that other person's conduct or that person's obtaining reward (see *R v. Bloxham* [1983] 1 A.C. 109).

Retention goes beyond mere use (*R v. Kanwar* [1982] 2 All E.R. 528) or transitory holding — it entails the keeping or safekeeping of the stolen property. Of course, retention is made much wider by the inclusion of "assisting" in the offence of retention, which need only consist of concealment of the fact that property is stolen or of where stolen property is being kept (*R v. Brown* [1970] 1 Q.B. 105). Removal is playing some part in moving or transporting the stolen goods. Disposal and realisation both probably mean the end stage of the dishonest dealing with stolen goods; they may pertain where the property is alienated from the thief, which may be by means of conversion to some other item of value. Thus, the offender may never physically handle the property, nor does he or she necessarily come into possession of it. In this context, McCutcheon suggests it is better to think of the offence as being directed towards dishonest dealings in stolen property (McCutcheon, paras 152–161). As Charlton puts it, "[t]he concept of handling, a continuing state of affairs, like possession, allows for a conviction upon an innocent receipt and a later discovery of the true facts" (Charlton, para. 10.141).

In effect the offence in this section is so conceptually wide that there must be some measure of caution in dealing with the present formulations. Exhaustive definition is a pipe-dream and we suffer inevitably the tendency to itemise possibilities where the possible scenarios or permutations of human (mis)conduct are not susceptible to delimitation. The avenues chosen, beginning with "receiving" and widened to include ephemeral concepts like "realisation", prompt the question whether it is not better to trust a generalised offence to judicial construal. This, with informed prosecutorial discipline and the vital check of defence scrutiny may achieve a balance which no amount of hypothesis can hope to achieve (see the endorsement by our own Law Reform Commission of *English* criticisms of s.22 of the English Theft Act 1968 (L.R.C. 23/87, para. 108)).

Mens Rea

It is handling where there are circumstances which allow, without reasonable doubt, the reasonable conclusion that the accused knew or was reckless as to whether the property was stolen. Case-law in support of argument must be drawn carefully to avoid confusion with the now obsolete common law genesis of handling stolen goods, for instance the old rule that to aid or abet in the disposal of stolen property would not qualify as an offence under the old common law of "receiving" (*Watson* [1916] 2 K.B. 385). The mental element must be understood in terms of either knowledge (which is now a well established criteria, see *Hanlon v. Fleming* [1981] I.R. 489) or recklessness, and any familiarity with the prior mental element must cede to the new formula. Thus, we may no longer see this offence in terms of accused persons "thinking that such property was probably stolen". At one time it was of paramount importance to "know" of the nature of the property at the time one came to "receive" it (see amendment of the Larceny Act 1916 by substitution for s.3 of s.33 of the Larceny Act 1990).

The Law Reform Commission has long since sought to broaden the offence to the extent that the offence now includes the notion of recklessness (L.R.C. 23/87; though, as pointed out by McCutcheon, the offence as first modified bore more resemblance to s.22 of the English Theft Act than to the recommendation of the Commission, see generally *The Larceny Act 1916* (Dublin, 1988), paras 152–161. It would seem that the Commission has now been vindicated). The draftsman was wary of the concept of recklessness (in 1990 preferring the concept of "belief" as one easier for juries to understand (see 392 *Dáil Debates* Cols. 963–965)) and has sought to define it in s.16 by the use of the concept of "substantial risk", which is unfortunately itself, a contingent notion. The accused must run a "substantial risk" that the property might *turn out to be* or be *discovered to be* stolen, which refers rather to one's potential of criminal liability than to moral culpability. To be reckless, arguably the issue must have presented itself in the mind of the accused. Though surely not the intention of the provision, the idea of risk, in this context, carries the unfortunate connotation of "being found out", rather than conscientiously to "find out" the true state of affairs. Recklessness may no longer be subjective in the manner it had previously been defined under the concept of belief (see *People (DPP) v. Balfe* [1998] 4 I.R. 50 at 63), and yet we should note the use of both belief and recklessness in s.21 concerning money laundering. Recklessness is defined in s.16 in the context of substantial risk, however Charlton phrases this rather more subjectively as "the conscious running of an unjustifiable risk" (para. 1.84). S.16 adds further to the objectivity of recklessness required with the formula "having regard to the circumstances in which the person acquired the property". One almost feels that the notion that sufficient disregard for an offence must involve "culpability of a high degree" is an apology for the introduction of dispassionate objectivity to a moral concept established and confirmed in this jurisdiction to be a subjective one (*People (DPP) v. Noel and Marie Murray* [1977] I.R. 360; *People (DPP) v. MacEoin* [1978] I.R. 27). The prior law in this regard does not relate to theft. True criminal offences carrying the stigma of crime are more than a regulatory penalty and properly "require a definition that is set in the concept of advertent fault" (*Re The Employment Equality Bill 1996* [1997] 2 I.R. 321; [1997] E.L.R. 185). In other words, what this writer refers to as dispassionate objectivity is not a test which should easily determine a conviction of ten years imprisonment and an unlimited fine.

Property

There is a significant change in the provision for the scope of goods to which this offence relates. The prior law, by virtue of the now abolished s.7 of the Larceny Act 1990, specifically extended the offence to include handling of property whether stolen, embezzled, fraudulently converted or obtained by false pretences, demanding money with menaces and extortion. There is conspicuously no equivalent provision in this Act, but the definition of "stolen property" in s.2 above includes property which has been unlawfully obtained otherwise than by stealing. There is also (if less relevantly), in s.16, in the context of the term "principal offender", reference to persons who have "stolen or otherwise unlawfully obtained the property alleged to have been handled". The decision in *Gomez* [1993]

A.C. 442 will probably lead to a wide application of the law of dishonesty, and perhaps acceptance that obtaining by deception is also a theft. The offences of burglary and robbery are likely to construed also as including in them the offence of theft (*Smythe* (1980) 72 Cr. App. R. 8 C.A.).

A defining distinction must be made between persons dealing with goods which are identifiable as stolen property or assumed to be those which are lawfully obtained. We might remember that it is often possible to trace the origin of a particular item, as records of such have been specifically catered for as admissible evidence (Criminal Evidence Act 1992). The goods which are said to have been handled and which are said to have been stolen need not be preserved in their original form, and indeed any property which directly or indirectly represents or consist of the proceeds of the original goods are covered by this section (see s.20 below). The property which is the subject of an investigation and prosecution may later transpire not to have been stolen at all; nevertheless the accused may have understood the property he or she handled or possessed to have been stolen. The similar wording chosen — "A person is guilty of handling stolen property …etc." replacing "A person who handles stolen property … etc." would seem to suggest that the rule that the property must in fact be stolen (*Walters v. Lunt* [1951] 2 All E.R. 645) remains. We will see below that this rule is now circumvented by s.17(3). There is, however, some grammatical distinction in the phrasing, and it is possible in the overall broadening of the offence that the wording now chosen refers to the wording of the *offence* (guilty of "handling stolen property") rather than the true nature of the goods (see comment of McCutcheon: "The changes effected by the 1990 Act are the product of a manifest legislative desire to expand the scope of the law dealing with dishonesty" (McCutcheon, *Revision of the Larceny Act* I.C.L.J. 1991), a trend which is continued, it is submitted, with the coming into force of the present Act). This would be a somewhat radical departure from the prior law (see *People (DPP) v. Noel Fowler,* unreported, Court of Criminal Appeal, February 24, 1995). *Forsyth* [1997] Crim L.R. 581 confirms that a thing in action may be the subject-matter of a prosecution under this section.

"Stolen Property"

It has become a principle of the offence of "handling" that it may now stand alone from the offence of stealing which arguably must precede it. S.17(3) provides that a person may be convicted of handling even if the actual thief is not. We are concerned here with two distinct issues:

1. Where the property is not actually stolen there can be no offence of handling it. We have seen, however, that under the primary interpretation section above the meaning of "stolen" extends to unlawfully obtained property. Nevertheless, the decision of the House of Lords in *Haughton v. Smith* [1975] A.C. 476 remains the current position, *i.e.* that in order to constitute the offence of handling, not only must the accused know or be reckless as to whether the goods specified in the particulars of the offence are stolen goods at the moment of handling, but they must actually be stolen at that time. Thus, s.20(3) is of particular relevance and from which we may assume that property may not be handled as of this offence once it has been restored to its proper owner or once putative owner ceases to have a right of ownership.

2. Where a person is shown to have known or to have been reckless as to whether he or she handled stolen property, it does not matter that the principal offender is convicted or not. Where the person alleged to have stolen the goods is ultimately found to be innocent of it, conceptually a person accused of handling those goods may be guilty of this offence irrespective of the guilt of the alleged thief (or principal offender *per* s.16 above). Thus the decision in *Walters v. Lunt* [1951] 2 All E.R. 645 is bypassed; though the principal offender might be a child and therefore inculpable, the handling of such goods may still be an offence. This is by express provision in s.17(3) which permits the trial of a person charged with handling stolen property whether or not the principal offender is or was convicted *and* (giving the matter novel breadth) whether or not the principal offender is amenable to justice. This may be to take account of the difficult English case of *Close* [1977] Crim L.R.

107, which unequivocally decided (perhaps unfortunately so given the facts) that a failure to convict the principal offender does not mean the offence of handling cannot stand. A simple way of looking at the proposition is that a not-guilty verdict in favour of the thief does not, therefore, mean that the property is not stolen (*cf. Cording* [1983] Crim. L.R. 175). Such offences which might have once depended on the conviction of the principal offender are not unknown to Irish law. Another example would be the provisions of the Criminal Law Act 1997 concerned with penalties for assisting offenders. A person who is charged in the first instance with the principal offence but is *not* found guilty of it, may be convicted in the alternative of assisting in that offence or any other offence for which that person *may have been* charged as a principal offender. Thus, where the offence is shown to have been committed, a person may be convicted even where no conviction is made for the principal offence (s.17(3)). The meaning of "amenable to justice" must refer to some circumstance relating to the principal offender which makes it impossible to convict that person, such as death, flight from the jurisdiction or immunity from prosecution due to co-operation in the investigation of offences or diplomatic immunity (*Madan* (1961) 45 Cr. App. R. 80).

It is worthy of note that the Irish Statute book contains no specific legislation concerned with attempts. Instead the legislature relies upon crimes of intent and crimes specifically inchoate such as handling. The English decision in *R v. Shivpuri* [1985] 1 All E.R. 143 at 146 concerned just such an attempt and effectively reverses the important decision in *Haughton v. Smith.* This may be relevant in illustrating that it was within the contemplation of the legislature that a person may be guilty of *attempting* to commit an offence where the facts are such that an essential ingredient of the substantive offence is missing. Thus the view of Walsh J. in *the People (A.G.) v. Sullivan* [1964] I.R. 169 may not be lost on our criminal law (on which, see McCutcheon ICLSA 90/9–07, 9–12). This issue may well arise in the future and it would not seem to be covered by the present statutory law (though there is the rather weak conceptual possibility that "undertake" in this section contemplates an attempt).

Liability

With the commencement of this Act handling stolen property received a reduction in penalty from 14 to 10 years as a maximum though it retains the unlimited fine and is subject to the common sense of the gravity of the penalty not being greater than the gravity of the penalty for the actual theft (see the repealed s.33 of the Larceny Act 1916, as substituted by s.3 of the Larceny Act 1990 now also repealed; see *Explanatory Memorandum,* p.5). The formulation of the offences for the purpose of prosecution, should retain some measure of generality. The reason for this is the very many possible permutations of the offence. As said above, it is a single offence which can be committed in many different ways. Case-law and academic commentary would advise caution on the part of the prosecutor in framing the indictment — as he or she is not likely to find favour in specifying handling by assisting in removing the property where the facts show handling by receiving (See *R. v. Nicklin* [1977] 2 All E.R. 444). Finally, the offence of handling should be as set out above and not with reference to its statutory antecedents. Though these are helpful in understanding the genesis of the provision, they may also create the difficulty of applying concepts which are not strictly applicable to this new, and hopefully improved, formula. Thus, recklessness should not be confused with belief, and the offence of handling is surely to be construed as creating one offence — handling — which may be committed in various different ways (receiving, retaining, removing, etc.). The use of prior law should not go so far as to emphasise "receiving" (which *is* the origin of this offence) to the extent of creating an offence within an offence (see *R v. Bloxham* [1983] 1 A.C. 109; see also the General Note on s.18 below).

Possession of stolen property

18.—(1) A person who, without lawful authority or excuse, possesses stolen property (otherwise than in the course of the stealing), knowing that the property was stolen or being reckless as to whether it was stolen, is guilty of an offence.

(2) Where a person has in his or her possession stolen property in such circumstances (including purchase of the property at a price below its market value) that it is reasonable to conclude that the person either knew that the property was stolen or was reckless as to whether it was stolen, he or she shall be taken for the purposes of this section to have so known or to have been so reckless, unless the court or the jury, as the case may be, is satisfied having regard to all the evidence that there is a reasonable doubt as to whether he or she so knew or was so reckless.

(3) A person to whom this section applies may be tried and convicted whether the principal offender has or has not been previously convicted or is or is not amenable to justice.

(4) A person guilty of an offence under this section is liable on conviction on indictment to a fine or imprisonment for a term not exceeding 5 years or both, but is not liable to a higher fine or longer term of imprisonment than that which applies to the principal offence.

GENERAL NOTE

Possession of stolen goods is similar and yet distinct from handling stolen goods. They both concern the complicity of persons willing to "deal" in items of suspicious origin. Possession, however, would usually relate to an end purchaser rather that the so-called middle-man. In the context of handling stolen property, it has been said that "evidence that the goods were stolen might be provided by the victim, by the thief ..., or from the circumstances in which the property was acquired by the accused". For instance, it is fair to infer theft where valuable jewellery was purchased from the proverbial "chap in the pub" or at a ridiculously low price (McCutcheon ICLSA 90/0–07, 0–09). As with s. 17 above, persons actually involved in the course of stealing are excluded as it would serve only to duplicate offences for which sentencing could not justifiably be duplicated. Defences include having lawful authority or (presumably "lawful") excuse to possess the otherwise incriminating items. Without such a defence, it is an offence either to know or to be reckless as to whether the property is stolen.

Whether or not a person is in possession of a thing is crucial, and this seems to be a separate issue to that of the circumstances which infer possession where there are circumstances which allow, without reasonable doubt, the reasonable conclusion that the accused was reckless as to whether the property was stolen. The offence revives the relevance of the old concept of "receiving stolen property", which was an offence only if possession could be shown (*Watson* [1916] 2 K.B. 385). This was formerly the only form of what is now known as "handling", and was said to be flawed in the requirement to establish possession where an offender may dishonestly deal with or handle stolen property without ever actually coming into possession (see Charlton, para. 10.140). It was a question of fact, then, whether from the presence of goods upon the accused's person or property it could be inferred that they were there with that person's knowledge and sanction (*Cavendish* [1916] 1 W.L.R. 1083). Knowledge has in the past been inferred from a variety of circumstance (see discussion in Charlton of the use of the old s.43 of the 1916 Larceny Act (now repealed) which permitted a person's previous convictions and relevant profile to be admitted in evidence (para. 10.142).

The current section now assists us with the formula in s.18(2): circumstances which, in the absence of reasonable doubt, allow for a reasonable conclusion that the accused knew the property was stolen or was reckless as to whether it was stolen. Such circumstances expressly include the old criteria that the property the subject of the prosecution was bought for a price below its market value. This formula can be seen in practice from the case of *Oglesby* where perhaps the better interpretation is that the price for the goods was "very much under their value" (*People (A.G.) v. Oglesby* [1966] I.R. 16; see Charlton, 10.142). Generally speaking, the temporal element may be decisive, the inference being that property received very soon after having been stolen imputes knowledge of its provenance (*Oglesby, ibid.*). Fundamentally, the test was subjective under prior law where "belief" was a criterion (*People (DPP) v. Balfe* [1998] 4 I.R. 50 at 63). Now that criterion is replaced by "recklessness" which is discussed in the General Note on s.17 above. As to possession, the distinction in the statute must therefore be pertinent: mere handling (or manual manipulation as it is phrased in this context in Charlton) does not constitute possession (see *Frost and Hale* (1964) 48 Cr. App. R. 481). The section is therefore likely to elucidate its meaning in the form of charge to juries as to what constitutes possession, with the gradual refinement such charges receive over time (see Charlton, para. 10.140 citing *Healy* [1965] 1 W.L.R. 1059; 49 Cr. App. R. 77). As Charlton states: "a continuing state of affairs [...] possession, allows for a conviction upon an innocent receipt and a later discovery of the true facts" (para. 10.141). S.18(3) provides that a person may be convicted of possession even if the actual thief is not. The penalty can be an unlimited fine and up to five years' imprisonment and is subject to the common sense of the gravity of the penalty not being greater than the gravity of the penalty for the actual theft (see *Explanatory Memorandum*, p. 5). See also the General Note on s.17 above.

Withholding information regarding stolen property

19.—(1) Where a member of the Garda Síochána—

   (a) has reasonable grounds for believing that an offence consisting of stealing property or of handling stolen property has been committed,

   (b) finds any person in possession of any property,

   (c) has reasonable grounds for believing that the property referred to in *paragraph* (b) includes, or may include, property referred to in *paragraph* (a) or part of it, or the whole or any part of the proceeds of that property or part, and

   (d) informs the person of his or her belief,

the member may require the person to give an account of how he or she came by the property.

(2) If the person fails or refuses, without reasonable excuse, to give such account or gives information that the person knows to be false or misleading, he or she is guilty of an offence and is liable on summary conviction to a fine not exceeding £1,500 or imprisonment for a term not exceeding 12 months or both.

(3) *Subsection* (2) shall not have effect unless the person when required to give the account was told in ordinary language by the member of the Garda Síochána what the effect of the failure or refusal might be.

(4) Any information given by a person in compliance with a requirement under *subsection* (1) shall not be admissible in evidence against that person or his or her spouse in any criminal proceedings, other than proceedings for an offence under *subsection* (2).

GENERAL NOTE

   This provision is couched in terms which have provoked the scrutiny which must always be brought to bear where the onus of proof in any matter is placed primarily upon the accused, (on which see General Note on s.16 above). The gardai are given power under this section to require any person to account for property in his or her possession where there are reasonable grounds for believing that an offence of theft or handling stolen property has been committed. The garda must first inform the person of his or her belief, and an offence of failure or refusal will only arise where the garda tells the person in ordinary language of the consequences of a failure or refusal. To cater for the constitutional right against self-incrimination (but running the gauntlet, perhaps, on other constitutional grounds), failure or refusal are the only offences for which any information provided can be used in criminal evidence against the person or the person's spouse.

Scope of offences relating to stolen property

20.—(1) The provisions of this Part relating to property which has been stolen apply—

(a) whether the stealing occurred before or after the commencement of this Act, and

(b) to stealing outside the State if the stealing constituted an offence where and at the time when the property was stolen,

and references to stolen property shall be construed accordingly.

(2) For the purposes of those provisions references to stolen property include, in addition to the property originally stolen and parts of it (whether in their original state or not)—

(a) any property which directly or indirectly represents, or has at any time represented, the stolen property in the hands of the person stole the property as being the proceeds of any disposal or realisation of the whole or part of the stolen property or of property so representing the stolen property, and

(b) any property which directly or indirectly represents, or has at any time represented, the stolen property in the hands of a handler or possessor of the stolen property or any part of it as being the proceeds of any disposal or realisation of the whole or part of the stolen property handled or possessed by him or her or of property so representing it.

(3) However, property shall not be regarded as having continued to be stolen property after it has been restored to the person from whom it was stolen or to other lawful possession or custody, or after that person and any other person claiming through him or her have otherwise ceased, as regards that property, to have any right to restitution in respect of the stealing.

General Note

Although this provision merely continues the prior law in s.7 of the Larceny Act 1990 (now repealed), it remains interesting that the Act applies retrospectively to offences occurring before the enactment of this Act. The scope of the offences in Pt 3 are ambitious in as far as they relate to property stolen anywhere in the world — the condition being that the stealing would constitute an offence where it occurred (*i.e. lex fori*, on which see General Note to s.60 below). Though originally contemplated by the legislature to eliminate the problems which arose in cases like *State (Gilsenan) v. McMorrow* [1978] I.R. 360, the provision should prove as interesting as it could prove difficult in practice. Certainly the State cannot be used to harbour illicit items, nor can offenders secure safe hiding or haven for themselves or for the yield of any theft committed abroad.

The proceeds of theft, in the context of offences under Pt 2, are also stolen property, which can be unlawfully handled or possessed. Moreover, both the property and such proceeds may be passed on to a third person, who also becomes liable under this Part as unlawful handler or possessor (thus overcoming doubtful jurisprudence like that in *A.G. v. Farnan* (1933) 67 I.L.T.R. 208). This "continued stolen property" brings with it liability for the offence as set out above until such time as the property is restored to the rightful owner or restitution rights in the property relinquish. In theory, the property remains, in substance, stolen property no matter how many re-manifestations it may undergo. The chain of transactions is only broken when a representative item is acquired innocently (McCutcheon, para. 9–16).

The evidential implications of this are clear, as they are also in relation to the dilution of illicit proceeds with property legally appropriated — the classic dilemma being sums representing mostly honest money (on which see *A.G.'s Reference (No. 4 of 1979)* [1981] 1 All E.R. 1193; see comments of McCutcheon, para. 9–16). As to s.19(3), see comments at s.17 above, in particular reference to the case of *Haughton v. Smith* [1975] A.C. 476 which held that in order to constitute the offence of handling, not only must the accused know or be reckless as to whether the goods specified in the particulars of the offence are stolen goods at the moment of handling — they must actually be stolen at that time. Thus, where the property is in the possession of persons intending the property's return to its rightful owner (the police, for example), there is an implied consent to this possession, so it is no longer stolen (*Minigall v. McCammon* [1970] S.A.S.R. 82).

Restitution arises where the original owner has a *bona fide* entitlement to the return of the property. This will not be the case where the claimant purports to be the owner through a voidable contract. Property obtained by deception, then, cannot be give a right of restitution, nor can a *bona fide* purchaser who was unaware of any such right be dispossessed. There are other civil law devices by which a claimant may be denied restitution, for example the equitable doctrine of *laches* and the ever present time limitation on civil claims contained in the Statute of Limitations 1957–91. The Sale of Goods and Supply of Services Acts 1893–1980 provide for restitution also; they provide that an innocent purchaser *does* obtain ownership but that title is restored to the *original* owner where the thief is apprehended. However, care should be taken in this civil law approach, as it is argued that the property does not cease to be stolen because the property passes *bona fide* and then becomes stolen again merely by virtue of the apprehension of the thief (see McCutcheon, 9–17).

Amendment of section 31 of Criminal Justice Act, 1994

21.—The Criminal Justice Act, 1994, is hereby amended by the substitution of the following section for section 31 (money laundering, etc.):

"**31.**—(1) A person is guilty of money laundering if, knowing or believing that property is or represents the proceeds of criminal conduct or being reckless as to whether it is or represents such proceeds, the person, without lawful authority or excuse (the proof of which shall lie on him or her)—

(*a*) converts, transfers or handles the property, or removes it from the State, with the intention of—

(i) concealing or disguising its true nature, source, location, disposition, movement or ownership or any rights with respect to it, or

(ii) assisting another person to avoid prosecution for the criminal conduct concerned, or

(iii) avoiding the making of a confiscation order or a confiscation co-operation order (within the meaning of section 46 of this Act) or frustrating its enforcement against that person or another person,

(*b*) conceals or disguises its true nature, source, location, disposition, movement or ownership or any rights with respect to it, or

(*c*) acquires, possesses or uses the property.

(2) A person guilty of money laundering is liable—

    (*a*) on summary conviction, to a fine not exceeding £1,500 or to imprisonment for a term not exceeding 12 months or to both, or

    (*b*) on conviction on indictment, to a fine or to imprisonment for a term not exceeding 14 years or to both.

(3) Where a person—

    (*a*) converts, transfers, handles or removes from the State any property which is or represents the proceeds of criminal conduct,

    (*b*) conceals or disguises its true nature, source, location, disposition, movement or ownership or any rights with respect to it, or

    (*c*) acquires, possesses or uses it,

in such circumstances that it is reasonable to conclude that the person—

    (i) knew or believed that the property was or represented the proceeds of criminal conduct, or

    (ii) was reckless as to whether it was or represented such proceeds,

the person shall be taken to have so known or believed or to have been so reckless, unless the court or jury, as the case may be, is satisfied having regard to all the evidence that there is a reasonable doubt as to whether the person so knew or believed or was so reckless.

(4) Where a person first referred to in subsection (1) of this section does an act referred to in paragraph (*a*) of that subsection in such circumstances that it is reasonable to conclude that the act was done with an intention specified in that paragraph, the person shall be taken to have done the act with that intention unless the court or jury, as the case may be, is satisfied having regard to all the evidence that there is a reasonable doubt as to whether the person did it with that intention.

(5) This section does not apply to a person in respect of anything done by the person in connection with the enforcement of any law.

(6) This Part shall apply whether the criminal conduct in question occurred before or after the commencement of this section and whether it was or is attributable to the person first mentioned in subsection (1) or another.

(7)(*a*) In this section—

    (i) 'criminal conduct' means conduct which—

        (I) constitutes an indictable offence, or

        (II) where the conduct occurs outside the State, would constitute such an offence if it occurred within the State and also constitutes an offence under the law of the country or territorial unit in which it occurs,

    and includes participation in such conduct;

    (ii) 'reckless' shall be construed in accordance with *section 16(2)* of the *Criminal Justice (Theft and Fraud Offences) Act, 2001*;

    (iii) references to converting, transferring, handling or removing any property include references to the provision of any advice or assistance in relation to converting, transferring, handling or removing it;

    (iv) references to believing that any property is or represents the proceeds of criminal conduct include references to thinking that the property was probably, or probably represented, such proceeds;

(v) references to any property representing the proceeds of criminal conduct include references to the property representing those proceeds in whole or in part directly or indirectly, and cognate references shall be construed accordingly.

(b) For the purposes of this section a person handles property if he or she, without a claim of right made in good faith—

(i) receives it, or

(ii) undertakes or assists in its retention, removal, disposal or realisation by or for the benefit of another person, or

(iii) arranges to do any of the things specified in subparagraph (i) or (ii).

(c) For the purposes of paragraph (a)(i)(II)—

(i) a document purporting to be signed by a lawyer practising in the state or territorial unit in which the criminal conduct concerned is alleged to have occurred and stating that such conduct is an offence under the law of that state or territorial unit, and

(ii) a document purporting to be a translation of a document mentioned in subparagraph (i) and to be certified as correct by a person appearing to be competent to so certify,

shall be admissible in any proceedings, without further proof, as evidence of the matters mentioned in those documents, unless the contrary is shown.

(8) Where—

(a) a report is made by a person or body to the Garda Síochána under section 57 of this Act in relation to property referred to in this section, or

(b) a person or body (other than a person or body suspected of committing an offence under this section) is informed by the Garda Síochána that property in the possession of the person or body is property referred to in this section,

the person or body shall not commit an offence under this section or section 58 of this Act if and for as long as the person or body complies with the directions of the Garda Síochána in relation to the property.".

GENERAL NOTE

S.31 of the Criminal Justice Act 1994 is replaced entirely with a new money laundering provision which makes it an offence, knowing or believing or being reckless as to whether an item or amount is the product or the proceeds of crime, to

1. convert,
2. transfer,
3. handle, or
4. remove it from the State.

Interestingly, retaining the old concept of belief and co-aligning (or confounding — which may be the effect) with it the concept of recklessness, as endorsed by the Supreme

Court in *People (DPP) v. Murray* [1997] I.R 360, "recklessness" has now a firm foothold in this jurisdiction (see General Note on s.4 above). The prosecution need not show intention *per se* but must show more than mere negligence. They must establish the deliberate or culpable ignoring or disregarding of circumstances indicating that the property represented the proceeds of crime. S.21 inserts also the precise context of knowledge and recklessness as extended to the source of the property. Concerns expressed above must also be pertinent to assumptions about intention of persons with regard to property. See General Note on s.17 above. The new s.31 deals with knowledge and recklessness as to the source of the property, assumptions about the intention of persons with regard to the property, definitions of words and phrases used in the section and the proof of foreign law where criminal conduct occurred outside the state. The conduct set out must be intentional, and the defendant must know that the assets in question represent the proceeds of criminal activity ("criminal activity", according to the Convention, means any crime either specified by the Member State implementing the Directive — which is done in s.31(7) — or any crime specified in Art. 3(1)(a) of the Vienna Convention (see General Introductory Note). The offence consists of doing so to conceal or disguise generally the true nature of the transaction or to acquire or possess the amount or item, thereby assisting another in avoiding prosecution or a confiscation order. As with s.20, the scope of this offence is ambitious in as far as it relates to money laundering arising from anywhere in the world — the condition being that the conduct would constitute an offence where it occurred (on *lex fori* see General Note on s.60 below). Awkwardly, the offence of participation is imposed on all such offences. See further discussion, including the political motivation behind this measure, in General Note on s.23 below.

Section 31(1)

The formula "proof of which shall lie on him or her" is an unfortunate wording of an accepted inroad into the presumption of innocence. We have acknowledged in s.16 that it is not viewed as a constitutional breach to shift the burden of proving "lawful authority or excuse," however the wording here does seem a little over-confident of this current position. We note that the words "indirectly represent" have been dropped from the original version but are included in the offence by s.31(7)(*a*)(v) below. It is also interesting to note that s.31(7)(*a*)(iv) below describes "belief" as believing that something was *probably* so, which is an important limitation. The meaning of "recklessness" is described in s.16 above. "Belief" is a lesser standard of awareness than *certainty*, but clearly a higher one than *possibility*. Thus, in the U.K. it was required that the defendant could have had "no other reasonable conclusion in the light of all the circumstances" (*R. v. Hall* (1985) 81 Cr. App. R. 260, 264). We note that the section draws a standard somewhat lower than this statement of the law in the U.K. Proof of intent may be approached from a great many angles under this very dynamic section. For instance, where an accused's motive is clearly not to assist, or to participate or even have regard to the source of monies, the accused in other jurisdictions would have to be acquitted (*United States v. Campbell* 977 F. 2d. 854 (1992)). However, the availability to the prosecutor of a charge based on handling and/or recklessness as to the origin of the property will avoid this lacuna. The essence of money laundering is to mix illicit funds with lawful funds; this will result, for the purpose of prosecution, in the "tainting" of the lawful money as s.31(7)(*a*)(v) includes "part" thereof (see Ashe & Reid, p.44). Property includes "money and all other property, real or personal, heritable or moveable including choses in action and other intangible or incorporeal property" (Criminal Justice Act 1994, s. 3(1); see also s.31 (7)(*a*)(v)). In paragraph (*a*) [s.31(1)(a)], we note that the offence of "handling" such property is now placed at the heart of the definition whereas it had formerly taken up a separate and later subsection of the unamended provision. The more pervasive reference in the new section to handling will doubtless make recourse to that more amenable misconduct easier. Nevertheless, "handling" carries with it the defence of "claim of right", which Ashe & Reid correctly state has some quality to it as a defence (p. 66, citing *R. v. Bernhard* [1938] 2 K.B. 264). It is first of all subjective and is also well recognised from a time when the modern sophistication of terminology did not exist. Thus, a claim of right is by no means a technical defence and one which will no doubt need some extensive argument in given cases. The defence in this section seems unqualified as elsewhere in this Act, and so the cases which suggest that no legal or factual claim of right need be established still hold sway (*People (A.G.) v. Grey*) [1944] I.R. 326; *People (DPP) v. O'Laughlin* [1979] I.R. 85). "Criminal conduct concerned" in s.31(1)(*a*)(ii) surely means the principal offence and not the money laundering offence, thus this does not specify that it is an offence to assist a person to avoid prosecution for money laundering. In s.31(1)(*a*)(iii) again, though this does criminalise the frustration of the confiscation order procedure, it does not *per se* cover the lacunae in subpara. (i) above. Oddly, the provision as a whole chose to order the section by placing the core or essence of money laundering ("conceal" or "disguise"; see Ashe & Reid, p. 1) second to the conversion, transfer, handling or removing of property in order to do so. In paragraph (*c*) we note that this particular provision is contained in Art. 1 of the Directive but was left out of the original unamended s.31. The reason might be that it is certainly one of the more far-reaching implications of the Directive. It would appear to contemplate the end user, the person at the very end of the chain of transaction, who, it is submitted, must be the defendant. The provision may also contemplate any person along the chain of transaction who simply uses the property. Again, the implications are far-reaching, as are the possible evidential problems. Costelloe notes that money laundering is not the same as "money spending" (at ICLSA 1994/15-39, citing *United States v. Sanders* 929 F. 2d. 1466 (1991)), although "money spending" would appear to be covered by the word "use". In *Sanders,* a couple purchased and used several cars, not attempting to conceal their identity in any way. The cars were purchased with illicit consideration which would qualify under this Act as the subject of money laundering. The Court of Appeal held, in acquitting the couple, that the legislative purpose was to reach transactions intended to disguise the relationship of the items purchased with the person purchasing, or to disguise the fact that the proceeds used to make the purchase were obtained from illegal activities. Thus, it seems, the defendant must act with the purpose of "avoiding prosecution for an offence ...."

Section 31(2)

The penalties remain as originally drafted except for an increase of £500 on the summary fine. It was beyond the competence of E.U. institutions to impose upon Member States a (uniform) penalty, and therefore it fell to the member state pursuant to Art. 14 of the Convention. As to the uniformity, effectiveness and sufficiency of the penalty, the same considerations will apply as those discussed above in the context of the Convention on the protection of the Community's financial interests.

Sections 31(3) and 31(4)

Ss. 31(3) and 31(4) compensate, somewhat, for the terse reference to a shifted burden of proof in the opening sentence of the section. It [opening sentence or s.31(3) and 31(4)] seeks to ensure the propriety of leaving it to the accused to prove that he or she did not know or believe or was not reckless as to whether the property with which he or she was associated was the proceeds of criminal conduct. By inference, this procedure is applicable to establish whether they had reasonable authority or excuse. It is not express in the section that the accused person knows the precise nature of the criminal origin of the property. However, in the U.S. an equally open formula, *i.e.* that the property represents the proceeds "of some criminal activity", has not been so widely construed. In *United States v. Campbell* 777 F. Supp. 1259 (1991), knowledge of the particular unlawful activity involved was required (see also United *States v. Waters* 850 F. Supp. 1550 (1994), as cited by Costelloe ICLSA 1994 15–38).

Section 31(5)

S.31(5) provides immunity for those who might be associated with goods with a view to investigating criminal conduct under this section. This is implicit in this provision, but *express* in s.31(8) below in relation to co-operation under s.57 as amended.

Section 31(6)

This potentially controversial provision could have been more precise. It is primarily a continuation provision, which, so far as it goes, is unproblematic. However, "another" may refer to those assisting in s.31(1)(*a*)(ii)? Importantly, assisting is an express requirement and may not automatically be inferred; an accused person may attempt to conceal proceeds without ever contemplating assisting another (*United States v. Campbell* 977 F. 2d. 854 (1992)).

Section 31(7)

It is clear that participation and assistance are culpable under the section and that any "criminal conduct" under this section is an indictable offence. This does not mean that it must be dealt with on indictment, only that it is capable of being so dealt with. S.31(7)(*b*) uses similar language in relation to handling as that used in s.17 above.

Amendment of section 56A of Criminal Justice Act, 1994

22.—Section 56A (inserted by section 15 of the Criminal Justice (Miscellaneous Provisions) Act, 1997), which deals with revenue offences, of the Criminal Justice Act, 1994, is hereby amended by the substitution, for "Part VII", of "Part IV or this Part".

GENERAL NOTE

This technical amendment was necessary with the changes effected by s.21 which deals with money laundering. References to an offence under the law of a country or territory outside Ireland in Pt IV of the Criminal Justice Act 1994 will now be taken also to mean reference to a revenue offence

Amendment of Criminal Justice Act, 1994

23.—The Criminal Justice Act, 1994, is hereby amended by the insertion of the following section after section 57:

"Designation of certain states or territorial units

57A.—(1) The Minister may by order, after consultation with the Minister for Finance, designate any state, or territorial unit within a state, that in his or her opinion has not in place adequate procedures for the detection of money laundering.

(2) Any person or body to whom or which section 32 of this Act applies (including any director, employee or officer thereof) shall report to the Garda Síochána any transaction connected with a state or territorial unit that stands designated under subsection (1).

(3) A person charged by law with the supervision of a person or body to whom or which section 32 of this Act applies shall report to the Garda Síochána if the person suspects that a transaction referred to in subsection (2) has taken place and that that subsection has not been complied with by the person or body with whose supervision the first-mentioned person is so charged.

(4) A report may be made to the Garda Síochána under this section in accordance with an internal reporting procedure established

by an employer for the purpose of facilitating the operation of this section.

(5) In the case of a person who was in employment at the relevant time, it shall be a defence to a charge of committing an offence under this section that the person charged made a report of the type referred to in subsection (2) or (3) of this section, as the case may be, to another person in accordance with an internal reporting procedure established for the purpose specified in subsection (4) of this section.

(6) A person who fails to comply with subsection (2) or (3) of this section is guilty of an offence and liable—

    (*a*) on summary conviction, to a fine not exceeding £1,000 or to imprisonment for a term not exceeding 12 months or both, or

    (*b*) on conviction on indictment, to a fine or to imprisonment for a term not exceeding 5 years or to both.

(7) In determining whether a person has complied with any of the requirements of this section, a court may take account of any relevant supervisory or regulatory guidance which applies to that person or any other relevant guidance issued by a body that regulates, or is representative of, any trade, profession, business or employment carried on by that person.

(8) Where a person or body discloses in good faith information in the course of making a report under subsection (2) or (3) of this section, the disclosure shall not be treated as a breach of any restriction on the disclosure of information imposed by statute or otherwise or involve the person or body making the disclosure (or any director, employee or officer of the body) in liability of any kind.

(9) The Minister may by order, after consultation with the Minister for Finance, amend or revoke an order under this section, including an order under this subsection.".

GENERAL NOTE

S.21 above criminalises various actions which amount to money laundering. It also protects any body which chooses or is obliged to report anything suspicious. It will henceforward be an offence where a person knows or is reckless as to whether property represents criminal proceeds and acquires, possesses, uses, or alternatively converts, transfers or handles this property to conceal its true nature or help another person avoid prosecution or have such property confiscated.

Since 1994, financial institutions have had certain obligations to detect and report suspicions of money laundering, including the rather vague obligation to "know their customers" (see s.32 of the Criminal Justice Act 1994; see also s.57). S.58 of the 1994 Act penalises third parties who tip off those subject to investigation. The catch might be that a conscientious institution in divesting a suspicious account may reveal that the account is under investigation — this section provides that no penalty will arise where there is compliance with Garda directions. The provision provoked considerable concern as it was coming to its final formulation (see 527 *Dáil Debates* Col. 913), but was welcomed during parliamentary debate, particularly in relation to (or on behalf of) those financial institutions thought to be complicit in off-shore non-resident accounts whilst not aware of the implications of the accounts they were operating (*ibid.*). It might be noted that the concept of recklessness was included specifically as part of broadening concern for vigilance in the face of international terrorism, and money laundering in support of such activities. S.23 inserts s.57A, which gives further power to deal with such concerns.

The Minister may designate territorial units or states which do not support comprehensive vigilance or control of the activities which this legislation hopes to prevent. Moreover, an obligation is placed on corporate bodies, their management and their employees to report even a suspicion of transactions connected with designated places. The section encourages such bodies to develop supervision procedures which may ultimately be used as a defence by an employee who can establish that he or she followed such procedures. The involvement of employment bodies such as trade unions is obviously contemplated, and the courts may take account of guidance provided by such bodies. In the context of this system as a whole, it is difficult to see how effective criminal supervision can be within the employment environment. Policing such obligations will depend largely on private motives — these were doubts also expressed in relation to enforcement measures under the Organisation of Working Time Act 1997. In other words, enforcement may ultimately depend on self-interest. It may be that such vigilance is necessary, but the trend towards tougher measures should not be construed so as to infringe upon inalienable rights of the accused, nor indeed of private enterprise (see *In re Article 26 Employment Equality Bill* [1997] E.L.R. 185).

PART 4

FORGERY

Interpretation (*Part 4*)

24.—In this Part—
"false" and "making", in relation to an instrument, have the meanings assigned to these words by *section 30*;
"instrument" means any document, whether of a formal or informal character (other than a currency note within the meaning of *Part 5*) and includes any—

- (*a*) disk, tape, sound track or other device on or in which information is recorded or stored by mechanical, electronic or other means,
- (*b*) money order,
- (*c*) postal order,
- (*d*) postage stamp issued or sold by An Post or any mark denoting payment of postage which is authorised by An Post to be used instead of an adhesive stamp,
- (*e*) stamp of the Revenue Commissioners denoting any stamp duty or fee, whether it is an adhesive stamp or a stamp impressed by means of a die,
- (*f*) licence or certificate issued by the Revenue Commissioners,
- (*g*) cheque, including traveller's cheque, or bank draft,
- (*h*) charge card, cheque card, credit card, debit card or any card combining two or more of the functions performed by such cards,
- (*i*) share certificate,
- (*j*) certified copy, issued by or on behalf of an tArd-Chláraitheoir, of an entry in any register of births, stillbirths, marriages or deaths or in the Adopted Children Register,
- (*k*) certificate relating to such an entry,
- (*l*) a certificate of insurance,
- (*m*) passport or document which can be used instead of a passport,
- (*n*) document issued by or on behalf of a Minister of the Government

and permitting or authorising a person to enter or remain (whether temporarily or permanently) in the State or to enter employment therein,

(*o*) registration certificate issued under Article 11(1)(*e*)(i) of the Aliens Order, 1946 (S.I. No. 395 of 1946),

(*p*) public service card,

(*q*) ticket of admission to an event to which members of the public may be admitted on payment of a fee;

"prejudice" and "induce", in relation to a person, have the meanings assigned to those words by *section 31*;

"share certificate" means a document entitling or evidencing the title of a person to a share or interest—

(*a*) in any public stock, annuity, fund or debt of the Government or the State or of any government or state, including a state which forms part of another state, or

(*b*) in any stock, fund or debt of a body (whether corporate or unincorporated), wherever established.

GENERAL NOTE

This is a further extensive definition section in which terms and phrases as used in Pt 4 are formally defined. S.23 defines "instrument" to exclude currency notes which are dealt with in Pt 5 below. Instrument does, however, include money orders. "Share certificate," which is an instrument showing title to a share or an interest in stocks, debts, funds or annuities, is also defined.

An instrument, then, includes *any* document, disk or tape (meaning media for storage of information), postage stamp or postage payment mark of An Post, revenue stamp (meaning a fee-stamp or authorisation document of the Revenue Commissioners), social services card, cheque (including travellers' cheques and bank drafts) or credit cards (including those with cheque, debit and charge facilities), certificates (including certified copies and certified entries) of birth, marriage and adoption, entry and residence documentation (including temporary residence cards issued to asylum seekers (which in any case are *not* evidence of identity), cards denoting public service and admission tickets available to members of the general fee-paying public.

The section does not include "travel document," which it might have, but chose instead to use the principal travel document, a passport, or any document which can be used as one. Examples are diplomatic authorisations and ministerial entry and exit permits. Neither does the section use the word "visa," but does cover work permits and business permission (no mention is made of "work visa" or "work authorisation"). It does not specify, as it might have, the designated Minister who issues such authorisation or permission (the Minister for Justice, Equality and Law Reform or the Minister of Enterprise, Trade and Employment).

Originally the word "document" was represented by the archaic use of the word "writing" (*Turner*, p.947). The original meaning is borne out by the present formula to the extent that it does not include works of art, an issue which was debated in the case of *Closs* (Dears & B. 460, 169 E.R. 1082 (1857)), thus consigning forgeries of classic works of art to the apocrypha of misapplied legal terminology. The notion of instrument is somewhat removed also from such items as product wrappers as debated under prior law in *Smith* (Deers & B. 566, 169 E.R. 1084 [1858]). In that case, Bramwell B. stated that forgery was something different: "[f]orgery supposes the possibility of a genuine document, and that the false document is not so good as the genuine document, and that the one is not so efficacious for all purposes as the other." It is submitted that this dicta is helpful today in as far as it remains the case that the efficacy is important in distinguishing forgery from copyright abuse and passing off. An instrument for the purpose of forgery is created for the purpose of illicit substitution of the original and, being effective in that substitution, its purpose is to effect some objective by that substitution. The instrument itself is of secondary importance to that objective. Thus a forgery is neither passing-off, because it must be an exact replica, precise in effecting replication it is not copyright abuse, because the forged item is utterly without importance, value or benefit except in the successful attainment of something else; nor does it require interpretation as it is precisely drafted for the purpose of effecting that objective. It has no utility (functional or aesthetic) aside from conveying information (Smith & Hogan (1st ed.), p.469, referring to Glanville Williams, "What is a document?" 11 *Modern L. Rev.* 150, p.160). It is an *instrument* for that purpose. Thus, the word instrument:

> "is of some help in carrying the idea of a document which is made for the purpose of creating or modifying or terminating a right. A wrapper or a label would not usually be considered an instrument in this sense but a certificate testifying to the authenticity of a painting, to a man's competency to drive a vehicle or even a football pools coupon would be considered instruments" (Smith & Hogan, p.469).

This is not to suggest that the word "instrument" is *narrower* than "document," rather it carries, as suggested in this passage, a different import. S.38 of the Forgery Act 1861, re-enacted by s.7 of the Forgery Act 1913 (now repealed), used the word "instrument." The L.R.C. suggested that this may have been intended to give the term document a narrower import (L.R.C. 43/92, p.81). They accepted that this was not the case, citing *Riley* [1896] 1 Q.B. 315.

The words "formal or informal" are intended to avoid the inference that only public documents (*Sturla v. Freccia* [1880] 5 App Cas 623), for example a public savings application (*R v. Gambling* [1975] Q.B. 207), are covered but also letters (*R. v. Cade* [1914] 2 K.B 209) and betting slips (*R. v. Butler* [1954] 38 Cr. App. Rep. 57).

As with the general definition of a document, the implications of technology must alter our conceptions in relation to instruments of forgery (see definition of document in the interpretation section above). The L.R.C. has indicated the direction in which the necessary adjustments must be made in their analysis of recorded sound and information proceeding from the human mind (L.R.C. 43/92, p.77; see also English Law Commission report No. 55, paras. 24 and 25).

Forgery

25.—(1) A person is guilty of forgery if he or she makes a false instrument with the intention that it shall be used to induce another person to accept it as genuine and, by reason of so accepting it, to do some act, or to make some omission, to the prejudice of that person or any other person.

(2) A person guilty of forgery is liable on conviction on indictment to a fine or imprisonment for a term not exceeding 10 years or both.

GENERAL NOTE

The Forgery Act 1913 is repealed by this Act. Nevertheless, the generality of the definition may be taken to incorporate its more specific legislative predecessor (see interpretation section above). It does avoid the onus on the prosecutor of choosing the class of document in proceeding to prosecute forgery; now it is simply a matter of showing that it was an instrument. This creates the difficulty of broadening the scope of the offence at the expense of clarity. There are two crucial steps the provisions relating to forgery seem to contemplate:

1. The (*actus reus*) making/copying/having custody/having control of a false instrument.
2. The (*mens rea*) intention to induce a person to:
   - accept the instrument as genuine and, because of this,
   - carry out an act or be attributed with an omission to that person's prejudice.

The prior law, which must be seen as the root of the present formula, was one, *inter alia,* of making a false document (*actus reus*) with intent to defraud or deceive (*mens rea*). With the introduction of the word "instrument," the external element remains fundamentally quite similar. The unhappy use of the alternative "or" in the mental element, however, had caused confusion (see *Re London and Global Finance Corporation* [1903] 1 Ch. 728, pp.732–733 and comments of Kenny, para. 377, as set out in L.R.C. 43/92, pp.79–80). The new provision relies instead upon the word "intention" with which there is no problem, and "induce", with which there is. "Induce" is not explained or defined by the Act. Where the prior law was at pains to extricate the words "deceit" and "defraud" from ambiguity, we are now left with an unfinished revision, a new formula which is, sadly, incomplete.

Where a person makes or alters an instrument, he or she may be guilty of forgery if he or she does so in order to make another person do something (or omit to do something) which causes prejudice. There must be an intention that the forged instrument will be tendered as if it were genuine and that the person to whom it is tendered accepts it as genuine and, *because of this*, effects a prejudice on some person. Only prejudice is required, which is far short of actual gain on the part of the forger. Indeed, the concept of prejudice, which is not defined, is perhaps excessively wide. It is, in essence, an offence of intent — no further *actus reus* being required once the instrument is made ("made" being defined at s.30 below). The *mens rea* requirement in forgery was always an intention to defraud. The current section is merely that the instrument be used to induce another person — accepting it as genuine — to effect prejudice. The concept of prejudice is defined in s.31 below. There is a conspicuous failure to define the word "induce." Prejudice exceeds the traditional limitation of "economic loss"; moreover, the nature of the prejudice may infer intent — which is generally benefit to the forger. The case of *People (DPP) v. Malocco* unreported, Court of Criminal Appeal, May 23, 1996 illustrates that there is no requirement that a benefit accrue to the forger; the accrual of such a benefit is evidence from which the intent to defraud may be inferred. The notion of prejudice proves to be quite suitable when applied to cases like that of *Noel Harrington* (unreported, Court of Criminal Appeal, July 31, 1990), in which intent could be inferred from the disadvantageous exchange rate of dollar bills. The dicta of Lord Denning in *Welham* [1961] A.C. 103, however, illustrates perhaps the limitations (or possibilities) of the word prejudice with the following example: "If a drug addict forges a doctor's prescription so as to enable him to get drugs from a chemist, he has an intent ... even though he intends to pay the chemist the full price and no one is a penny worse off." The definition in *East*, Common Pleas of the Crown, Vol. 2, p. 852, cited by Keane J. contained in *Malocco* is more pertinent:

> "To *forge* (a metaphorical expression borrowed from the occupation of a smith, means, properly speaking, no more than to make or form: but in our law it is always taken in an evil sense; and therefore Forgery at common law denotes a false making (which includes every alteration of or addition to a true instrument), a making *malo animo*, of any written instrument for the purpose of fraud and deceit" (*Common Pleas of the Crown*, Vol. 2, p. 852).

It remains the case that the prosecution does not have to show that the intended inducement related to any particular person (in the context of prior law, see Kenny, para. 394, as cited by L.R.C. 43/92, p.80). Honesty and claim of right were defences to that offence (L.R.C 43/92, 6.16; Smith & Hogan (1st ed.), p.476, citing *Forbes* 7 C&P 224, 173 ER (1835) and *Parker* (1910) 74 JP 208), and in the light of the general importance given to the concept of dishonesty in the present Act, this is probably still the case

In the common case of a person impersonating the endorsement of a cheque which is not made out to them, the rightful payee of the cheque is bound by a duty of care to the bank to report the loss or suspected forgery as soon as he or she becomes aware of it and also to conduct his or her affairs so as not to facilitate any such forgery (*Tai Hing Cotton Mill Ltd v. Liu Chong Hing Bank Ltd* [1985] 2 All E.R. 344; *London Joint Stock Bank Ltd v. McaMillan and Arthur* [1918] A.C. 777; *Greenwood v. Martins Bank Ltd* [1933] A.C. 51). Unlike the prior law, the penalty for the offence of forgery under this section does not *expressly* depend on the type of document which is forged. This does not preclude this as a criterion in the apportionment of gravity by penal sanction.

Using false instrument

26.—(1) A person who uses an instrument which is, and which he or she knows or believes to be, a false instrument, with the intention of inducing another person to accept it as genuine and, by reason of so accepting it, to do some act, or to make some omission, or to provide some service, to the prejudice of that person or any other person is guilty of an offence.

(2) A person guilty of an offence under this section is liable on conviction on indictment to a fine or imprisonment for a term not exceeding 10 years or both.

GENERAL NOTE

This is a repetition of the definition of forgery in s.25 with the addition of the verb "to use" and the mental element of "knowledge" or "belief." The prior common law offence of uttering a forged document required it to be passed over or shown (Charlton, para. 10.181). Simple possession is not enough (Smith & Hogan, p.477). Passive acquiescence in the perpetration of forgery by another — even where benefit results to the onlooker — is not use (Charlton, 10.184). The onlooker, however, may be guilty of using where a forgery, whether successful or not (Charlton, 10.184), is effected by him or her through a third party who may or may not have knowledge of it (*Russell on Crime*, p.1285, citing *Palmer v. Hudson* (1804) 127 E.R. 395). The concept of uttering is effectively replaced with the simple use of the word "use." Whether or not this is simplification or an invitation to the broadest of interpretations remains to be seen. It is true that the word "utter" has always meant to "use" and therefore offers nothing new. Prior law suggests that "use" means to use, offer, publish, deliver, dispose or, tender in payment, evidence or exchange, expose for sale or exchange, or put off (Forgery Act 1913, s.6(2)). To produce an instrument is to show it, however briefly (Charlton, para. 10.184, citing *Radford* (1844) 1 Cox CC 168; *Ion* (1852) 6 Cox CC 1). The geographical limitations of the word "use" are not specified in the Act, but provisions elsewhere in the Act, such as ss.21 and 17, extend to conduct outside the State — therefore one assumes that this applies here also (*Owen* [1957] 1 K.B. 174; [1956] 3 W.L.R. 739).

Copying false instrument

27.—(1) A person who makes a copy of an instrument which is, and which he or she knows or believes to be, a false instrument with the intention that it shall be used to induce another person to accept it as a copy of a genuine instrument and, by reason of so accepting it, to do some act, or to make some omission, or to provide some service, to the prejudice of that person or any other person is guilty of an offence.

(2) A person guilty of an offence under this section is liable on conviction on indictment to a fine or imprisonment for a term not exceeding 10 years or both.

GENERAL NOTE

S.27 is to avoid doubt and extends the meaning of false instrument to copies of a false instrument where there is the attendant knowledge or belief. This section will also cover copy-and-paste situations such as that in the case of *Chow Sik Wah and Quon Hong* [1964] 1 O.R. 410, discussed in Charlton, para. 10.187.

Using copy of false instrument

28.—(1) A person who uses a copy of an instrument which is, and which he or she knows or believes to be, a false instrument with the intention of inducing another person to accept it as a copy of a genuine instrument and, by reason of so accepting it, to do some act, or to make some omission, or to provide some service, to the prejudice of that person or another person is guilty of an offence.

(2) A person guilty of an offence under this section is liable on conviction on indictment to a fine or imprisonment for a term not exceeding 10 years or both.

GENERAL NOTE

The comments at ss.26 and 27 are largely applicable here.

Custody or control of certain false instruments, etc.

29.—(1) A person who has in his or her custody or under his or her control an instrument which is, and which he or she knows or believes to be, a false instrument with the intention that it shall be used to induce another person to accept it as genuine and, by reason of so accepting it, to do some act, or to make some omission, or to provide some service, to the prejudice of that person or any other person is guilty of an offence.

(2) A person who, without lawful authority or excuse, has an instrument which is, and which he or she knows or believes to be, a false instrument in his or her custody or under his or her control is guilty of an offence.

(3) A person who makes or has in his or her custody or under his or her control a machine, stamp, implement, paper or any other material, which to his or her knowledge is or has been specially designed or adapted for the making of an instrument with the intention—

    (*a*) that it would be used in the making of a false instrument, and

    (*b*) that the instrument would be used to induce another person to accept it as genuine and, by reason of so accepting it, to do some act, or to make some omission, or to provide some service, to the prejudice of that person or any other person,

is guilty of an offence.

(4) A person who, without lawful authority or excuse, has in his or her custody or under his or her control any machine, stamp, implement, paper or material which to his or her knowledge is or has been specially designed or adapted for the making of an instrument with the intention that it would be used for the making of a false instrument is guilty of an offence.

(5) In *subsections (3)* and *(4)*, references to a machine include references to any disk, tape, drive or other device on or in which a program is recorded or stored by mechanical, electronic or other means, being a program designed or adapted to enable an instrument to be made or to assist in its making, and those subsections shall apply and have effect accordingly.

(6) A person guilty of an offence under this section is liable on conviction on indictment to a fine or imprisonment for a term not exceeding—

    (*a*) in the case of an offence under *subsection (2)* or *(4)*, 5 years,

    (*b*) in the case of an offence under *subsection (1)* or *(3)*, 10 years,

or both.

GENERAL NOTE

It was formerly an offence to possess a forged document knowing it to be forged. This idea is continued with the current section. Knowledge can be inferred from circumstances once they are established by the prosecution. S.29(2), however, places the onus on the accused to show lawful authority or excuse for having it, which is a device of established law (see discussion in General Note on s.16 above). This section not only provides for the offence of possession of instruments themselves but also of items used to make or procure such an instrument. Smith & Hogan suggest that the possession of a forged bank note would not be defensible on the basis that that the possessor kept it as a *curio* (p.479). Indeed, collectors are unlikely to receive any indulgence from the courts (see *Dickens v. Gill* [1896] 2 Q.B. 310).

Meaning of "false" and "making"

30.—(1) An instrument is false for the purposes of this Part if it purports—

    (*a*) to have been made in the form in which it is made by a person who did not in fact make it in that form,

    (*b*) to have been made in the form in which it is made on the authority of a person who did not in fact authorise its making in that form,

    (*c*) to have been made in the terms in which it is made by a person who did not in fact make it in those terms,

    (*d*) to have been made in the terms in which it is made on the authority of a person who did not in fact authorise its making in those terms,

    (*e*) to have been altered in any respect by a person who did not in fact alter it in that respect,

    (*f*) to have been altered in any respect on the authority of a person who did not in fact authorise the alteration in that respect,

    (*g*) to have been made or altered on a date on which, or at a place at which, or otherwise in circumstances in which, it was not in fact made or altered, or

    (*h*) to have been made or altered by an existing person where that person did not in fact exist.

(2) A person shall be treated for the purposes of this Part as making a false instrument if he or she alters an instrument so as to make it false in any respect (whether or not it is false in some other respect apart from that alteration).

GENERAL NOTE

An instrument is false as to its:
- form,
- terms, or
- alterations

where these are said to have been effected by someone who did not effect them or were effected on a person's authority who did not so authorise. Otherwise a document is false where it was not in fact made when and/or where and/or in circumstances in which it purports to have been. Finally, an instrument is false where the person who made it or altered it does not exist. An instrument is made once it is made false in any way, and it does not matter that it was already false in some respect. The use of the word "purport" would seem to cover situations where a person assumes a name, knowing it to be the name of another, but crucially, the "existing person" requirement leaves us with the issue of whether assumed names refer to existing persons, which arguably they do (see L.R.C. 43/1992, p.277; *Moore* [1987] 3 All E.R. 825. See discussion at paras 10.187 *et seq.* of Charlton). Offences, therefore which seem to be forgery may more easily fall to be dealt with under ss.6 and 7 above. The prior law of this specific provision is to be found in s.1(2) of the repealed Forgery Act 1913, which is sought to be simplified and improved upon in this section. The new section generally follows the same sequence, making sure to add the word "circumstances" in paragraph (*g*). This will take account of the principle in *Donnelly* [1984] 1 W.L.R. 1017 which considered and rejected the concept of "automendacity," *i.e.* that the instrument must not only contain false information but must itself be false. This would appear to extend the law far beyond those instruments purporting to be what they are not (on which see J.C. Smith (1984) Crim. L.R. pp. 491–492). Oddly, the new section omits the "whole or any material part" formula in the prior provision but is unlikely to be any less effective for that. The prior requirement that a document be false in any part that is *material* or at a time or place which was *material* is a limitation which is not included in the new section. Instead the new section uses inclusive terminology like "form" or "terms" and in para. *(e)* uses the widest possible formula, "alter in any respect" and s.30(2) refers to altering an instrument so as "to make it false in any respect." The notion is, however, limited by the opening clause of the section, that the instrument is false only if it *purports* any of the given criteria. Thus, meaningless and inconsequential alterations should not expose the maker to any liability.

Paras (*a*) & (*b*) mean that the document is a pretence in form because it is not in fact made by the person by whom it is said to have been made, nor is it made with that person's authority.

Paras (*c*) & (*d*) mean that the document is a pretence as to its terms because it is not in fact made by whom it is said to have been made by, nor is it made with that person's authority.

Paras (*e*) & (*f*) mean that the document is a pretence in as far as it purports to have been altered because it has not in fact been altered by the person it is said to have been altered by, nor was it altered with that person's authority.

Para. (*g*) means the alteration is a pretence in as far as it was not in fact altered on the date, or in the place or in the circumstance it is said to have been altered.

S.30(2) would appear to cover situations where a person may compound a forgery by "adding their own touch" to an already defiled original.

Meaning of "prejudice" and "induce"

31.—(1) Subject to *subsections* (*2*) and (*4*), for the purposes of this Part, an act or omission intended to be induced shall be to a person's prejudice if, and only if, it is one which, if it occurs—

(*a*) will result, as respects that person—

    (i) in temporary or permanent loss of property,

    (ii) in deprivation of an opportunity to earn remuneration or greater remuneration, or

    (iii) in deprivation of an opportunity to gain a financial advantage otherwise than by way of remuneration,

or

(*b*) will result in another person being given an opportunity—

    (i) to earn remuneration or greater remuneration from him or her, or

    (ii) to gain a financial advantage from him or her otherwise than by way of remuneration,

or

(*c*) will be the result of his or her having accepted any false instrument as genuine, or any copy of it as a copy of a genuine instrument, in connection with his or her performance of any duty.

(2) An act which a person has an enforceable duty to do and an omission to do an act which a person is not entitled to do shall be disregarded for the purposes of this Part.

(3) In this Part references to inducing a person to accept a false instrument

as genuine, or a copy of a false instrument as a copy of a genuine one, include references to inducing a machine to respond to the instrument or copy as if it were a genuine instrument or copy of a genuine one.

(4) Where *subsection (3)* applies, the act or omission intended to be induced by the machine responding to the instrument or copy shall be treated as an act or omission to a person's prejudice.

GENERAL NOTE

This is a definition section in which the terms "prejudice" and "induce" are formally defined. The section is a replication of s.10 of the English Forgery and Counterfeiting Act 1981. One first of all wonders whether a good lawyer needed the words "and only if" in the opening sally of this section. The words "if it occurs" may create the difficulty of ruling out attempts. Furthermore, on the face of it s.31(1)(c) seems to be somewhat contradictory of s.31(2).

Prejudice occurs where a person loses property or is deprived of an opportunity to earn (or where another is given such an opportunity) or to otherwise gain financial advantage. "Prejudice" was a word favoured by the English Law Commission in the Report on Forgery and Counterfeit Currency. The concept is applied to situations where a person or a machine is induced to accept a false document as genuine. As discussed in the context of forgery at s.25 above, an example given by Lord Denning perhaps usefully illustrates the limitations (or possibilities) of the word prejudice: "If a drug addict forges a doctor's prescription so as to enable him to get drugs from a chemist, he has, an intent ... even though he intends to pay the chemist the full price and no one is a penny worse off" *Welham* [1961] A.C. 103. Such a scenario would now seem to be covered.

If, as is suggested by the title to this section, the word "induce" is to be defined in this provision, there is clearly some want of efficacy in doing so. Neither is the concept defined in the interpretation section. This is a lacuna which may require legislative steps to be taken, and yet the English Act seems to have survived unamended. The focus in that jurisdiction has been on the word "prejudice", which seems to have been very broadly drawn to include liability in situations where, it is submitted, the concept is somehow manufactured. In *Campbell, The Times*, July 31, 1984 the defendant foolishly (as it turned out), to oblige a friend, endorsed a cheque made out to another which she lodged to her bank account, withdrew the sum and gave it over to that friend. There appeared to be no prejudice to another, but Lord Ackner on appeal found that the *bank* had been prejudiced by having had to accept a false instrument where it was under a duty to pay out only on a valid instrument (see also *Horsey v. Hutchings, The Times*, November 8, 1984). Whilst it might be a valid claim that the bank had been abused in some way, perhaps amenable to civil liability, it seems harsh that a criminal conviction should result.

PART 5

COUNTERFEITING

Interpretation (*Part 5*)

32.—(1) In this Part—

"currency note" and "coin" mean, respectively, a currency note and coin lawfully issued or customarily used as money in the State or in any other state or a territorial unit within it and include a note denominated in euro and a coin denominated in euro or in cent and also any note or coin which has not been lawfully issued but which would, on being so issued, be a currency note or coin within the above meaning; and

"lawfully issued" means issued—

    (*a*) by or under the authority of the European Central Bank,

    (*b*) by the Central Bank of Ireland or the Minister for Finance, or

    (*c*) by a body in a state (other than the State) or a territorial unit within it which is authorised under the law of that state or territorial unit to issue currency notes or coins.

(2) For the purposes of this Part, a thing is a counterfeit of a currency note or coin—

    (*a*) if it is not a currency note or coin but resembles a currency note or coin (whether on one side only or on both) to such an extent that it is reasonably capable of passing for a currency note or coin of that description, or

    (*b*) if it is a currency note or coin which has been so altered that it is reasonably capable of passing for a note or coin of some other description.

(3) For the purposes of this Part—

    (*a*) a thing consisting of or containing a representation of one side only of a currency note, with or without the addition of other material, is capable of being a counterfeit of such a currency note, and

    (*b*) a thing consisting—

        (i) of parts of two or more currency notes, or

        (ii) of parts of a currency note, or of parts of two or more currency notes, with the addition of other material,

is capable of being a counterfeit of a currency note.

GENERAL NOTE

The definitions of what is generally referred to as money, legal tender or notes and coins are defined. More technically speaking, we refer to "currency notes" and "coins" which are *either* (which is somewhat surprising) lawfully issued *or* customarily used or *would* be so issued. The English Counterfeit Act uses a further criteria — "is payable on demand" — which is not included here (s.27(1)(*a*)(iii)). This seems to include currencies awaiting issue or in reserve and currencies such as the U.S. dollar which are customarily used in countries where the native currency is unstable due to inflation. The regular definition (if we might use that phrase) of currency note or coin is that which is lawfully issued. Again this is *either* by our own Department of Finance or Central Bank or the Central Bank of the European Union, but also by an authorised issuing body in another state or territorial unit. The L.R.C. recommended "the extension of protection to all officially recognised international currencies and recommend that a similar provision be adopted" (L.R.C. 43/92, para. 33.5). The other state, however, must not be "the State" which must logically mean Ireland, as otherwise this phrase would exclude the "other State" but would not expressly exclude an "other territorial unit". The explanatory memorandum explains that "currency note" and "coin" mean those lawfully issued or customarily used in the State [capitalised] or in any other state.

The formula "reasonably capable" of passing for a currency note or coin of that description" falls short of the Law Reform Commission recommendation which was in favour of liability attaching even where the counterfeit note or coin was not reasonably capable of passing as genuine (L.R.C. 43/92, p.289), or at least falls short of specifically providing that in such circumstances the offence of attempt should lie against the accused. The English Law Commission had also been of the view that those attempting and not succeeding particularly well in producing a counterfeit should be liable to the same penalty as their more adept fellows.

As to the meaning of counterfeit, it is anything containing a representation of at least one side of a genuine currency note which is capable of being counterfeit. This is very wide

— considerably wider than the explanatory memorandum suggests — and would also *not* apply to coin. The memo explains it to mean things which resemble currency notes *or* coins. It would appear that a single incomplete currency note cannot be counterfeit; according to s.32(3), though it is sufficient that a note be complete on one side only, an incomplete note of itself must either be composed of parts of two or more notes or of part of one note with the addition of other material. Therefore, to tender a genuine but incomplete note is not an offence, nor — as is conceivable — would it be an offence to tender parts of the same note separately unless the note were literally spliced so as to represent two complete faces.

Counterfeiting currency notes and coins

33.—(1) A person who makes a counterfeit of a currency note or coin, with the intention that he or she or another shall pass or tender it as genuine, is guilty of an offence.

(2) A person guilty of an offence under this section is liable on conviction on indictment to a fine or imprisonment for a term not exceeding 10 years or both.

GENERAL NOTE

The offence here is to make counterfeit currency or coins with the intention of passing them off as genuine notes or coins. It was an interesting comment of the L.R.C. that intention is not of paramount importance here, as most people engaged in these practices will have no legitimate reason for their industry (L.R.C. 43/92, para. 33.6). The counterfeit need only be intended to pass as genuine within the European Union irrespective of where it was made (see *Explanatory Memorandum*). The intention, as elsewhere, may be inferred from the circumstances as established by the prosecution. As pointed out by Charlton, inference naturally arises from possession of numerous or a series of counterfeits which are unlikely to pass through innocent commercial transaction (Charlton, para. 10.210).

Passing, etc. counterfeit currency notes or coins

34.—(1) A person who—

    (*a*) passes or tenders as genuine any thing which is, and which he or she knows or believes to be, a counterfeit of a currency note or coin, or

    (*b*) delivers any such thing to another person with the intention that that person or any other person shall pass or tender it as genuine,

is guilty of an offence.

(2) A person who, without lawful authority or excuse, delivers to another person anything which is, and which he or she knows or believes to be, a counterfeit of a currency note or coin is guilty of an offence.

(3) A person guilty of an offence under this section is liable on conviction on indictment to a fine or imprisonment for a term not exceeding—

    (*a*) in the case of an offence under *subsection (1)*, 10 years, or

    (*b*) in the case of an offence under *subsection (2)*, 5 years,

or both.

GENERAL NOTE

The offence here is to "pass" or to "tender" counterfeit currency or coins with the intention of passing it as a genuine note or coin. This includes delivery of such counterfeits, and again there is an onus upon the accused to offer a reasonable or lawful excuse for doing so (see Genearl Note on s.16 above).

Custody or control of counterfeit currency notes and coins

35.—(1) A person who has in his or her custody or under his or her control any thing which is, and which he or she knows or believes to be, a counterfeit of a currency note or coin, intending either—

    (*a*) to pass or tender it as genuine, or

    (*b*) to deliver it to another with the intention that that person or any other person shall pass or tender it as genuine,

is guilty of an offence.

(2) A person who, without lawful authority or excuse, has in his or her custody or under his or her control any thing which is, and which he or she knows or believes to be, a counterfeit of a currency note or coin is guilty of an offence.

(3) A person guilty of an offence under this section is liable on conviction on indictment to a fine or imprisonment for a term not exceeding—

    (*a*) in the case of an offence under *subsection (1)*, 10 years, or

    (*b*) in the case of an offence under *subsection (2)*, 5 years,

or both.

GENERAL NOTE

This offence will not apply to persons accidentally coming into possession of isolated counterfeits through the normal course of commercial transaction. It is an offence under this section either to have custody or control *with intent to pass, tender or deliver* (s.35(1)), or of having custody or control of counterfeits which are known to be counterfeits (s.35(2)).

Materials and implements for counterfeiting

36.—(1) A person who makes, or has in his or her custody or under his or her control, any thing which he or she intends to use, or to permit any other person to use, for the purpose of making a counterfeit of a currency note or coin with the intention that it be passed or tendered as genuine is guilty of an offence.

(2) A person who, without lawful authority or excuse, has in his or her custody or under his or her control any thing which is or has been specially designed or adapted for making a counterfeit of a currency note or coin is guilty of an offence.

(3) A person guilty of an offence under this section is liable on conviction on indictment to a fine or imprisonment for a term not exceeding—

    (*a*) in the case of an offence under *subsection (1)*, 10 years, or

    (*b*) in the case of an offence under *subsection (2)*, 5 years,

or both.

GENERAL NOTE

It was a recommendation of the Law Reform Commission that not only the offence of counterfeiting but also the attempt be subject to criminal charge (L.R.C. 43/92, p.289). This is not specifically included in the offence at s.33 above. As to possession of the materials and instruments necessary to commit the offence of counterfeiting currency note or coin, it had, however, already been an offence to be in possession of forged seals and dyes (s.8 of the Forgery Act 1913) and paper or implements for forgery (s.9 of the Forgery Act 1913 — entirely repealed by this Act). In keeping with this broad approach, the possession of implements for counterfeiting remains an offence under s.36. It is both an offence to have in one's custody and control "anything," intending to use it oneself *or* to permit another to us it to make a counterfeit. This is extraordinarily imprecise. One hopes that a certain discipline in charging and reserve in judicial interpretation will prevent this imprecision becoming problematic. More focused and workable is the offence of having in one's custody or control anything *which has been specially designed or adapted.* One difficulty that arises is that the offence of custody or control with intent is punishable by a measure which is double that of the offence of custody or control of anything adapted or specially designed. Arguably, having in one's control a specialised device is more culpable than with "anything" that can be deemed to be an instrument whether or not it would be ineffectual or useless for the objective intended.

Import and export of counterfeits

37.—(1) A person who without lawful authority or excuse imports into, or exports from, a member state of the European Union a counterfeit of a currency note or coin is guilty of an offence.

(2) A person guilty of an offence under this section is liable on conviction on indictment to a fine or imprisonment for a term not exceeding 10 years or both.

GENERAL NOTE

Here again we see the formula "without lawful authority or excuse" as discussed in the General Note on s.16 above. This provision is limited to the European Union.

Certain offences committed outside the State

38.—(1) A person who outside the State does any act referred to in *section 33, 34, 35, 36* or *37* is guilty of an offence and liable on conviction on indictment to the penalty specified for such an act in the section concerned.

(2) *Section 46* shall apply in relation to an offence under *subsection (1)* as it applies in relation to an offence under *section 45*.

GENERAL NOTE

The effect of this provision is best analysed from the *penalties* section located at the end of the General Introductory Note above. S.38(1) is a significant extension of the scope of the offences in Pt 5. S.46 refers to the forfeiture of seized property and s.45 refers to the obstruction of the gardai acting on foot of a warrant.

Measures to detect counterfeiting

39.—(1) In this section—
"designated body" means:
   (*a*) a body licensed to carry on banking business under the Central Bank Act, 1971, or authorised to carry on such business under the ACC Bank Acts, 1978 to 2001, or regulations under the European Communities Acts, 1972 to 1998,
   (*b*) a building society within the meaning of the Building Societies Act, 1989,
   (*c*) a trustee savings bank within the meaning of the Trustee Savings Banks Acts, 1989 and 2001,
   (*d*) An Post,

    (*e*) a credit union within the meaning of the Credit Union Act, 1997,

    (*f*) a person or body authorised under the Central Bank Act, 1997, to provide *bureau de change* business,

    (*g*) a person who in the course of business provides a service of sorting and redistributing currency notes or coins,

    (*h*) any other person or body—

        (i) whose business consists of or includes the provision of services involving the acceptance, exchange, transfer or holding of money for or on behalf of other persons or bodies, and

        (ii) who is designated for the purposes of this section by regulations made by the Minister after consultation with the Minister for Finance; and

"recognised code of practice" means a code of practice drawn up for the purposes of this section—

    (*a*) by a designated body or class of designated bodies and approved by the Central Bank of Ireland, or

    (*b*) by the Central Bank of Ireland for a designated body or class of such bodies.

  (2) A designated body shall—

    (*a*) withdraw from circulation any notes or coins received by it or tendered to it which it knows or suspects to be counterfeit, and

    (*b*) transmit them as soon as possible to the Central Bank of Ireland with such information as to the time, location and circumstances of their receipt as may be available.

  (3) Counterfeit or suspect currency notes or coins may be transmitted to the Garda Síochána under *subsection* (2) in accordance with a recognised code of practice.

  (4) A recognised code of practice may include provision for—

    (*a*) procedures to be followed by directors or other officers and employees of a designated body in the conduct of its business,

    (*b*) instructions to them on the application of this section,

    (*c*) standards of training in the identification of counterfeit notes and coins,

    (*d*) procedures to be followed by them on perceiving or suspecting that currency notes or coins are counterfeit,

    (*e*) different such procedures to be followed in respect of different currencies,

    (*f*) the retention of documents required for the purposes of criminal proceedings.

  (5) Without prejudice to *section 58*, a designated body which contravenes a provision of *subsection* (2) of this section or who provides false or misleading information on matters referred to in those subsections is guilty of an offence under this section and liable—

    (*a*) on summary conviction, to a fine not exceeding £1,500 or imprisonment for a term not exceeding 12 months or both, or

    (*b*) on conviction on indictment, to a fine or imprisonment for a term not exceeding 5 years or both.

  (6) It shall be a defence in proceedings for an offence under this section—

    (*a*) for a designated body to show—
        (i) that it had established procedures to enable this section to be complied with, or
        (ii) that it had complied with the relevant provisions of a recognised code of practice,
    and
    (*b*) for a person employed by a designated body to show that he or she transmitted the currency notes or coins concerned, or gave the relevant information, to another person in accordance with an internal reporting procedure or a recognised code of practice.

(7) Where a designated body, a director, other officer or employee of the body—

    (*a*) discloses in good faith to a member of the Garda Síochána or any person concerned in the investigation or prosecution of an offence under this Part a suspicion that a currency note or coin is counterfeit or any matter on which such a suspicion is based, or
    (*b*) otherwise complies in good faith with *subsection* (2) or with a recognised code of practice,

such disclosure or compliance shall not be treated as a breach of any restriction imposed by statute or otherwise on the disclosure of information or involve the person or body making the disclosure in liability in any proceedings.

(8) Every regulation made under this section shall be laid before each House of the Oireachtas as soon as may be after it is made and, if a resolution annulling it is passed by either such House within the next 21 days on which that House has sat after the regulation is laid before it, the regulation shall be annulled accordingly, but without prejudice to the validity of anything previously done under it.

GENERAL NOTE

    This section, in similar fashion to the measures taken in s.21 above, criminalises various acts or failures to act where certain corporate or administrative bodies do not assist in the detection of the offence of counterfeiting. As with s.21, the provision provides immunity for those designated bodies disclosing or complying with the section (s.39(7)). Though the money laundering provision in s.21 above provoked considerable concern (see 545 *Dáil Debates* Col. 913), this provision passed without such comment. Designated bodies under the section are listed in s.39(1) but are considerably wider than this due to the extension of application to "any person or body whose business consists or includes the provision of services involving the acceptance, exchange, transfer or holding of money" (s.39(1)(*h*)(i)). The Minister also may designate further bodies or persons. An obligation is placed on the designated corporate bodies, their management and their employees to report even a suspicion (s.39(6)(*b*)). The section encourages such bodies to develop supervision procedures which may ultimately be used as a defence by bodies which can establish they followed such procedures. The issue of duties upon *victims* of fraud to disclose the misdealing is dealt with more fully in the General Note on s.59 below.

PART 6

CONVENTION ON PROTECTION OF EUROPEAN COMMUNITIES' FINANCIAL INTERESTS

Interpretation (*Part 6*)

40.—(1) In this Part—

"active corruption" has the meaning given to it by Article 3.1 of the First Protocol;

"Community official" has the meaning given to it by Article 1.1(*b*) of the First Protocol;

"Convention" means the Convention drawn up on the basis of Article K.3 of the Treaty on European Union, on the protection of the European Communities' financial interests done at Brussels on 26 July 1995;

"First Protocol" means the Protocol drawn up on the basis of Article K.3 of the Treaty on European Union to the Convention on the protection of the European Communities' financial interests done at Brussels on 27 September 1996;

"fraud affecting the European Communities' financial interests" has the meaning given to it by Article 1.1 of the Convention;

"money laundering" has the meaning given to it by section 31 (as substituted by *section 21* of this Act) of the Criminal Justice Act, 1994;

"national official", for the purposes of the application in the State of Article 1.1(*c*) of the First Protocol, means any one of the following persons:

> (*a*) a Minister of the Government or Minister of State;
> (*b*) an Attorney General who is not a member of Dáil Éireann or Seanad Éireann;
> (*c*) the Comptroller and Auditor General;
> (*d*) a member of Dáil Éireann or Seanad Éireann;
> (*e*) a judge of a court in the State;
> (*f*) the Director of Public Prosecutions;
> (*g*) any other holder of an office who is remunerated wholly or partly out of moneys provided by the Oireachtas;
> (*h*) any person employed by a person referred to in any of *paragraphs (d)* to (*g*) in the performance of that person's official functions; and
> (*i*) a director of, or an occupier of a position of employment in, a public body as defined in the Ethics in Public Office Act, 1995,

and, for the purposes of the application in the State of Article 4.2 of the First Protocol, any one of the following persons shall be treated as a national official:

> (i) a member of the Commission of the European Communities;
> (ii) a member of the European Parliament;
> (iii) a member of the Court of Justice of the European Communities;
> (iv) a member of the Court of Auditors of the European Communities;

"official" has the meaning given to it by Article 1.1(*a*) of the First Protocol;

"passive corruption" has the meaning given to it by Article 2.1 of the First Protocol;

"Protocol on Interpretation" means the Protocol drawn up on the basis of Article K.3 of the Treaty on European Union, on the interpretation, by way of preliminary rulings, by the Court of Justice of the European Communities of the Convention on the protection of the European Communities' financial interests done at Brussels on 29 November 1996; and

"Second Protocol" means the Protocol drawn up on the basis of Article K.3 of the Treaty on European Union, to the Convention on the protection of the European Communities' financial interests done at Brussels on 19 June 1997.

(2) For the purposes of *sections 42(c)* and *45(1)(a)*—

    (*a*) a person benefits from fraud or money laundering if he or she obtains property as a result of or in connection with the commission of an offence under either of those provisions, and

    (*b*) a person derives a pecuniary advantage from fraud or money laundering if he or she obtains a sum of money as a result of or in connection with the commission of such an offence.

GENERAL NOTE

The concepts defined under this section include active and passive corruption — and community and national official. Crucially in s.40(2) there is a criteria setting out the circumstances in which a person will be deemed to have derived pecuniary advantage from or otherwise benefited from fraud or money laundering.

"Fraud affecting the European Communities' financial interests" is defined broadly. Nevertheless, it finds precision in what has been called its symmetrical definition, covering fraud as to revenue and expenditure. It extends to the Community budget and also to other budgets managed or controlled by or on behalf of the European Communities. The definition includes non-disclosure of information where such information is specifically required and has the effect set out below. Misappropriation must also be understood in the context of misapplying funds for purposes other than those for which they were granted (expenditure) or using them to obtain a benefit (revenue). Fraud is defined as "any act or omission relating to the use or presentation of false, incorrect or incomplete documents or statements". Such act or omission must have the effect of either:
– as to expenditure;
    • misappropriation, or
    • wrongful retention of Community funds.
– as to revenue;
    • illegal diminution of Community resources.

Convention and Protocols to have force of law

41.—(1) Subject to the provisions of this Part, the Convention (other than Article 7.2), the First Protocol, the Protocol on Interpretation (other than Article 2(*b*)) and the Second Protocol (other than Articles 8 and 9) shall have the force of law in the State and judicial notice shall be taken of them.

(2) Judicial notice shall also be taken of any ruling or decision of, or expression of opinion by, the Court of Justice of the European Communities on any question as to the meaning or effect of any provision of the Convention, the First Protocol, the Protocol on Interpretation and the Second Protocol.

(3) For convenience of reference there are set out in *Schedules 2* to *9* respectively—

    (*a*) the text in the English language of the Convention;

    (*b*) the text in the Irish language of the Convention;

    (*c*) the text in the English language of the First Protocol;

    (*d*) the text in the Irish language of the First Protocol;

    (*e*) the text in the English language of the Protocol on Interpretation;

(*f*) the text in the Irish language of the Protocol on Interpretation;

(*g*) the text in the English language of the Second Protocol;

(*h*) the text in the Irish language of the Second Protocol.

GENERAL NOTE

The First Protocol will have force of law, as will, for the most part, the Convention and the Second Protocol and Protocol on Interpretation. For ease of reference, then, they are referred to simply here as the Convention, First Protocol, the Protocol on Interpretation and the Second Protocol. Ireland chose not to be bound by the *ne bis in idem* rule as set out and qualified by Art. 7 of the Convention, the jurisdiction in certain areas of the E.C.J. on the interpretation of these measures under Art. 2(2) of the Protocol on Interpretation [2(*b*) surely being a misprint or typographical error] and finally data protection and publication provisions under Arts. 8 and 9 of the Second Protocol.

Though the Convention and associated Protocols have been adopted within the frame-work of the European Union, they do not automatically become part of Irish law. Unlike countries like the Netherlands or Luxembourg, Ireland persists in the view that supra-national institutions consist in a separate (though not necessarily superior) sovereign system (the contradiction in terms is clear). This so-called dualist approach means that the Convention and Protocols had to be specifically enacted into Irish law to ensure that the obligations imposed, and rights conferred, by them can be enforced in the Irish courts. In other words, the Convention and Protocols, of themselves, have the status of international law but are not necessarily directly effective provisions of European Community law. This is not to say that the superior law is *not* that contained in the Convention. What is not clear, however, is the applicability of comparative concepts under domestic corruption laws (see for example *Arlidge & Parry,* Chap. 7; Sullivan, *Proscribing Corruption – Some Comments on the Law Commission's Report* [1998] Crim. L.R. 547).

This section gives the Convention and associated Protocols the required force of law in this State. This legal status purports to be subject to the provisions of the Act itself. The specific stipulation that judicial notice shall be taken of the Convention and Protocols must be superfluous, since judicial notice is implicit in the fact that they have the force of law in the State (Walsh, Annotations to the Europol Act, ICLSA 1999).

In s.41(3) we see that the Convention and Protocols are scheduled to the Act for ease of reference. There are two versions of each, the English and Irish version. The text of the Act itself by contrast (but which is the current practice) is in English only.

Fraud affecting European Communities' financial interests

42.—A person who—

(*a*) commits in whole or in part any fraud affecting the European Communities' financial interests,

(*b*) participates in, instigates or attempts any such fraud, or

(*c*) obtains the benefit of, or derives any pecuniary advantage from, any such fraud,

is guilty of an offence and is liable on conviction on indictment to a fine or imprisonment for a term not exceeding 5 years or both.

GENERAL NOTE

A major concern of this novel semi-direct legislative action by the Community is that the offence and penalty be sufficiently effective and proportionate, but also *dissuasive* in order to achieve harmonised protection of Community finances (*Commission v. Greece,* Case 68/88, 21/9/89, Reports p.2985 point 23 and 24; see also *Milchwerke Köln/Wuppertal v. Hauptzollamt Köln-Rheinau,* Case C–352/92, July 14, 1994, Reports I p. 3400 point 23). Though the Irish criminal law may have had some existing limited provision to cover the kind of fraud with which we are here concerned, it was certainly necessary to create new criminal offences with penalties according to the principle as exemplified in cases such as *Michwerke* (see Kuhl, pp. 324–5). Even if our law could have sufficiently protected Community finances, it is probably for the best, in the interest of consensus that all Member States now have a centralised specific offence (see the approach of Spain, which managed to amend its new Penal Code before it came in to force on June 1, 1996 to include fraud offences in respect of Community revenue and expenditure (Arts. 306 and 309)).

Art. 1 of the Convention requires that the culpable act be committed *intentionally*. The Council rejected any lesser mental element such as recklessness or gross negligence (Commission Proposal, [1994] O.J. C216, Art. 1.2). Some commentators feel this is unfortunate as it lays too easily at the door of any company the defence of incompetence, mistake, negligence and so on (Kuhl, 326). More importantly, it lays wide open to defendants to claim that they were unaware of the origin or genesis of the transaction. This might be true, but only because it suited them to be unaware of a conspicuously good business opportunity. It seems not incumbent on such persons to look behind such opportunities or, indeed, question irregularities.

Art. 1 of the convention provides several "verbs" by which the *actus reus* of the offence of fraud can be committed:
- "presentation" of incorrect, incomplete or false representations (through documents or statements),
- "non-disclosure" of information specifically required, and
- "misapplication" of funds.

We may note that the Act as a whole introduces in some respects an entirely new (some might say English) perspective on fraud. Thus, it might be tempting to embark upon a consideration of whether dishonesty or deception is required in the "presentation" or "non-disclosure" (misapplication containing the inherent "misdeed" or element of wrongdoing). However, the Convention does not concern itself with either deception or dishonesty. Thus it is not a necessary element of this kind of fraud for the defendant to have actually concealed anything. It is interesting to note that the English perspective which we have chosen to follow in this Act as a whole was pressed upon the Council but was rejected (U.K. "Joint Action" proposal, Council Document 10700/94 JUSTPEN 84, November 9, 1994). Also interesting is the comment, with reference to the English proposal, that:

> "The very detailed definition of fraud in the Convention also allows the requirements of the legality principle (*null poena sine lege*) to be satisfied and deliberately avoids a vague and uncertain and consequently informal and rather programmatic language" (Kuhl, p. 329).

This might be a lesson indeed from the preponderance of civil law (and therefore codification) traditions to the Irish legislature which so easily adopts the English perspective.

S.42(*b*) confirms that participation, instigation and, most importantly, attempts only can constitute fraud. Art. 1 of the convention makes it an offence to do any of the aforesaid irrespective of whether it is done in co-operation with others or alone. No particular accord is required by a person participating in or instigating a fraud with other defendants in the same fraudulent transaction (*cf.* s.45(1)(*b*)). The importance of listing not only attempts, and not only participation or instigation but all three is that a fraud may be committed, for example in the preparation of false documents where there is no real agreement or conspiracy between different defendants, they may not succeed and may even be at cross purposes but remain, under the section quite open to prosecution.

Active corruption

43.—A person who commits active corruption is guilty of an offence and is liable on conviction on indictment to a fine or imprisonment for a term not exceeding 5 years or both.

General Note

Active corruption is defined in Art. 3 of the First Protocol. It may be summarised as deliberate action of the defendant to provide, directly or indirectly, an advantage of any kind either to himself or to an official so that the official or a third party breaches an official duty which in some way damages the Communities' financial interests. The closest relevant analogy we may draw from is the English Law Commission on Proscribing Corruption (Law Com., No 248). That document identifies the core of corruption in the context of "an 'agent' tempted" by some form of advantage to betray the trust owed to his or her principal (5.14). Sullivan's analysis of the Commission's proposals focuses on the seeking of influence over conduct of agents but correctly points out that seeking influence may not be of itself corrupt ([1998] Crim. L.R. 550). Therefore, legitimate influences must be distinguished from the advantage set out in the First Protocol. The English Law Commission recommended that an advantage will not be corrupt if it is conferred "by or on behalf of the principal as remuneration or reimbursement ... ". However, where wages are fixed in the case of an officer, and perks are clearly not the norm or taken account of by that office, these comments are harder to apply. Is it not clear from such accepted enticements as "corporate stadium seating" and "tickets to the game" that perks and advantage are part of our culture? In ironic contrast the section seems foreign. The language is awkward and unclear, perhaps as a result of translation. See General Note on s.42 above.

Passive corruption

44.—An official who commits passive corruption is guilty of an offence and is liable on conviction on indictment to a fine or imprisonment for a term not exceeding 5 years or both.

GENERAL NOTE

Art. 2 of the First Protocol defines passive corruption. Again, action is mentioned but only as an alternative to the more central *actus reus* of this particular section, *i.e.* the acceptance of a promise of advantage in return for acting or refraining from acting in breach of official duties in a way which damages or is likely to damage Community financial interests. The language is difficult and unclear, as suggested above as a result of translation not only in the literal sense but in the legalese. See General Note on ss.42 and 43 above.

Extra-territorial jurisdiction in case of certain offences

45.—(1) It is an offence for a person to commit fraud affecting the Communities' financial interests or to commit the offence of money laundering, or to participate in, instigate or attempt any such fraud or offence, outside the State if—

    (*a*) the benefit of the fraud or offence is obtained, or a pecuniary advantage is derived from it, by a person within the State, or

    (*b*) a person within the State knowingly assists or induces the commission of the fraud or offence, or

    (*c*) the offender is an Irish citizen, a national official or a Community official working for a European Community institution or a body set up in accordance with the Treaties establishing the European Communities which has its headquarters in the State.

(2) Active or passive corruption committed by a person outside the State is an offence if—

    (*a*) the offender is an Irish citizen, a national official or a Community official working for a European Community institution or a body set up in accordance with the Treaties establishing the European Communities which has its headquarters within the State, or

    (*b*) in the case of active corruption, it is directed against an official, or a member of one of the institutions mentioned in *paragraphs (i)* to *(iv)* of the definition of "national official" in *section 40*, who is an Irish citizen.

(3) A person guilty of an offence under this section is liable on conviction on indictment to a fine or imprisonment for a term not exceeding 5 years or both.

GENERAL NOTE

Each Member State must, pursuant to Art. 4 of the Convention, establish its own juris-diction for fraud committed in whole or in part within its territory. It was open to Ireland to decline to apply the so-called rule of "active personality" where offences committed by one of its nationals are punishable in the country where they occurred. The U.K. insisted on this opt-out clause (see comments of Kuhl, pp. 329–330). Thus Ireland retains an interest in the prosecution of its nationals where the offence occurs outside its domestic jurisdiction whilst at the same time requires co-operation and transfer where other states may express interest. Art. 5 of the Convention requires Ireland to prosecute the offence where it cannot extradite the proposed defendant.

Restriction on certain proceedings

46.—(1) Where a person is charged with an offence under *section 45*, no further proceedings (other than a remand in custody or on bail) shall be taken except by or with the consent of the Director of Public Prosecutions.

(2) Where the Director of Public Prosecutions considers that another mem-ber state of the European Union has jurisdiction to try a person charged with an offence under *section 45*, the Director shall cooperate with the appropriate authorities in the member state concerned with a view to centralising the pros-ecution of the person in a single member state where possible.

(3) Proceedings for an offence to which this section applies may be taken in any place in the State, and the offence may for all incidental purposes be treated as having been committed in that place.

(4) Proceedings shall not be taken under section 38 of the Extradition Act, 1965, in respect of an act that is an offence under both that section and *section 45* of this Act.

GENERAL NOTE

S.45 above allows the Irish prosecutorial authorities to retain seisin, as it were, of the prosecution of persons the subject of charges under this Act. This section regulates the restriction on the extradition of persons by other states who feel an offence has been committed within their remit or jurisdiction. Provision is already made in s.38 of the Extradition Act 1965 as amended for a request to be made by such a state for the alleged offender to be prosecuted here in Ireland. Importantly this is only where Ireland refuses to extradite that person. The new approach provided here contemplates a centralised notion of prosecuting intra-Community fraud: centralised, however, to the point that it should no longer be important *where* an offence is tried; thus once a person is charged with an offence under this Act, arguably he or she should remain here to be prosecuted. The other interested state(s), however, can avail of the co-operation of the DPP but only with a view to "centralising the prosecution". This remains vague, but clearly extradition (or transfer) may still occur, with the consent of the DPP, where such would facilitate this nebulous the idea of "centralising" of prosecutions under this Part.

Extradition for revenue offences

47.—For the purposes of the application in the State of Article 5.3 of the Convention, as applied by Article 12.1 of the Second Protocol, extradition for the offence of fraud against the European Communities' financial interests or money laundering shall not be refused, notwithstanding section 13 of the Extradition Act, 1965, solely on the ground that the offence constitutes a revenue offence as defined in that Act.

GENERAL NOTE

This section is an implementation of the principle in Art. 5.3 of the Convention which states: "A Member State may not refuse extradition in the event of fraud affecting the European Communities' financial interest for the sole reason that it concerns a tax or customs duty offence."

PART 7

INVESTIGATION OF OFFENCES

Search warrants

48.—(1) This section applies to an offence under any provision of this Act for which a person of full age and capacity and not previously convicted may be punished by imprisonment for a term of five years or by a more severe penalty and to an attempt to commit any such offence.

(2) A judge of the District Court, on hearing evidence on oath given by a member of the Garda Síochána, may, if he or she is satisfied that there are reasonable grounds for suspecting that evidence of, or relating to the commission of, an offence to which this section applies is to be found in any place, issue a warrant for the search of that place and any persons found there.

(3) A warrant under this section shall be expressed and shall operate to authorise a named member of the Garda Síochána, alone or accompanied by such other persons as may be necessary—

(*a*) to enter, within 7 days from the date of issuing of the warrant (if necessary by the use of reasonable force), the place named in the warrant,

(*b*) to search it and any persons found there,

(*c*) to examine, seize and retain any thing found there, or in the possession of a person present there at the time of the search, which the member reasonably believes to be evidence of or relating to the commission of an offence to which this section applies, and

(*d*) to take any other steps which may appear to the member to be necessary for preserving any such thing and preventing interference with it.

(4) The authority conferred by *subsection* (*3*)(*c*) to seize and retain any thing includes, in the case of a document or record, authority—

(*a*) to make and retain a copy of the document or record, and

(*b*) where necessary, to seize and, for as long as necessary, retain any computer or other storage medium in which any record is kept.

(5) A member of the Garda Síochána acting under the authority of a warrant under this section may—

    (*a*) operate any computer at the place which is being searched or cause any such computer to be operated by a person accompanying the member for that purpose, and

    (*b*) require any person at that place who appears to the member to have lawful access to the information in any such computer—

        (i) to give to the member any password necessary to operate it,

        (ii) otherwise to enable the member to examine the information accessible by the computer in a form in which the information is visible and legible, or

        (iii) to produce the information in a form in which it can be removed and in which it is, or can be made, visible and legible.

(6) Where a member of the Garda Síochána has entered premises in the execution of a warrant issued under this section, he may seize and retain any material, other than items subject to legal privilege, which is likely to be of substantial value (whether by itself or together with other material) to the investigation for the purpose of which the warrant was issued.

(7) The power to issue a warrant under this section is in addition to and not in substitution for any other power to issue a warrant for the search of any place or person.

(8) In this section, unless the context otherwise requires—

"commission", in relation to an offence, includes an attempt to commit the offence;

"computer at the place which is being searched" includes any other computer, whether at that place or at any other place, which is lawfully accessible by means of that computer;

"place" includes a dwelling;

"thing" includes an instrument (within the meaning of *Part 4*), a copy of such instrument, a document or a record.

GENERAL NOTE

Art. 40.5 of the Constitution preserves as inviolable the dwelling of every citizen which shall not be forcibly entered into save in accordance with law. And this recognition of a sacred private preserve extends beyond the dwelling to a person's property (see *Simple Imports Ltd v. Revenue Commissioners* [2000] 2 I.R. 243 at 250). However, it is accepted that a member of the gardai may effect a non-consensual entry in order to arrest a person suspected of having committed a *felony* (now an abolished term which may roughly equate to the term "arrestable offence"). Much reservation, nevertheless, has traditionally surrounded the entry and search of one's private premises. No general right exists which permits entry and search of private property. Instead, the law has created piecemeal exceptions to this Constitutional inviolability. At one time the power was restricted to the home where stolen goods might be found (*Entick v. Carrington* [1765] 2 Wills 275 at 291; *Leach v. Money* [1765] 19 St. Tr. 1001). The modern law with respect to search warrants took recognisable form in s.42(1) of the Larceny Act 1916, which is effectively replaced and broadened by this section. Nowadays, the power to search is nothing unusual and is found in common law doctrine (see *DPP v. Forbes* [1993] I.L.R.M. 817 and *Minister for Justice v. Wang Zhu Jie* [1991] I.L.R.M. 823) and in many statutory provisions. It reaches its more extreme manifestation, however, in such acts as the Criminal Law Act 1976, which concerns offences against the State and which allows search and seizure irrespective of which power, offence or thing in respect of which the warrant issued (see ss.5 and 9). This, it is submitted, should be seen as the exceptional case by which the present provision is to be limited (*cf.* Ryan & Magee, p.151). Nor is it irrelevant to note that Ireland will retain its particular constitutional values in spite of influential foreign developments (see Morris J., *DPP v. Delaney* [1996] 1 I.L.R.M. 536).

In order to effect what would in the ordinary course be an unconstitutional entry and search of a person's premises, there must be a valid warrant so to do. The warrant is valid where it issues lawfully upon a statutory or common law power of entry and search; thus it is a written legal authority to someone to search a *specified* place and/or to do *specified* things there, such as seize relevant items or search occupants. It was formerly the procedure for a District Court judge to consider "sworn information" before issuing such a warrant to search. The express requirement of a judge's consideration, in this procedure, makes it implicitly a judicial act to bypass the constitutional inviolability of the person and of the home. It was formerly the position that the issue of a warrant could be made in favour of non-judicial personages and was therefore an executive decision (*Ryan v. O'Callaghan* unreported, High Court, July 22, 1987; *Byrne v. Grey* [1981] I.R. 31; *Farrell v. Farelly* [1988] I.R. 655, [1989] I.L.R.M. 309). The power here, however, is to issue to gardaí only, though it is true that they may be accompanied. What was decisive in constitutional terms in the wider powers expressed in the 1976 Act was what the learned writers in Kelly call the "imprimatur of any judicial authority." That Act did not require a District judge to "hear" evidence on oath but permitted a superintendent or an officer of the gardaí of higher ranking to authorise the search. Thus, in *DPP v. O'Leary* (1988) 3 Frewen 163, it was unsuccessfully argued that warrants issued under that Act were broad sweeping so as to be warrants "at large" (a phrase used in *Entick* discussed above).

Where any irregularity occurs, evidence which is obtained by such irregular search may be excluded unless it is established there was no intention to ignore the constitutional mandate or where there are extraordinarily excusing circumstances (*People (DPP) v. Kenny* [1990] 2 I.R. 110). However, in the case of *Delaney* [1997] 3 I.R. 453 it was held that the inviolability of the dwelling may be encroached upon where the gardai (or, indeed, some other person) have a *bona fide* belief that it is necessary to enter in order to safeguard life and limb. In any event, the decision in *DPP v. Rooney* [1993] I.L.R.M. 61 establishes that a person stopped under any statutory power must be told of the reason for the action and the nature and description of the power invoked. A person against whom a search warrant is executed should be given an opportunity to see the warrant and to examine it. However, it is current practice for legal representatives to have to seek to obtain it by request from the investigating authorities. It goes without saying that in the interest of the defendant and the checks and balances which scrutinise such encroachments to the constitutional rights of citizens, the warrant should be available to be examined as to its authorisation and compliance with this section. Where the gardai have lawful authority to search, they may use reasonable force to effect entry for that purpose; a request for consent, however, should, where possible, be made (*DPP v. Corrigan* [1986] I.R. 290, [1987] I.L.R.M. 575; *McMahon v. McDonald*, High Court, May 3, 1988; unreported, Supreme Court, *The Irish Times*, July 27, 1988).

The section itself provides for new garda powers to obtain search warrants for evidence of offences of fraud and dishonesty. Indeed, the power extends to any offence under the Act provided it is an arrestable offence as defined in the Criminal Law Act 1997. A District Court judge must be satisfied that there are reasonable grounds to suspect that evidence relating to an offence under this Act is to be found in any such place or (subject to comments below) on the person or any person found at that place. The warrant must be executed within seven days of its issue and must specifically authorise a named member of the Garda Siochána and such other persons as may be necessary to effect the search for evidence which the *member reasonably believes to be evidence of or relating to* the commission of an offence under this Act. This express authority must include reference to any search of "persons" who might be at that place "at the time of the search". As Ryan & Magee would have it, such an Act "does not demand that a Garda entertain any suspicion whatsoever in relation to any person whom he proposes to search" (p.144, citing Leigh, *Police Powers in England and* Wales, pp.182–183).

If properly issued, the warrant not only authorises the search, but also seizure and retention of anything of substantial value to the investigation *for the purpose of which the warrant was issued.* It also authorises the copying of documents or records, the seizure of computers containing records and the operation of a computer by the gardai including the provision to the gardai of passwords and copies of records, etc. However, items subject to legal privilege may not be seized (see explanatory memorandum).

The section is operable under a warrant only; this does not preclude, however, that the search may be effected in the course of a lawful arrest (either for an arrestable offence or by arrest warrant). In *Dillon v. O'Brien* (1887) 20 L.R. (Ir.) 300 Palles C.B. stated that police investigative powers are: "of no value if the law is powerless to prevent the abstraction or destruction of [...] evidence, without which a trial would be no more than an empty form."

In *Jennings v. Quinn* [1968] I.R. 305, O'Keefe J. (Ó Dálaigh and Walsh JJ. concurring) set out the following position:

> "In my opinion the public interest requires that the police, when effecting a lawful arrest, may seize, without a search warrant, property in the possession or custody of the person arrested when they believe it *necessary to do so to avoid the abstraction or destruction of that property* [emphasis added] and when the property is–
> (a) evidence in support of the criminal charge upon which the arrest is made, or
> (b) evidence in support of any other criminal charge against the person then in contemplation, or
> (c) reasonably believed to be stolen property or to be property unlawfully in the possession of that person".

This is a very broad statement of the law, and it is subject to possible abuse unless discipline is shown by all concerned in the interpretation of the right to search (especially, perhaps, in the interpretation of the emphasised words. It is submitted that the Constitution envisaged, where possible, the statutory power as endorsed by the legislature as preferable to an over-zealous recourse to the common law. Where an entry to effect an arrest is contemplated, any revocation of authority to enter will render the arrest made, upon the premises and without warrant, unlawful (*DPP v. Gaffney* [1987] I.R. 173, [1989] I.L.R.M. 39). However, see comments above on reasonable force and entry to effect an arrest.

S.48(2) refers to "any place", which could not, it seems, be wider, but in fact is extended to the person of anyone found there. Furthermore, the former requirement that it "*appear* by information on oath before a justice that there is reasonable cause to believe ..." [emphasis added] (Larceny Act 1916, s.42(1), now abolished by this Act) is now replaced with "on *hearing* evidence on oath given by a member of the Garda Síochána may, if he or she is satisfied that there are reasonable grounds for suspecting ..." (emphasis added). The requirement under the new law, then is that the evidence be actually sworn in front of the District Court. This was not the position, however, as envisaged in the Report of the Government Advisory Committee on Fraud (para. 5.12). But the original procedure had conceivably been susceptible to challenge on constitutional grounds (see *King v. A.G.* [1981] I.R. 233; *cf. Ryan v O'Callaghan* unreported, High Court, Barr J., July 22, 1987). This, it must be remembered, is in the context of a conclusion by a District Court judge which is not subject to challenge by certiorari (*State (Batchelor) v. O'Floinn* [1958] I.R. 155). The new procedure reflects the importance of procedural propriety where such an immunity obtains.

S.48(3) requires care to be taken in drawing up the warrant, in order for it to be operable, for it to express an authority for a member of the gardai alone or with "such persons as may be necessary" to act upon it. Such other persons as may be necessary is not defined but given the nature of the possible breaches of constitutional rights to which these searches bear very close relation, it is submitted, this notion is to be construed strictly. Under s.2(7) of the English Criminal Justice Act 1987, the equivalent of other person is "appropriate person" and is confined to members of their Serious Fraud Office (which has no equivalent here) or someone approved by the Director to accompany the searching police officer. The provision seems to contemplate the member of the Garda Síochána being *accompanied* by such persons. However, the actual authority for such other persons is to enter only. The other powers, seizure, examination, etc., are vested in the member only.

It would appear that the search may include the persons of those present "at the time of the search" only. This would appear to contemplate innocents being searched by mere virtue of their being at the wrong place at the wrong time. More invidiously, however, this would suggest that the person searching the place may not lay in wait for any person to return or to enter that place. The provision presumes, as mentioned elsewhere, some knowledge of what may reasonably be believed to be evidence; it also should be given effect to with some focus upon what it is that is required to further an investigation. The provision cannot surely permit of confiscation and retention of broad categories of documentation simply because the searcher does not know what he or she is looking for. S.48(6) requires that anything seized and retained by the searching member be of "substantial" value to the investigation. If we still retain the principle of minimum interference — even after the passing of the almost free-for-all provision in s.9 of the Criminal Law Act — the courts should permit, as they did traditionally, only the seizure of items within specified parameters in the warrant and perhaps items reasonably believed, albeit mistakenly, to be within those parameters (*Price v. Messanger* 2 Bos & P 158, as cited by Ryan & Magee, p. 151). Thus "evidence relating to the commission of an offence" under the Act, though it appears wide, should be construed with discipline. In one sense, the broad framing of the word *relating* is sensibly wide because the power cannot be taken to go beyond that word. It remains to be seen, however, how sensible will be the interpretation of the term. One of the few statements on the law on a more restricted (common law) power of search extended the power to a similarly wide frame,

> "[W]]hen a constable enters a house by virtue of a search warrant for stolen goods, he may seize not only the goods which he reasonably believes to be covered by the warrant, but also any other goods which he believes on reasonable grounds to have been stolen and to be material evidence on a charge of stealing or receiving against the person in possession or anyone associated with him" (*Chic Fashions (West Wales) Ltd v. Jones, per* Denning L.J. [1968] 2 Q.B. 299, as set out in *Ryan & Magee,* p.152).

It is submitted that this dicta goes no further than to state the law as set out in this provision. Furthermore, it might be practically necessary for the searcher to have some knowledge of computers to avoid unnecessary seizure of entire computer systems where the necessary information can be retrieved with less infringement to property. Thus, it may be that the legislature intended that a computer technician *must* by necessity accompany a member to avoid such infringement under the "such other persons as may be necessary" provision. Alternatively, the member may require a person found at the place being searched to operate any information retrieval system on his behalf. Failure to do so is not provided for in this section (but see s.49 below).

The word "removed" is awkward in the context of computers. Surely what was intended was "downloaded" or "retrieved" or perhaps the information is in fact to be removed to prevent it being used.

Obstruction of Garda acting on warrant

49.—(1) A person who—

(*a*) obstructs or attempts to obstruct a member of the Garda Síochána acting under the authority of a warrant issued under this Part, or

(*b*) is found in or at the place named in the warrant by a member of the Garda Síochána so acting and fails or refuses to give the member his or her name and address when required by the member to do so or gives the member a name and address that is false or misleading, or

(*c*) fails without lawful authority or excuse to comply with a requirement under *paragraph* (*b*) or *section 48(5)(b)*,

is guilty of an offence and is liable on summary conviction to a fine not exceeding £500 or imprisonment for a term not exceeding 6 months or both.

(2) A member of the Garda Síochána may arrest without warrant any person who is committing an offence under this section or whom the member suspects, with reasonable cause, of having done so.

GENERAL NOTE

This section also provides for the penalty for the preceding section (s.48(5)(*b*)) where a person is found at the place being searched and fails to enable the searching member to examine information in pursuance of the search.

S.49(2) makes obstruction of a Garda acting on a warrant an arrestable offence. This is in conflict with the general parameters of an arrestable offence, namely an offence punishable by a term of imprisonment of at least five years. It will be an offence under this section to obstruct a Garda executing a warrant to search any place as deemed fit by a District Court judge under s.48 above. It is a specific offence for persons found at that place to refuse to properly identify themselves or to enable a searching member of the Garda Síochána to examine information under the warrant. The person found at the relevant place who refuses properly to give his or her name *and* address is guilty of the offence, which is not insubstantial in its penalty. This is interesting in the context of any issue of privilege. We note that under s.2(9) of the English Criminal Justice Act 1987, a person in similar circumstances is not obliged to provide information subject to privilege "except that a lawyer may be required to furnish the name and address of his client." There is no mention whatever, in any section of this Act, of access to a lawyer, which is inherent as a constitutional norm. It is provided in s.2 as cited, that:

> "if it is represented or appears to a person proposing to seize or retain a document under this section that the document was, or may have been, made for the purpose of obtaining, giving or communicating legal advice from or by a barrister or solicitor, that person shall not seize or retain the document unless he suspects with reasonable cause that the document was not made, or is not intended, solely for any of the purposes aforesaid."

Forfeiture of seized property

50.—(1) This section applies to any thing which has been seized by a member of the Garda Síochána (whether the seizure was effected by virtue of a warrant under *section 48* or otherwise) and which the member suspects to be—

    (*a*) any thing used (whether before or after the commencement of this section), or intended to be used, for the making of any false instrument, or any copy of a false instrument, in contravention of *section 25* or *27* respectively,

    (*b*) any false instrument or any copy of a false instrument used (whether before or after the commencement of this section), or intended to be so used, in contravention of *section 26* or *28* respectively,

    (*c*) any thing the custody or control of which, without lawful authority or excuse, is an offence under *section 29*,

    (*d*) any thing which is a counterfeit of a currency note or coin,

    (*e*) any thing used, whether before or after the commencement of this section, or intended to be used, for the making of any such counterfeit.

(2) A member of the Garda Síochána may, at any time after the seizure of any thing to which this section applies, apply to the judge of the District Court for the time being assigned to the district in which the seizure was effected for an order under this subsection with respect to it; and the judge may, if satisfied both that the thing is one to which this section applies and that it is in the public interest to do so, subject to *subsection (4)*, make such order as the judge thinks fit for its forfeiture and subsequent destruction or disposal.

(3) Subject to *subsection (4)*, the court by or before which a person is convicted of an offence under *Part 4* or *5* may order any thing shown to the satisfaction of the court to relate to the offence to be forfeited and either destroyed

or dealt with in such other manner as the court may order.

(4) The court shall not order any thing to be forfeited under *subsection (3)* or *(4)* where a person claiming to be the owner of or otherwise interested in it applies to be heard by the court, unless an opportunity has been given to the person to show cause why the order should not be made.

GENERAL NOTE

This section applies (and applies retrospectively) in relation to anything used to make false instruments, or forgeries or counterfeits under this Act. The provision concerns property seized by the gardai which they suspect is being used in connection with forgery or counterfeiting. On application, a District Court judge may, if satisfied that it is a thing to which this section applies *and* it is in the public interest to do so, make an order for its forfeiture and subsequent destruction or disposal. However, where a person is convicted, this requirement of "public interest" does not seem to apply (s.50(3)), the thing need only relate to the offence to the satisfaction of the District Court judge who convicts the offender.

S.50(4) would appear to require the court to put the owner, if capable of being known, on notice of the possibility of its destruction.

Concealing facts disclosed by documents

51.—(1) Any person who—
   (*a*) knows or suspects that an investigation by the Garda Síochána into an offence under this Act is being or is likely to be carried out, and
   (*b*) falsifies, conceals, destroys or otherwise disposes of a document or record which he or she knows or suspects is or would be relevant to the investigation or causes or permits its falsification, concealment, destruction or disposal,
is guilty of an offence.

(2) Where a person—
   (*a*) falsifies, conceals, destroys or otherwise disposes of a document, or
   (*b*) causes or permits its falsification, concealment, destruction or disposal,
in such circumstances that it is reasonable to conclude that the person knew or suspected—
   (i) that an investigation by the Garda Síochána into an offence under this Act was being or was likely to be carried out, and
   (ii) that the document was or would be relevant to the investigation,
he or she shall be taken for the purposes of this section to have so known or suspected, unless the court or the jury, as the case may be, is satisfied having regard to all the evidence that there is a reasonable doubt as to whether he or she so knew or suspected.

(3) A person guilty of an offence under this section is liable on conviction on indictment to a fine or imprisonment for a term not exceeding 5 years or both.

GENERAL NOTE

This section is a reproduction in similar terms of s.2(16) of the English Criminal Justice Act 1987. It is an offence under s.51, knowingly or suspecting that the gardai are investigating or are likely to investigate an offence under the Act, to falsify, conceal or destroy any

document relevant to the investigation. This extends to "causing" or "permitting" such to be done. Importantly, it is where it is "reasonable to conclude" that this person knew or suspected:
1. that an investigation was being carried out or was likely to be carried out, and
2. that the document was relevant.
that the person will be taken to have known or suspected, unless the judge (or jury, as the case may be) is satisfied otherwise (see explanatory memorandum). Interestingly, only s.51(1) refers to "record"; it would appear then that computer records — or the concealing of such — does not have any recourse to or benefit of s.51(2).

This section contemplates concealment post-complaint; the duty already on certain persons to disclose information at s.59 is somewhat extended by this provision, as failure to report is now broadened to "permitting" falsification, destruction or disclosure of a document. This could be interpreted to mean that knowledge of any such impending falsification, destruction or disposal places a duty on persons with such knowledge (or maybe suspicion only) to disclose — thereby actively not "permitting" it.

Order to produce evidential material

52.—(1) This section applies to any offence under this Act which is punishable by imprisonment for a term of five years or by a more severe penalty.

(2) A judge of the District Court, on hearing evidence on oath given by a member of the Garda Síochána, may, if he or she is satisfied that—

    (*a*) the Garda Síochána are investigating an offence to which this section applies,

    (*b*) a person has possession or control of particular material or material of a particular description, and

    (*c*) there are reasonable grounds for suspecting that the material constitutes evidence of or relating to the commission of the offence,

order that the person shall—

    (i) produce the material to a member of the Garda Síochána for the member to take away, or

    (ii) give such a member access to it,

either immediately or within such period as the order may specify.

(3) Where the material consists of or includes information contained in a computer, the order shall have effect as an order to produce the information, or to give access to it, in a form in which it is visible and legible and in which it can be taken away.

(4) An order under this section—

    (*a*) in so far as it may empower a member of the Garda Síochána to take away a document, or to be given access to it, shall also have effect as an order empowering the member to take away a copy of the document (and for that purpose the member may, if necessary, make a copy of the document),

    (*b*) shall not confer any right to production of, or access to, any document subject to legal privilege, and

    (*c*) shall have effect notwithstanding any other obligation as to secrecy or other restriction on disclosure of information imposed by statute or otherwise.

(5) Any material taken away by a member of the Garda Síochána, under this section may be retained by the member for use as evidence in any criminal proceedings.

(6)(*a*) Information contained in a document which was produced to a member of the Garda Síochána, or to which such a member was given access, in accordance with an order under this section shall be admissible in any criminal proceedings as evidence of any fact therein of which direct oral evidence would be admissible unless the information—

    (i) is privileged from disclosure in such proceedings,

    (ii) was supplied by a person who would not be compellable to give evidence at the instance of the prosecution,

    (iii) was compiled for the purposes or in contemplation of any—

        (I) criminal investigation,

        (II) investigation or inquiry carried out pursuant to or under any enactment,

        (III) civil or criminal proceedings, or

        (IV) proceedings of a disciplinary nature,

or unless the requirements of the provisions mentioned in *paragraph* (*b*) are not complied with.

(*b*) References in sections 7 (notice of documentary evidence to be served on accused), 8 (admission and weight of documentary evidence) and 9 (admissibility of evidence as to credibility of supplier of information) of the Criminal Evidence Act, 1992, to a document or information contained in it shall be construed as including references to a document mentioned in *paragraph* (*a*) and the information contained in it, and those provisions shall have effect accordingly with any necessary modifications.

(*c*) The Criminal Procedure Act, 1967, is amended both in section 6(1)(*e*) (as amended by section 10 of the Criminal Evidence Act, 1992) and in section 11 (as so amended) by the insertion, after "1992", of "or *section 52(6)(b)* of the *Criminal Justice (Theft and Fraud Offences) Act, 2001*,".

(7) A judge of the District Court may, on the application of any person to whom an order under this section relates or a member of the Garda Síochána, vary or discharge the order.

(8) A person who without reasonable excuse fails or refuses to comply with an order under this section is guilty of an offence and liable on summary conviction to a fine not exceeding £1,500 or imprisonment for a term not exceeding 12 months or both.

GENERAL NOTE

This section applies to arrestable offences as defined under the Criminal Law Act 1997. Thus it refers to the more serious range of offences. Nevertheless, the investigative power here is not of the "dawn raid" variety, though there is reference to "immediate" production. This provision is a more constrained version of s.2 of the English Criminal Justice Act 1987. We note that, significantly, the Irish version does not contain a power to have a person classified as a "person under investigation" and have that person attend before an investigator for questioning. In any event, the chosen regime might be more effective than such a power, as answers given in such interviews could not be used in evidence (see s. 2(8) of the English Act).

S.52(6)(*a*)(i)-(iii) seem to suggest that the gardai may have access to material which ultimately may not be produced at trial. This would appear to be at variance with the decisions in *Dunne*, unreported, Supreme Court, April 25, 2002 and *Braddish*, unreported, Supreme Court, May 18, 2001. This provision is replete with imprecision. For an order to issue, a District Court judge must first of all be satisfied that an investigation is underway and that it is an investigation of an offence which attracts a punishment of at least five years imprisonment under this Act. In addition, the judge must be satisfied the subjects of any order have in their possession or control "material" of a particular kind or description. This is unfortunate in the context of information which is often intellectual rather than redacted or material in form. In addition, the garda must satisfy the judge that the evidence is material upon reasonable grounds. There is no delegation of the power of search to any person other than a judge of the District Court as exists in England. It is interesting that they have in that jurisdiction a similar immunity for legal professional privilege, but they also have a specified requirement of approval for an order to produce a document in respect of which the producer might owe an obligation of confidence by virtue of carrying on any banking business. This may provide some guidance as to relevant matters to be taken into account by the District Court in granting such an order. Such a document may be produced where the person to whom the duty is owed consents to its production.

S.52(3) remedies the "material" dilemma in the preceding subsection, but again stretches the natural meaning of the word "material."

Legal privilege applies but supersedes any other obligation as to secrecy or other restriction on disclosure of information imposed by statute or otherwise. This is extremely wide and cannot be understood to mean constitutional privacy. How precisely the Garda is to make a copy remains to be seen — is he or she to use the office copier at the office's expense or will he or she bring the wherewithal to do so?

S.52(5) must be understood in the context of the recent Supreme Court decisions of *Braddish* and *Dunne*. It is incumbent upon the gardai, given their unique investigative role, not only to retain and preserve evidence (of guilt or innocence) but actively to seek it out.

The Criminal Evidence Act 1992 is endorsed by the approach that any information contained in a document will be admissible as evidence of any fact contained in it of which direct oral evidence would be admissible. The limitations on this principle are listed; admissibility is subject to:

1. privilege,
2. compellability,
3. any alternative evidential purpose for which the information was compiled, and
4. those conditions contained in the Criminal Evidence Act 1992

S.52(8) provides that an application can be made by the subject of such an order to have it varied or discharged. This application is to be made to a judge of the District Court

PART 8

Trial of Offences

Summary trial of indictable offences

53.—(1) The District Court may try summarily a person charged with an indictable offence under this Act if—

    (a) the Court is of opinion that the facts proved or alleged constitute a minor offence fit to be tried summarily,

    (b) the accused, on being informed by the Court of his or her right to be tried with a jury, does not object to being tried summarily, and

    (c) the Director of Public Prosecutions consents to the accused being tried summarily for the offence.

(2) On conviction by the District Court for an indictable offence tried summarily under *subsection (1)* the accused shall be liable to a fine not exceeding

£1,500 or imprisonment for a term not exceeding 12 months or both such fine and imprisonment.

GENERAL NOTE

This is a restatement of the "fully-constituted" rules in relation to summary trial of indictable offences, in other words the conditions to have an offence capable of going forward to a higher court dealt with in the District Court. The first condition is the opinion of the District Court; if it is of the opinion on the facts "proved" or alleged that the offence is a minor one, then; subject to the DPP and the accused, the matter may be dealt with in the District Court. It appears from the use of the word "proved" that the District Court judge may "refuse jurisdiction" even *after* he or she has assumed jurisdiction to hear the case actually argued and has come to a determination. The next condition is the "election" of the accused. In cases which are indictable (*i.e.* capable of trial on indictment), it must be made clear to the accused the implications of choosing to have his or her case heard in the District Court if he or she so wishes, *i.e.* that the case will be determined by a judge alone, sitting without a jury. It is normally the case that the accused is advised to seek legal advice on the decision, which invariably will be to opt for District Court determination because of the lower ceiling on the penalties within that court's competence, as set out in s.53(2). The third and often determinative condition is that the DPP is satisfied that the case be dealt with in a summary fashion. Thankfully, the position favoured by the L.R.C. was that the matter of venue not be left to the DPP. Though it is a viable argument that no accused should be entitled to a full jury trial for what is termed "petty theft", equally the constitutional right to judge and jury in Art. 38 of the Constitution may not so easily be deprived (see L.R.C. 43/92, p. 347, in particular the comments of Michael McDowell, S.C.).

S. (3 of the Prosecution of Offences Act 1974 provides the DPP with a broad discretion in relation to the institution of criminal proceedings. Whether or not this decision (which used to be taken by the Attorney General) is subject to judicial scrutiny has been doubted (*State (Killian) v. Attorney General* [1957] 92 I.L.T.R. 182; *State (Ennis) v. Farrell* [1966] I.R. 107; *cf. R. v. DPP ex p. C.* [1995] Cr. App. R. 136). The consent of the DPP must be express and clear and is "no mere empty form" (*R. v. Downey* [1971] N.I. 224; see Ryan & Magee, p.78).

Trial procedure

54.—(1) In any proceedings for an offence or attempted offence under any of *sections 6* and *7* and *sections 9* to *11* it shall not be necessary to prove an intention dishonestly to cause a loss to, or make a gain at the expense of, a particular person, and it shall be sufficient to prove that the accused did the act charged dishonestly with the intention of causing such a loss or making such a gain.

(2) Any number of persons may be charged in one indictment, with reference to the same theft, with having at different times or at the same time handled or possessed all or any of the stolen property, and the persons so charged may be tried together.

(3) Any person who—
    (*a*) is a member of a partnership or is one of two or more beneficial owners of any property, and
    (*b*) steals any property of or belonging to the partnership or such beneficial owners,
is liable to be dealt with, tried and punished as if he or she had not been or was not a member of the partnership or one of such beneficial owners.

(4) If on the trial of a person for stealing any property it appears that the property alleged to have been stolen at one time was taken at different times,

the separate takings may, unless the trial judge directs otherwise, be tried to-gether, to a number not exceeding 3, provided that not more than 6 months elapsed between the first and the last of the takings.

(5) Charges of stealing, handling or possessing any property or any part thereof may be included in separate counts of the same indictment and such counts may be tried together.

(6) Any person or persons charged in separate counts of the same indict-ment with stealing any property or any part thereof may be severally found guilty of stealing, handling or possessing the property or any part thereof.

(7) On the trial of two or more persons indicted for jointly handling or pos-sessing any stolen property the court or jury, as the case may be, may find any of the accused guilty if satisfied that he or she handled or possessed all or any part of such property, whether or not he or she did so jointly with the other accused or any of them.

GENERAL NOTE

This section applies to the trial procedure — or more correctly, the prosecutorial re-quirements — for the trial of the following offences:
1. making gain or causing loss by deception,
2. obtaining services by deception,
3. unlawful use of a computer,
4. false accounting, and
5. suppression of documents.

This provision makes it clear that no particular victim need be contemplated in the above offences. There are two requirements to establish the necessary mental element. They are:
1. an intention to cause loss or make gain, and
2. dishonesty.

This and other sections in this Part have sought to facilitate prosecution of offences by making the offences of stealing to a certain extent interchangeable with those of handling and possession.

S.54(2) allows any number of persons to be charged in the same indictment with han-dling or possessing stolen property at the same or at different times. This represents a con-tinuation of the provision in the prior law, s.40 of the Larceny Act 1916 as amended by s.4 of the Larceny Act 1990 (now repealed). The origin of the offence of handling derives from the offences of receiving stolen goods. It was with that offence that the court was concerned in *R. v. Tizard* [1962] 2 Q.B. 608 where it was held that the equivalent section was not confined to cases of successive offences of receiving (as it then was). Thus it was possible to charge a number of defendants on the same indictment of handling (as it now is) whether or not they did so from the same thief or from one another.

S.54(3) ensures that it is no defence for an accused simply to claim that he or she was joint beneficial owner of the property alleged to have been stolen, or that he or she was a partner of the alleged victim.

S.54(4) allows up to three separate takings to be tried together provided they occurred within a six-month period. S.54(4) is either awkward wording of the general principle that dishonest appropriations at different times can be joined for the purpose of trial, or express provision for amendments to the indictment during the course of the trial. This will depend on when exactly "it appears" that there is a temporal difficulty. From the provision, it seems that this will be "on the trial"; in either case this provision is to overcome any such temporal difficulty within a six-month lapse between appropriations and to a total number of three different appropriations. This facilitation of the trial of general theft offences together is contained in s.54(5).

S.54(5) provides that stealing, handling or possession may be included in separate counts on the same indictment, but may be tried together.

S.54(6) permits a person charged with theft to be found guilty of handling or possession if the facts prove the latter, and if charged with handling or possession to be found guilty of theft if the facts prove theft; thus this provision will apply to all persons charged with theft, who may now clearly be found guilty of handling or possession if the facts prove these offences. Alternatively, if charged with handling or possession, the person charged may be tried and found guilty of theft. This will bring clarity to the difficulties which gave rise to *People (DPP) v. Fowler*, unreported, Court of Criminal Appeal, February 24, 1995 (resolved to some effect by the decision in *People (DPP) v. Peter O'Neill* unreported, Court of Criminal Appeal, July 24, 1995). This provision operates irrespective of the original counts or charges.

S.54(7) uses the phrase "jointly accused" where they are indicted on the same facts. This provision allows them to be found guilty of handling or possession regardless of whether or not they did so jointly with the other accused.

Alternative verdicts

55.—(1) If, on the trial of a person for theft or for unlawfully obtaining property otherwise, it is proved that the person handled or possessed the property in such circumstances as to constitute an offence under *section 17* or *18*, he or she may be convicted of that offence.

(2) If, on the trial of a person for an offence under *section 17* or *18* of handling or possessing stolen or otherwise unlawfully obtained property, it is proved that the person stole or otherwise unlawfully obtained the property, he or she may be convicted of the theft of the property or of the offence consisting of unlawfully obtaining the property.

GENERAL NOTE

Though awkward, the wording of this section should not prove unworkable. The section surely refers to offences under this Act (see commentary on "unlawfully obtained" and on "stolen property" in the General Note on s.2 above), and makes all such offences amenable to conviction upon proof. The offences contemplated are those under ss. 17 or 18 of handling or possession of property "unlawfully obtained" which can be difficult to separate from the actual stealing (or otherwise unlawfully obtaining). S.55 allows the substitution of verdicts of handling or possession for theft, for example under s.4. S.55(2) makes the section operable in reverse. The defendant is not, however, exposed to only one of the alternatives but is in jeopardy in respect of both offences; he or she cannot be acquitted on the principal charge and subsequently be charged with the alternative (McCutcheon, 9–17, citing *People (A.G.) v. Heald* [1954] I.R. 58. This provision is a restatement of the prior law under s.8 of the Larceny Act 1990 (now repealed by this Act). It is accepted, then, that verdicts can be substituted (*People (A.G.) v. O'Brien* [1963] I.R. 65; *cf. Kenny*, para. 335). Where such facility is not permissive of imprecision on the part of the prosecutor, nor prejudicial to the accused, there should be no difficulty.

Orders for restitution

56.—(1) Where property has been stolen and either—
    (*a*) a person is convicted of an offence with reference to the theft (whether or not the stealing is the essential ingredient of the offence), or
    (*b*) a person is convicted of any other offence but the first-mentioned offence is taken into consideration in determining his or her sentence,

the court by or before which the person is convicted may on the conviction (whether or not the passing of sentence is in other respects deferred)—
    (i) order anyone having possession or control of the property to restore

it to any person entitled to recover it from the convicted person,

   (ii) on the application of a person entitled to recover from the convicted person any other property directly or indirectly representing the first-mentioned property (as being the proceeds of any disposal or realisation of the whole or part of it or of property so representing it), order that other property to be delivered or transferred to the applicant, or

   (iii) order that a sum not exceeding the value of the first-mentioned property shall be paid, out of any money of the convicted person which was taken out of his or her possession when arrested, to any person who, if that property were in the possession of the convicted person, would be entitled to recover it from him or her.

(2) Where the court has power on a person's conviction to make an order against him or her under both *paragraph (ii)* and *paragraph (iii)* of *subsection (1)* with reference to the stealing of the same property, the court may make orders under both paragraphs, if the person in whose favour the orders are made does not thereby recover more than the value of that property.

(3) Where—

   (a) the court makes an order under *subsection (1)(i)* for the restoration of any property, and

   (b) it appears to the court that the convicted person has sold the property to a person acting in good faith or has borrowed money on the security of it from a person so acting,

then, on the application of the purchaser or lender the court may order that there shall be paid to the applicant, out of any money of the convicted person which was taken out of his or her possession when arrested, a sum not exceeding the amount paid for the purchase by the applicant or, as the case may be, the amount owed to the applicant in respect of the loan.

(4)(a) The court shall not exercise the powers conferred by this section unless in its opinion the relevant facts sufficiently appear from evidence given at the trial or the available documents, together with admissions made by or on behalf of any person in connection with any proposed exercise of the powers.

   (b) In *paragraph (a)* "available documents" means—

      (i) any written statements or admissions which were made for use, and would have been admissible in evidence, at the trial,

      (ii) any depositions taken in any proceedings before the trial, and

      (iii) any written statements or admissions used as evidence at the trial or in any such proceedings.

(5) The provisions of *section 20* in relation to property which has been stolen shall have effect also in relation to the property referred to in this section.

(6) This section is without prejudice to the Police (Property) Act, 1897 (disposal of property in the possession of the Garda Síochána).

GENERAL NOTE

Where:
1. property is stolen,
2. a person is convicted of an offence,
3. there is some "reference to theft" in that offence, or

4. such an offence is at least taken into consideration in sentencing that person,

the court may — on the date of conviction (not necessarily the date of sentence, though how this is possible where an offence must first be taken into account is unclear) — make an order for restitution. Such an order may consist in the return of the actual property taken, any other property representing the property taken or a sum not exceeding the value of the property stolen, to be taken out of monies seized from the person convicted when arrested. The English Theft Act provides for similar powers of restoration of property that has been wrongfully appropriated. That instrument uses the same "entitled to recover" formula as this provision. The C.L.R.C. seemed to feel that this procedure should be used only in clear cases (para. 164). This indicates that the formula for restitution now set out in the law of theft and fraud offences contemplates distinct proceedings in cases which are not clearly meritorious.

S.56(2) makes it possible to combine restitution orders of, for example, property into which the original stolen property has been converted, plus any money seized to make up the original value.

S.56(3) makes an interesting facility available to a person who has unwittingly purchased stolen goods. They may apply to court to have monies paid over to them from the same source as the victim. This does give rise to the issue of priority (which no doubt will be in the primary victim's favour). A second issue which arises is the method of proving the loss to the purchaser — this will not be difficult where a loan is taken out to cover the purchase, but cash purchases are not easily amenable to such a provision. Issues of such proofs are provided for to some extent in s.56(4), but clearly may often not be conclusive, though they do give an outline of the lengths to which a District Court is expected to go in determining such applications.

Stolen property is extended the benefit of the definition provided in s.20 and the section as a whole should not prejudice any police property application taken under the Police Property (Act) 1897.

Provision of information to juries

57.—(1) In a trial on indictment of an offence under this Act, the trial judge may order that copies of any or all of the following documents shall be given to the jury in any form that the judge considers appropriate:

(*a*) any document admitted in evidence at the trial,

(*b*) the transcript of the opening speeches of counsel,

(*c*) any charts, diagrams, graphics, schedules or agreed summaries of evidence produced at the trial,

(*d*) the transcript of the whole or any part of the evidence given at the trial,

(*e*) the transcript of the closing speeches of counsel,

(*f*) the transcript of the trial judge's charge to the jury,

(*g*) any other document that in the opinion of the trial judge would be of assistance to the jury in its deliberations including, where appropriate, an affidavit by an accountant summarising, in a form which is likely to be comprehended by the jury, any transactions by the accused or other persons which are relevant to the offence.

(2) If the prosecutor proposes to apply to the trial judge for an order that a document mentioned in *subsection (1)(g)* shall be given to the jury, the prosecutor shall give a copy of the document to the accused in advance of the trial and, on the hearing of the application, the trial judge shall take into account any representations made by or on behalf of the accused in relation to it.

(3) Where the trial judge has made an order that an affidavit mentioned in *subsection (1)(g)* shall be given to the jury, the accountant concerned—

(a) shall be summoned by the prosecutor to attend at the trial as an expert witness, and

(b) may be required by the trial judge, in an appropriate case, to give evidence in regard to any relevant accounting procedures or principles.

GENERAL NOTE

The trial of issues of fraud and dishonesty in general have proven to be some of the more lengthy, complex and difficult of processes. Jurors, it must be emphasised, cannot be assumed to know about such things as accounting practices (*R. v. Sundhers* [1998] Crim. L.R. 497 C.A.), and yet they are required to consider vast tracts of evidence and countless exhibits which they are as likely as not cannot fathom without guidance. In Charlton, the learned authors cite the example of the Britannia Park fraud as a particularly (but not surprisingly) long, complex and drawn-out trial which took 17 months to hear (Charlton, para. 10.26-1). However, one is tempted to suggest that the many politically charged tribunals set up specifically to embark upon such investigations might be another case in point — though they are quite distinct in their constitutional role and jurisdiction. It is instructive, nonetheless, to read some of the observations cited in such cases:

"The awesome time-scale of the trial, the multiplicity of the issues, the distance between evidence, speeches and retirement and not least the two prolonged periods of absence by the jury (amounting to 126 days) could be regarded as combining to destroy a basic assumption. This assumption is that a jury determine guilt or innocence upon evidence which they are able as humans both to comprehend and remember, and upon which they have been addressed at a time when the parties can reasonably expect the speeches to make an impression upon the deliberations." (*Kellard* [1995] 2 Cr. App. R. 134, *per* Mann L.J. at 144–145)

At one point the Law Reform Commission was in favour of preliminary hearings to deal with such complexities (L.R.C. 55/1997, p.342), and it remains a valid argument that pre-trial preparation can save time and expense as well as clarify many of the problems in relation to juries (see comments in respect of s.57(4) contained in the General Introductory Note). Indeed, Corker examines the merits of dispensing with the jury altogether in fraud cases (Corker, "Trying Fraud Cases Without Juries" [2002] Crim. L.R. 283). The constitutional position, however, is clear in this jurisdiction. Art. 38.5 provides as follows: "save in the case of trial of offences under section 2, section 3 or section 4 of the Article no person shall be tried on any criminal charge without a jury."

It is submitted that none of these alternatives could conceivably relate to crimes of serious fraud. S.2 concerns minor offences; s.4 relates to military courts; and finally, though s.3 refers to offences in respect of which the ordinary courts are inadequate to secure the effective administration of justice (which might be relevant), that section goes on to qualify this with the objective of preservation of public peace and order. Though it might be said that the public at large are disturbed by high profile cases of serious fraud, none of these scenarios apply. Indeed, the Report of the Government Advisory Committee on Fraud, 1992 firmly recommend that no matter what doubts there may be over the ability of juries to cope with serious fraud trials, that public peace and order are hardly at risk" (para. 8.2). The only other option available would be to truncate or divide s.3 by referendum, which might not seem so unreal a proposition given:

1. the resurgent cycles of sensation amongst the public at scandals arising out of misappropriation of funds, and

2. the inferior constitutional position of quasi-judicial bodies to deal with matters of distinct and exigent judicial function.

The Report of the Government Advisory Committee on Fraud, 1992 also recommended agreement on and summaries of evidence to assist the jury (paras 7.9–7.11 and 7.17). This report and the section itself is probably a result of one of the recommendations in *Simmonds* [1969] 1 Q.B. 685; Arlidge and Parry summarise the relevant recommendation as follows (para. 15–009):

"Schedules of evidence which it is anticipated will be given should be prepared in advance of the trial. Not all evidence can or should be scheduled …. In a fraud case, however, there will often be repetitive evidence based on documents which need not be produced if a schedule is made of them. This can be done by agreement between counsel, and often by admission. It is rarely suitable to schedule evidence which is at the heart of the case and is disputed by the defence. The written word may have an unduly persuasive effect. Often, however, a schedule may by agreement replace the evidence on which it is based if the defence admits it. If it is not admitted and the judge takes the view that disputes on it are minor matters, there would seem to be no reason why he should not order it to go before the jury, even if the defence objects; but the evidence supporting the schedule would have to be called, and the jury warned strongly that the schedule itself is not evidence."

The section was conspicuously the only section yet to be commenced at the time of final edit.

PART 9

Miscellaneous

Liability for offences by bodies corporate and unincorporated

58.—(1) Where—

    (*a*) an offence under this Act has been committed by a body corporate, and

    (*b*) the offence is proved to have been committed with the consent or connivance of, or to have been attributable to any neglect on the part of, a person who was either—

        (i) a director, manager, secretary or other officer of the body corporate, or

        (ii) a person purporting to act in any such capacity,

that person, as well as the body corporate, is guilty of an offence and liable to be proceeded against and punished as if he or she were guilty of the first-mentioned offence.

(2) Where the affairs of a body corporate are managed by its members, *subsection (1)* shall apply in relation to the acts and defaults of a member in connection with the member's functions of management as if he or she were a director or manager of the body corporate.

(3) The foregoing provisions shall apply, with the necessary modifications, in relation to offences under this Act committed by an unincorporated body.

General Note

The Minister introduced the Bill of this Act at Second Stage addressing the concern that legislation often:

"… only catches the small time criminal or the unfortunate individual who engages in crime to feed a drug habit …. [s. 58, however] deals with a situation where an offence is committed by a company with the consent or connivance of a director or manager of the company. In those circumstances, the person as well as the company will be guilty of an offence" (527 *Dáil Debates* Col. 247).

Therefore, where an offence under the Act is committed by a company, certain persons, *e.g.* a director or manager, who have connived in the commission of the offence will be guilty of the offence along with the company. The distinction with "bodies corporate" is that it may be managed by its members — who also may be personally liable in criminal law.

As a general principle, as Card put it:

> "The conviction of a corporation does not in itself involve any person in criminal liability. On the other hand, of course, where a corporation is criminally liable for an offence, a natural person involved may also be convicted of it, as a joint perpetrator (if he is the person who physically committed the offence) or as an accomplice (if he added, abetted, counselled or procured its commission" (*Card Cross & Jones* (15th ed.), para. 20.63).

He goes on to put provisions like s. 58 in context:

> "in addition, many statutes now provide for the guilt of controlling officers of the corporation who should not be criminally liable under ordinary principles, or whose guilt it would otherwise be hard to prove. This makes it easier to get at those who are really responsible for the corporation's offence" (*ibid.*).

Under this section, it is provided that the individual found to have connived, consented, etc., (which are mental perspectives which must be accompanied at least by acquiescence) so as to attract liability *with* the company by which the offence was committed will be punished "as if" they had also committed the offence committed by the body corporate. The general principles of corporate liability will apply to prosecutions of corporations as defendants under this Act. These principles are honed by the *personal* criteria of consent and connivance taken from s.18 of the English Theft Act 1968. Consent infers awareness of and agreement in the alleged misdealings (C.L.R.C., para. 104 (1966); *Huckerby* [1970] 1 All E.R. 18). Connivance is less than this but is equally an offence, described in *Somerset v. Hart* (1884) 12 Q.B. 360 as "wilful blindness to the misdealings". Thus, by connivance and consent the individual defendant is assigned the effective status of accomplice. S.58, however, is wider still to add "attributable neglect" to the formula. This addition in our statute, absent from s.18 of the English model, invites circumspection. It is a very broad requirement — almost certainly so wide as to be inappropriate to principal (as opposed to attributed) criminal liability. On deliberate failure on the part of management, see *Tamm* [1973] Crim. L.R. 115; *cf.* Smith & Hogan (10th ed.), p.584; see below. Two cases are apposite. *Wilson* [1997] 1 All E.R. 119 would be authority for the proposition that s.58 is in effect an imposition of liability on an officer for negligence in failing to *prevent* an offence; *Bland* [1985] R.T.R. 171 would suggest that this will only be so where there is a duty on the individual defendant to check the *actual conduct* of the *actual perpetrator* of the misdealings. This second case will be of considerable import in assuaging management-wide paranoia. It is not required to keep a constant check, in the ordinary course, on members of staff who have sufficient competence, standing and experience to be capable of their own respective sphere of control. Further, it is interesting that the English C.L.R.C. took the position before the passing of the English Act that the measure should follow:

> "a form of provisions commonly included in statutes, where an offence is of a kind to be committed by bodies corporate and where it is desired to put the management under a positive obligation to prevent irregularities, if aware of them. Passive acquiescence does not, under the general law, make a person liable as a party to the offence, but there are clearly cases (of which we think this is one) where the director's responsibilities for his company require him to prevent fraud and where consent or connivance amount to guilt" (para. 104).

The clear view, then, of the original commentators on the draft English model was that *passive acquiescence* was not sufficient. In contrast, the draftsman has chosen to include the now common form on corporate liability with extension to its controlling members. But then, liability by virtue of the phrase "attributable neglect" can only apply to an offence of strict liability, and arguably that kind of liability is out of order in criminal cases (A.T.H. Smith, p.774), and yet the word negligence is expressly chosen in a criminal statute. Where negligence is not compatible with the criminal law, it should at least be subject to something more than objective analysis; Hart would ask (*Oxford Essays in Jurisprudence* 29):

> "1. Did the accused fail to take those precautions which any reasonable man with normal capacities would in the circumstances have taken?
> 2. Could the accused, given his mental and physical capacities have taken those precautions?"

But then, as we noted above, no offence is created by the formula, instead it creates an extended form of secondary liability. No criminal offence can incur personal liability under a test of mere negligence without strict liability. Thus the offence here applies automatically to the individual, but is not of itself an offence. In other words, an individual who is liable under the section is guilty of the same offence as that committed by the corporation, but he does not commit a separate offence by virtue of s.58 (*cf. Wilson*).

It is a matter of fact for the jury to decide whether in the circumstances the individual defendant was an officer. We have considered this and the merits of corporate liability above (see General Introductory Note). Finally, it is for the prosecution to establish the duty purported to have been neglected (*Huckerby*).

Reporting of offences

59.—(1) In this section—

"firm" means a partnership, a corporate or unincorporated body or a self-employed individual;

"relevant person" means a person—

  (*a*) who audits the accounts of a firm, or

  (*b*) who otherwise with a view to reward assists or advises a firm in the preparation or delivery of any information, or of any declaration, return, account or other document, which the person knows will be, or is likely to be, used for the purpose of keeping or auditing the accounts of the firm,

but does not include an employee of a firm who—

  (i) in that capacity so assists or advises the firm, and

  (ii) whose income from so doing consists solely of emoluments chargeable to income tax under Schedule E, as defined in section 19 of the Taxes Consolidation Act, 1997.

(2) Where the accounts of a firm, or as the case may be any information or document mentioned in *subsection (1)(b)*, indicate that—

  (*a*) an offence under this Act (other than *sections 8, 12 to 15, 49(1)* and *52(8)*) may have been committed by the firm concerned, or

  (*b*) such an offence may have been committed in relation to its affairs by a partner in the firm or, in the case of a corporate or unincorporated body, by a director, manager, secretary or other employee thereof, or by the self-employed individual concerned,

the relevant person shall, notwithstanding any professional obligations of privilege or confidentiality, report that fact to a member of the Garda Síochána.

(3) A disclosure in a report made in good faith by a relevant person to a member of the Garda Síochána under *subsection (2)* shall not be treated as a breach of any restriction imposed by statute or otherwise or involve the person in liability of any kind.

(4) A person who fails, without reasonable excuse, to comply with the duty imposed by *subsection (2)* is guilty of an offence and is liable on summary conviction to a fine not exceeding £1,500 or imprisonment for a term not exceeding 12 months or both.

GENERAL NOTE

The L.R.C. in 1992 felt that:

"Good internal auditing is the best bulwark against fraud and we would recommend that any auditor who discovers fraud or any form of criminal appropriation in a company's accounts should be required to report same to the gardai" (L.R.C. 43/92, para. 37.9).

In seeking to do so, this section provides for assistance in the investigation and prosecution of the bulk of the offences under this Act, requiring certain persons to report to the gardai matters which indicate that the company or those responsible for its operation may have committed such an offence. It was stated by the Commission that: "The board of a company may be tempted not to report an employee found engaging in fraudulent conduct; this may result in financial loss to shareholders" (*ibid.* at para. 37.2). The provision as set out here, however, goes beyond that to include the employee who might suspect that an "indication" that an offence under this act "may" have been committed, must report this to the gardai. The category of persons expected to report, or "relevant persons," is confined to those with some part to play in the auditing process, extending to those who provide information in the auditing of the accounts of a firm. The issue of duties upon *victims* of fraud to disclose the misdealing was considered by the Law Reform Commission in its Report on the Law Relating to Dishonesty (L.R.C. 43/92, Chap. 37). The provision eventually arrived at goes somewhat beyond the L.R.C.'s view that "[t]he person upon whom the duty to disclose might lie would, almost certainly, be a person who had a supervisory role and, therefore, a vested interest in covering up" (*ibid.* at para. 37.2).

S.59(1) defines both "firm" and "relevant person". The L.R.C. commented that though "[m]uch fraud is engaged in by company directors and occasionally accountants," it went on to say "[t]hey frequently enlist the aid of bookkeepers, computer operators or other employees in perpetrating fraud either by giving a share in the proceeds or by intimidation with regard to their keeping their jobs" (*ibid.* at para. 37.10). Interestingly, "relevant person" excludes the employee as defined by his or her tax status. This has long been a point of much debate in employment law (*i.e.* whether or not, in fact, tax categorisation bears out the true nature of one's employment). Few will argue, however, that classification under Sched. E of the Tax Acts and generally the concomitant having *pro rata* insurance taken care of by one's employer is indeed a characteristic which indicates that the worker is an employee. This may be for no better reason than the mere fact that he or she has taken no active role in organising his or her own tax and insurance affairs with a view to perhaps maximising financial position. Indeed, this might be the very attitude which this section as a whole intends to scrutinse.

S.59(2). Neither confidentiality nor privilege will be considered for the purpose of this section where any offence under this Act other than:
1. making off without payment,
2. burglary,
3. aggravated burglary,
4. robbery,
5. possession of articles,
6. obstruction of a Garda acting on a warrant, or
7. failure to comply with an order to produce evidential material
may have been committed. Under this section it is incumbent upon a partner, director, manager, secretary or other employee of the firm, or upon the self-employed individual concerned to report any information which indicates that any such offence may have been committed. This does appear to relate to offences already committed and carries with it no pre-emptive obligation.

S.59(3) allows a relevant person to disclose information without risk of liability or breach of statute. The duty to disclose may not easily be imposed upon members of a firm; apart from inherent difficulties of proof is the general motivation and efficacy of application which has proven to be lacking (see *Fraud Trial Report* (HMSO, 1986 – *the Roskill Report*, para. 2.5; see also L.R.C. 43/92, para. 37.5)

Interestingly, the L.R.C. also raises the issue of dealing with any assistance to offences under this Act by the traditional means of being an "accessory after the fact" and misprison (*ibid.* at para. 37.3). They expressly recommended that the law in relation to accessories should be reviewed rather than making piecemeal attempts to provide for them. The position at present is that the law in relation to accessories has been reviewed. S.7 of the Criminal Law Act, repealed entirely by s.8 of the Accessories and Abettors Act 1861, merely gave legislative recognition to the common law recognition of such categories of offenders. The main purpose of the Criminal Law Act 1997 was to abolish the concepts of misdemeanour and felony. Among the effects this had was to leave without basis those certain sophistications of the criminal law which referred only to felonies. Felonies attracted this more elaborate system of offence, because the crimes were more serious. These particularised offences are somewhat more developed. Simple misdemeanours involved no such concepts, and those accused of "aiding, abetting, counselling or procuring" were treated alike as principal offenders. Now that the concepts of "felony" and "misdemeanour" had been removed, it was to be likewise with accessoror, as the law would now treat all aiders, abettors, counsellors and procurers as principal offenders. Thus the Act retains the misdemeanour rule, now extending it to cover those offences that were previously classed as felonies.

Evidence in proceedings

60.—(1) For the purposes of any provision of this Act relating to specified conduct outside the State—

> (*a*) a document purporting to be signed by a lawyer practising in the state or a territorial unit within it where the conduct is alleged to have occurred and stating that the conduct is an offence under the law of that state or territorial unit, and
>
> (*b*) a document purporting to be a translation of a document mentioned in *paragraph (a)* and to be certified as correct by a person appearing to be competent to so certify,

shall be admissible in any proceedings, without further proof, as evidence of the matters mentioned in those documents, unless the contrary is shown.

(2) For the purposes of *section 45* a document purporting to be signed by an officer of the Department of Foreign Affairs and stating that a passport was issued by the Department to a specified person on a specified date and that, to the best of the officer's knowledge and belief, the person has not ceased to be an Irish citizen shall be admissible in any proceedings, without further proof, as evidence that the person was an Irish citizen on the date on which the offence under that section with which the person is charged was committed, unless the contrary is shown.

GENERAL NOTE

Remarkable in its reliance upon a private professional, or someone "purporting to be" such, this section facilitates matters of evidence for the prosecution of offences with an extra-territorial dimension under the Act. Foreign documents might be admissible in the relevant foreign court, but would not normally be admissible here unless they complied with Irish law. In the absence of this statutory provision, a question of evidence would arguably have to be determined in accordance with the *lex fori* (*i.e.* the law of the forum, or of the place where the document would ordinarily be recognised by law), and not by Irish law (*Bain v. Whitehaven Ry.* (1850) 3 H.L.C. 1 at 19; *Hamlyn v. Talisker* [1894] A.C. 202 at 213). Foreign law must be proved as a fact by skilled witnesses (*F&K Jabbour v. Custodian of Israeli Absentee Property* [1954] 1 W.L.R. 139; see also *O'Callaghan v. O'Sullivan* [1925] 1 I.R. 90). Interpretation of the document does not seem to fall under any recognised principle, though in civil law it would be the proper law of contract, after proof of translation and of the local meaning of the terms (*Cahtenay v. Brazilian Co.* [1891] 1 Q.B. 89, as cited in *Phipson on Evidence* (15th ed., 2000), para. 1–20). The established means by which an offence is deemed to be an extradition offence, however, would make it necessary to look at the evidence supplied by the requesting state (*Neilson* [1984] A.C. 606). Conspicuously there is no such requirement here.

Jurisdiction of District Court in certain proceedings

61.—For the purposes of the exercise of jurisdiction by a judge of the District Court in proceedings for an offence under this Act committed on a vessel or hovercraft or on an installation in the territorial seas or in a designated area (within the meaning of the Continental Shelf Act, 1968) the offence may be treated as having been committed in any place in the State.

GENERAL NOTE

This section provides quite literal meaning to the term "off-shore" funds, which have resulted in so much public debate both here and in other jurisdictions. It is sufficient, generally, that only part of an offence is effected within the State for the jurisdiction of the criminal courts to apply (*R. v. Baxter* [1972] Q.B. 1). Specific to territorial waters, however, we have the Maritime Jurisdiction Act 1959 which provides that every offence committed within the territorial seas or internal waters of the State is an offence within the jurisdiction of the State and may be dealt with by a court of competent jurisdiction even if committed on board or by means of a foreign ship. By virtue of s.10 of that Act a person may be arrested on suspicion of any offence. The inclusion of s.61, then, would appear to cover ground (or sea) already covered, but is probably a measure to remove doubt that the prior law in s.15 of the Larceny Act 1916 could assume extra-territorial jurisdiction (*State (Foley) v. Director of Public Prosecutions*, unreported, High Court, June 23, 1979).

Amendment of section 9 of Married Women's Status Act, 1957

62.—Section 9 of the Married Women's Status Act, 1957, is hereby amended by the substitution for subsection (3) of the following subsection:

"(3) No criminal proceedings referred to in subsection (1) or (2) shall be taken by a spouse against the other spouse except by or with the consent of the Director of Public Prosecutions.".

GENERAL NOTE

A partner can steal from a partner, and a fraud consists of making a gain or causing loss by deception, it should be no surprise then that marriage gives no immunity to the offences under this Act. The permission of the DPP, however, is required for criminal proceedings to be taken in such circumstances by virtue of this section. The wording suggests that the spouse actually take criminal proceedings against a spouse. Though possible, it is very unusual for a private citizen to prosecute an offence. In any event, this precondition, presumably on the "making of a complaint", will have to be based on strong policy grounds for the common good, otherwise it is susceptible to possible constitutional challenge for discrimination on the grounds of marital status; but then again, it might be the constitutional protection of the institution of marriage which founds this pre-condition. It is nevertheless relevant to note that it is an established principle of law that spouses may be restricted in the evidence which they might give against one another at trial.

Amendment of Defence Act, 1954

63.—The Defence Act, 1954, is hereby amended by the substitution for section 156 (as substituted by the Larceny Act, 1990) of the following section:

"156.—(1) Every person subject to military law who—

    (*a*) steals or otherwise unlawfully obtains any property belonging to a person subject to military law or any public service property or service property, or

    (*b*) handles or possesses (within the meaning of *section 17* or *18* of the *Criminal Justice (Theft and Fraud Offences) Act, 2001*) any such property,

is guilty of an offence against military law and shall, on conviction by court-martial, be liable to suffer imprisonment for any term not exceeding two years or any less punishment awardable by a court martial.

(2) The said *sections 17* and *18* shall apply to the offences of handling and possessing under subsection (1)(*b*) of this section as they apply to the offences of handling and possessing stolen or otherwise unlawfully obtained property.".

GENERAL NOTE

This amendment brings into existence a parallel criminal code to the one to which civilians are subject. Penalties under that parallel code can be seen in ss.209 and 210 of the Defence Act 1954

Amendment of Bail Act, 1997

64.—The Schedule to the Bail Act, 1997, is hereby amended by the substitution, for the matter contained in paragraph 17, of "Any offence under the *Criminal Justice (Theft and Fraud Offences) Act, 2001.*" and by the deletion of the section headed "Forgery etc. offences.".

GENERAL NOTE

In keeping with the current system of incremental amendment of even relatively new statutes, these consequential amendments are made to synchronise legislation which pertains to relevant procedures in the present Act.

Effect of Act and transitional provisions

65.—(1) This Act, save as otherwise provided by it, shall, as regards offences under any of its provisions, have effect only in relation to offences wholly or partly committed on or after the commencement of any such provision.

(2) No repeal or amendment by this Act of any enactment relating to procedure or evidence or to the jurisdiction or powers of any court or to the effect of a conviction shall affect the operation of the enactment in relation to offences committed before the commencement of this Act or to proceedings for any such offence.

(3) If—

(*a*) a person is charged in the alternative with having committed an offence under a statute or rule of law in force immediately before the commencement of this Act and an offence under this Act, and

(*b*) it is proved that the person did acts which would constitute either of the offences charged, but it is not proved whether those acts were done before or after such commencement,

the person may be convicted of the first-mentioned offence but shall not be liable to a penalty greater than the lesser of the maximum penalties provided for the two offences with which the person was charged.

(4) Except as regards offences committed before the commencement of this Act and except where the context otherwise requires—

    (*a*) references in any enactment passed before this Act to an offence abolished by this Act shall, subject to any express amendment or repeal made by this Act, have effect as references to the corresponding offence under this Act, and

    (*b*) without prejudice to *paragraph* (*a*), references, however expressed, in any enactment, whenever passed, to theft or stealing (including references to stolen goods) or related offences, and references to robbery, burglary, aggravated burglary, receiving or handling stolen property, forgery or counterfeiting shall be construed in accordance with the provisions of this Act, and any such enactment shall have effect accordingly, with any necessary modifications.

(5)(*a*) The repeal by *section 3(1)* of sections 23 (robbery), 23A (burglary) and 23B (aggravated burglary) of the Larceny Act, 1916, shall not affect the operation of those sections for the purposes of section 2 of, and paragraph 9 of the Schedule to, the Criminal Law (Jurisdiction) Act, 1976, and accordingly that section and that paragraph shall have effect as if *section 3(1)* had not been enacted.

    (*b*) References in *paragraph* (*a*) to sections 23, 23A and 23B of the Larceny Act, 1916, are to those sections as substituted, or as the case may be inserted, by sections 5 to 7 of the Criminal Law (Jurisdiction) Act, 1976.

(6) On the commencement of this subsection—

    (*a*) *subsection* (5) shall cease to have effect,

    (*b*) sections 5 to 7 of the Criminal Law (Jurisdiction) Act, 1976, shall be repealed, and

    (*c*) the following paragraph shall be substituted for paragraph 9 of the Schedule to the Criminal Law (Jurisdiction) Act, 1976:

"Robbery and burglary

9. Any offence under the following provisions of the *Criminal Justice (Theft and Fraud Offences) Act, 2001*:

    (*a*) *section 13* (aggravated burglary);

    (*b*) *section 14* (robbery).".

GENERAL NOTE

The legislature has adopted the now normal practice in criminal statutes of seamless continuation, from offences replaced, to the new offence. This is achieved by deeming reference to the former offences to be those under the new statute. Where penalties differ, the defendant is given the benefit of the doubt, and the lesser penalty is imposed. It is intended that no change made by this Act is to disturb any effect (especially conviction) of any enactment which might be altered or affected by this Act.

S.65(1) provides that only offences committed (at least partly) after the relevant commencement date in this Act will be treated as "offences under its provisions", unless the Act specifically provides otherwise. Ss. 23, 53, 58 and 60(1) as well as all of Pts 5 and 7 will come into effect on the passing of the Act. The Minister appointed the operative date or dates for the remainder, which in the case of s.23 (which inserts an new s.57A into the Criminal Justice Act 1994) was April 2, 2002, and for the remainder (except s.57), August 1, 2002. Commencement of s.57, concerning the provision of information to juries, remained outstanding at the time of writing.

S.65(2) states, for the purpose of removing doubt, that any repeal or amendment effected by this Act with respect to procedure or evidence or to the jurisdiction or powers of any court, or to the effect of a conviction will not affect the operation of that amended or repealed enactment in relation to offences committed before the commencement of this Act or to proceedings for any such offence.

S.65(3) ensures that where any person is charged with alternative offences, and one of them is an offence under this Act, any doubt as to the commencement of the Act and the date of that offence should not prejudice the proceedings against that accused save as far as maximum penalties, which must not be higher than that provided for the relevant alternative charge under this Act. The wording is cautionary in the use of "acts which would constitute either" an offence under the new Act or prior law. No reference is made to offences which are now abolished (on which see comments in General Note on s.3 above). This is left to be dealt with in s.64(4).

S.65(4) allows the weight of statutory reference to abolished offences which may have a corresponding offence under this Act to refer instead to the corresponding offence (as it is here amended) in this Act. This does not apply to offences committed before commencement. There is difficulty in what constitutes a "corresponding offence." No problem arises for offences like burglary or robbery, but those types of prohibited conduct which have received considerable restructuring in the way they are to be criminalised do not necessarily fall to be considered as a "corresponding offence". The inevitable question will be whether larceny is now theft, which generally speaking it is, but strictly speaking is far from necessarily so. Equally, offences of false pretences do not, strictly speaking, "correspond" to offences of deception. Finally, if larceny corresponds to theft, does this mean that all the offences attributed to the general term "larceny" can be said to be a corresponding offence to that of theft? On the difficulty of transition where common law offences are abolished, see General Note on s.3 above.

S.65(5) preserves the schedule, amendments and references to certain offences under the Criminal Law (Jurisdiction) Act 1976. This is possible because of the existence of corresponding offences under this Act. The 1976 Act extended the criminal law of the State to certain acts done in Northern Ireland, and reformed the criminal law in other respects, *inter alia*, significant amendments of the Larceny Act 1916 which are now repealed by this Act.

S.65(6) is a trigger mechanism (by Ministerial order) to the removal of what is preserved by s.65(5) above. The necessary amendment of the 1976 Act is effected by the substitution of a new para. 9 in the Schedule.

Bibliography with key:

Arlidge & Parry on Fraud (2nd ed., Sweet & Maxwell, London, 1996)

Ashe & Reid, *Money Laundering, Risks and Liabilities* (Roundhall Sweet and Maxwell, Dublin, 2000).

Braddish v. DPP, unreported, Supreme Court, May 18, 2001.

Charlton, McDermott and Bolger, *Criminal Law* (Butterworths, Ireland, 1999)

CLRC – Criminal Law Revision Committee (England) Eighth Report on *Theft and Related Offences*, Cmnd 2977 (1966).

Dunne v. DPP, unreported, Supreme Court, April 25, 2002.

Ghosh [1982] 2 All E.R. 689.

Gomez [1993] A.C. 442.

Hinks [2000] 3 W.L.R. 1590.

Kelly: The Irish Constitution (Hogan and White eds, (3rd ed., Butterworths, 1994)).

Kenny, *Outlines of Criminal Law* (1st ed., 1902).

Kuhl, "The Criminal Law Protection of the Communities' Financial Interests against Fraud" (1998) Criminal Law Review Crim. L.R. Pt 1, 259; Pt 2, 323.

L.R.C. 43/92, Law Reform Commission Report on the Law relating to Dishonesty.

L.R.C. 23/87, Law Reform Commission Report on Receiving Stolen Property.

McCutcheon, *The Larceny Act 1916* (Dublin, 1988).

McCutcheon ICLSA 1990.

Model Penal Code and Commentaries, American Law Institute *(Official Draft and Revised Comments)*, P.W. Low ed., 1980) Part II, Vol. 2.

Morris [1984] A.C. 320.

Rowell, *Counterfeiting and Forgery, A Practical Guide to the Law* (Butterworths, London, 1986).

Ryan & Magee, *The Irish Criminal Process* (Mercier Press, Dublin and Cork, 1983).

Shute, "Appropriation and the Law of Theft" (2002) Crim. L.R. 445.

Smith, A.T.H., *Property Offences, The Protection of Property through the Criminal Law* (Sweet and Maxwell, London, 1994).

Smith, J.C., *The Law of Theft* (8th ed., Butterworths, London 1997)

Smith & Hogan, *Criminal Law* (1st. ed., Butterworths, London, 1965)

Smith & Hogan, *Criminal Law* (10th ed., Butterworths Lexus Nexus, London, 2001)

Turner, *Documents in the law of Forgery* 32 Va. L. Rev. 939 (1946)

Vervaele, *Fraud Against the Community, The Need for European Fraud Legislation* (Kluwer Law and Taxation Publishers, Deventer, The Netherlands, 1992.

Wells, "Corporations: Culture, Risk and Criminal Liability" [1993] Crim. L.R. 551.

Section 3

SCHEDULE 1

ENACTMENTS REPEALED

Session and Chapter or Number & Year (1)	Short Title (2)	Extent of repeal (3)
24 & 25 Vict., c. 96	Larceny Act, 1861	The whole Act, except sections 12 to 16 and 24 and 25
24 & 25 Vict., c. 98	Forgery Act, 1861	The whole Act
24 & 25 Vict., c. 99	Coinage Offences Act, 1861	The whole Act
24 & 25 Vict., c. 50	Summary Jurisdiction (Ireland) Act, 1862	Sections 4 to 8
35 & 36 Vict., c. 57	Debtors (Ireland) Act, 1872	Section 13
38 & 39 Vict., c. 24	Falsification of Accounts Act, 1875	The whole Act
56 & 57 Vict., c. 71	Sale of Goods Act, 1893	Section 24
3 & 4 Geo. 5, c. 27	Forgery Act, 1913	The whole Act
6 & 7 Geo. 5, c. 50	Larceny Act, 1916	The whole Act
No. 2 of 1951	Criminal Justice Act, 1951	Sections 10 and 13 and ref. nos. 8, 11, 14, 15 and 20 of First Schedule
No. 2 of 1956	Gaming and Lotteries Act, 1956	Section 11
No. 1 of 1963	Official Secrets Act, 1963	Sections 7 and 8
No. 22 of 1984	Criminal Justice Act, 1984	Section 16
No. 9 of 1990	Larceny Act, 1990	The whole Act

Section 41   SCHEDULE 2

TEXT IN THE ENGLISH LANGUAGE OF THE CONVENTION DRAWN UP ON THE BASIS OF
ARTICLE K.3 OF THE TREATY ON EUROPEAN UNION, ON THE PROTECTION
OF THE EUROPEAN COMMUNITIES' FINANCIAL INTERESTS DONE AT BRUSSELS
ON 26 JULY 1995

CONVENTION

**Drawn up on the basis of Article K.3 of the Treaty on European Union,
on the protection of the European Communities' financial interests**

THE HIGH CONTRACTING PARTIES to this Convention, Member States
of the European Union,

REFERRING to the Act of the Council of the European Union of 26 July
1995;

DESIRING to ensure that their criminal laws contribute effectively to the protection of the financial interests of the European Communities;

NOTING that fraud affecting Community revenue and expenditure in many
cases is not confined to a single country and is often committed by organized
criminal networks;

CONVINCED that protection of the European Communities' financial interests calls for the criminal prosecution of fraudulent conduct injuring those interests and requires, for that purpose, the adoption of a common definition;

CONVINCED of the need to make such conduct punishable with effective,
proportionate and dissuasive criminal penalties, without prejudice to the possibility of applying other penalties in appropriate cases, and of the need, at least
in serious cases, to make such conduct punishable with deprivation of liberty
which can give rise to extradition;

RECOGNIZING that businesses play an important role in the areas financed
by the European Communities and that those with decision-making powers in
business should not escape criminal responsibility in appropriate circumstances;

DETERMINED to combat together fraud affecting the European Communities' financial interests by undertaking obligations concerning jurisdiction, extradition, and mutual cooperation,

HAVE AGREED ON THE FOLLOWING PROVISIONS:

Article 1

General provisions

1. For the purposes of this Convention, fraud affecting the European Communities' financial interests shall consist of:

(*a*) in respect of expenditure, any intentional act or omission relating to:

— the use or presentation of false, incorrect or incomplete statements or documents, which has as its effect the misappropriation or wrongful retention of funds from the general budget of the European Communities or budgets managed by, or on behalf of, the European Communities,

— non-disclosure of information in violation of a specific obligation, with the same effect,

— the misapplication of such funds for purposes other than those for which they were originally granted;

(*b*) in respect of revenue, any intentional act or omission relating to:

— the use or presentation of false, incorrect or incomplete statements or documents, which has as its effect the illegal diminution of the resources of the general budget of the European Communities or budgets managed by, or on behalf of, the European Communities,

— non-disclosure of information in violation of a specific obligation, with the same effect,

— misapplication of a legally obtained benefit, with the same effect.

2. Subject to Article 2(2), each Member State shall take the necessary and appropriate measures to transpose paragraph 1 into their national criminal law in such a way that the conduct referred to therein constitutes criminal offences.

3. Subject to Article 2(2), each Member State shall also take the necessary measures to ensure that the intentional preparation or supply of false, incorrect or incomplete statements or documents having the effect described in paragraph 1 constitutes a criminal offence if it is not already punishable as a principal offence or as participation in, instigation of, or attempt to commit, fraud as defined in paragraph 1.

4. The intentional nature of an act or omission as referred to in paragraphs 1 and 3 may be inferred from objective, factual circumstances.

Article 2

Penalties

1. Each Member State shall take the necessary measures to ensure that the conduct referred to in Article 1, and participating in, instigating, or attempting the conduct referred to in Article 1 (1), are punishable by effective, proportionate and dissuasive criminal penalties, including, at least in cases of serious fraud, penalties involving deprivation of liberty which can give rise to extradition, it being understood that serious fraud shall be considered to be fraud involving a minimum amount to be set in each Member State. This minimum amount may not be set at a sum exceeding ECU 50 000.

2. However in cases of minor fraud involving a total amount of less than ECU 4 000 and not involving particularly serious circumstances under its laws, a Member State may provide for penalties of a different type from those laid down in paragraph 1.

3. The Council of the European Union, acting unanimously, may alter the amount referred to in paragraph 2.

Article 3

Criminal liability of heads of businesses

Each Member State shall take the necessary measures to allow heads of businesses or any persons having power to take decisions or exercise control within a business to be declared criminally liable in accordance with the principles defined by its national law in cases of fraud affecting the European Community's financial interests, as referred to in Article 1, by a person under their authority acting on behalf of the business.

Article 4

Jurisdiction

1. Each Member State shall take the necessary measures to establish its jurisdiction over the offences it has established in accordance with Article 1 and 2 (1) when:
   — fraud, participation in fraud or attempted fraud affecting the European Communities' financial interests is committed in whole or in part within its territory, including fraud for which the benefit was obtained in that territory,
   — a person within its territory knowingly assists or induces the commission of such fraud within the territory of any other State,
   — the offender is a national of the Member State concerned, provided that the law of that Member State may require the conduct to be punishable also in the country where it occurred.

2. Each Member State may declare, when giving the notification referred to in Article 11 (2), that it will not apply the rule laid down in the third indent of paragraph 1 of this Article.

Article 5

Extradition and prosecution

1. Any Member State which, under its law, does not extradite its own nationals shall take the necessary measures to establish its jurisdiction over the offences it has established in accordance with Articles 1 and 2 (1), when committed by its own nationals outside its territory.

2. Each Member State shall, when one of its nationals is alleged to have committed in another Member State a criminal offence involving the conduct described in Articles 1 and 2 (1), and it does not extradite that person to that other Member State solely on the ground of his or her nationality, submit the case to its competent authorities for the purpose of prosecution if appropriate. In order to enable prosecution to take place, the files, information and exhibits relating to the offence shall be transmitted in accordance with the procedures laid down in Article 6 of the European Convention on Extradition. The requesting Member State shall be informed of the prosecution initiated and of its outcome.

3. A Member State may not refuse extradition in the event of fraud affecting the European Communities' financial interests for the sole reason that it concerns a tax or customs duty offence.

4. For the purposes of this Article, a Member State's own nationals shall be construed in accordance with any declaration made by it under Article 6 (1) (*b*) of the European Convention on Extradition and with paragraph 1 (*c*) of the Article.

Article 6

Cooperation

1. If a fraud as defined in Article 1 constitutes a criminal offence and concerns at least two Member States, those States shall cooperate effectively in the investigation, the prosecution and in carrying out the punishment imposed by means, for example, of mutual legal assistance, extradition, transfer of proceedings or enforcement of sentences passed in another Member State.

2. Where more than one Member State has jurisdiction and has the possibility of viable prosecution of an offence based on the same facts, the Member States involved shall cooperate in deciding which shall prosecute the offender or offenders with a view to centralizing the prosecution in a single Member State where possible.

Article 7

Ne bis in idem

1. Member States shall apply in their national criminal laws the 'ne bis in idem' rule, under which a person whose trial has been finally disposed of in a Member State may not be prosecuted in another Member State in respect of the same facts, provided that if a penalty was imposed, it has been enforced, is actually in the process of being enforced or can no longer be enforced under the laws of the sentencing State.

2. A Member State may, when giving the notification referred to in Article 11 (2), declare that it shall not be bound by paragraph 1 of this Article in one or more of the following cases:

   (*a*) if the facts which were the subject of the judgement rendered abroad took place on its own territory either in whole or in part; in the latter case this exception shall not apply if those facts took place partly on the territory of the Member State where the judgement was rendered;

   (*b*) if the facts which were the subject of the judgment rendered abroad constitute an offence directed against the security or other equally essential interests of that Member State;

   (*c*) if the facts which were the subject of the judgment rendered abroad were committed by an official of the Member State contrary to the duties of his office.

3. The exceptions which may be the subject of a declaration under paragraph 2 shall not apply if the Member State concerned in respect of the same

facts requested the other Member State to bring the prosecution or granted extradition of the person concerned.

4. Relevant bilateral or multilateral agreements concluded between Member States and relevant declarations shall remain unaffected by this Article.

Article 8

Court of Justice

1. Any dispute between Member States on the interpretation or application of this Convention must in an initial stage be examined by the Council in accordance with the procedure set out in Title VI of the Treaty on European Union with a view to reaching a solution.
If no solution is found within six months, the matter may be referred to the Court of Justice of the European Communities by a party to the dispute.

2. Any dispute between one or more Member States and the Commission of the European Communities concerning the application of Article 1 or 10 of this Convention which it has proved impossible to settle through negotiation may be submitted to the Court of Justice.

Article 9

Internal provisions

No provision in this Convention shall prevent Member States from adopting internal legal provisions which go beyond the obligations deriving from this Convention.

Article 10

Transmission

1. Member States shall transmit to the Commission of the European Communities the text of the provisions transposing into their domestic law the obligations imposed on them under the provisions of this Convention.

2. For the purposes of implementing this Convention, the High Contracting Parties shall determine, within the Council of the European Union, the information to be communicated or exchanged between the Member States or between the Member States and the Commission, and also the arrangements for doing so.

Article 11

Entry into force

1. This Convention shall be subject to adoption by the Member States in accordance with their respective constitutional requirements.

2. Member States shall notify the Secretary-General of the Council of the

European Union of the completion of their constitutional requirements for adopting this Convention.

3. This Convention shall enter into force 90 days after the notification, referred to in paragraph 2, by the last Member State to fulfil that formality.

Article 12

Accession

1. This Convention shall be open to accession by any State that becomes a member of the European Union.

2. The text of this Convention in the language of the acceding State, drawn up by the Council of the European Union, shall be authentic.

3. Instruments of accession shall be deposited with the depositary.

4. This Convention shall enter into force with respect to any State that accedes to it 90 days after the deposit of its instrument of accession or on the date of entry into force of the Convention if it has not already entered into force at the time of expiry of the said period 90 days.

Article 13

Depositary

1. The Secretary-General of the Council of the European Union shall act as depositary of this Convention.

2. The depositary shall publish in the Official Journal of the European Communities information on the progress of adoptions and accessions, declarations and reservations, and also any other notification concerning this Convention.

Section 41   SCHEDULE 3

<small>TEXT IN THE IRISH LANGUAGE OF THE CONVENTION DRAWN UP ON THE BASIS OF
ARTICLE K.3 OF THE TREATY ON EUROPEAN UNION, ON THE PROTECTION
OF THE EUROPEAN COMMUNITIES' FINANCIAL INTERESTS DONE AT BRUSSELS
ON 26 JULY 1995</small>

COINBHINSIÚN

arna dhréachtú ar bhonn Airteagal K.3 den Chonradh ar an Aontas Eorpach maidir le leasanna airgeadais na gComhphobal Eorpach a chosaint

TÁ NA hARDPHÁIRTITHE CONARTHACHA sa Choinbhinsiún seo, Ballstáit den Aontas Eorpach,

AG TAGAIRT DÓIBH do Ghníomh ó Chomhairle an Aontais Eorpaigh an ?? Meitheamh 1995;

ÓS MIAN LEO a áirithiú go gcuidíonn a ndlíthe coiriúla go héifeachtach le leasanna airgeadais na gComhphobal Eorpach a chosaint;

AG TABHAIRT DÁ nAIRE DÓIBH nach bhfuil calaois a dhéanann difear d'ioncam agus do chaiteachas an Chomhphobail teoranta do thír amháin i mórán cásanna, agus gur minic gur gréasáin choiriúla eagraithe údar na calaoise sin;

ÓS DEIMHIN LEO go n-éilíonn cosaint leasanna airgeadais na gComhphobal Eorpach go ndéanfar iompar calaoiseach a dhéanann díobháil do na leasanna sin a ionchúiseamh agus gur gá chun na críche sin sainmhíniú coiteann a ghlacadh;

ÓS DEIMHIN LEO gur gá iompar den sórt sin a dhéanamh inphionóis le pionóis choiriúla atá éifeachtach, comhréireach agus athchomhairleach, gan dochar don fhéidearthacht pionóis eile a chur i bhfeidhm i gcásanna iomchuí, agus gur gá ar a laghad i gcásanna tromchúiseacha iompar den sórt sin a dhéanamh inphionóis le cailleadh saoirse a bhféadfaidh eiseachadadh teacht as;

AG AITHINT DÓIBH go bhfuil ról tábhachtach ag gnóthais i réimsí arna maoiniú ag na Comhphobail Eorpacha agus nár chóir go n-éalóidís siúd a bhfuil cumhachtaí cinnteoireachta i ngnóthais acu óna bhfreagracht choiriúil in imthosca iomchuí;

ÓS É A RÚN DAINGEAN calaois a dhéanann díobháil do leasanna airgeadais na gComhphobal Eorpach a chomhrac le chéile trí oibleagáidí a ghlacadh ar láimh maidir le dlínse, eiseachadadh agus comhar frithpháirteach,

TAR ÉIS COMHAONTÚ AR NA FORÁLACHA SEO A LEANAS:

Airteagal 1

Forálacha ginearálta

1. Chun críocha an Choinbhinsiúin seo, is éard é calaois a dhéanann díobháil do leasanna airgeadais na gComhphobal Eorpach:

    (*a*) maidir le caiteachas, aon ghníomh nó neamhghníomh intinneach a bhaineann:

        — le húsáid nó tíolacadh ráiteas nó doiciméad atá bréagach, neamhbheacht nóneamhiomlán, arb é a n-éifeacht mídhílsiú nó

146

coinneáil éagórach cistí as buiséad ginearálta na gComhphobal Eorpach nó as buiséid arna mbainisteoireacht ag na Comhphobail Eorpacha nó thar a gceann,

— le neamhnochtadh faisnéise de shárú ar oibleagáid shonrach ar a bhfuil an éifeacht chéanna,

— le sraonadh cistí den sórt sin chun críocha eile seachas na críocha ar deonaíodh i dtosach báire chucu iad;

(b) maidir le hioncam, aon ghníomh nó neamhghníomh intinneach a bhaineann:

— le húsáid nó tíolacadh ráiteas nó doiciméad atá bréagach, neamhbheacht nó neamhiomlán, arb é a n-éifeacht acmhainní bhuiséad ginearálta na gComhphobal Eorpach nó buiséad arna mbainisteoireacht ag na Comhphobail Eorpacha nóthar a gceann a laghdú go neamhdhíthiúil,

— le neamhnochtadh faisnéise de shárú ar oibleagáid shonrach ar a bhfuil an éifeacht chéanna,

— le sraonadh sochair arna fháil go dlíthiúil ar a bhfuil an éifeacht chéanna.

2. Faoi réir Airteagal 2(2), glacfaidh gach Ballstát na bearta is gá agus is iomchuí chun forálacha mhír 1 a thrasuí ina dhlí coiriúil inmheánach ar dhóigh go ndéanfar cionta coiriú la den iompar dá dtagraítear sna forálacha sin.

3. Faoi réir Airteagal 2(2), glacfaidh gach Ballstát freisin na bearta is gá chun a áirithiú go ndéanfar cionta coiriúla de tharraingt suas nó soláthar intinneach ráiteas nó doiciméad bréagach, neamhbheacht nó neamhiomlán ar a bhfuil an éifeacht atá luaite i mír 1 mura bhfuil siad inphionóis cheana mar phríomhchion nó mar rannpháirteachas i gcalaois, gríosú chuici nó iarracht uirthi, mar atá calaois sainmhínithe i mír 1.

4. Féadfar cineál intinneach gnímh nó neamhghnímh dá dtagraítear i míreanna 1 agus 3 a infeiriú ó imthosca fíorasacha oibiachtúla.

Airteagal 2

Pionóis

1. Glacfaidh gach Ballstát na bearta is gá chun a áirithiú go mbeidh an t-iompar dá dtagraítear in Airteagal 1, maille le rannpháirteachas san iompar dá dtagraítear in Airteagal 1(1), gríosú chuige nó iarracht air, inphionóis le pionóis atá éifeachtach, comhréireach agus athchomhairleach lena n-áirítear, ar a laghad i gcásanna tromchúiseacha calaoise, pionóis lena mbaineann cailleadh saoirse a bhféadfaidh eiseachadadh teacht astu, ar an mbun tuisceana nach foláir a mheas mar chalaois thromchúiseach gach calaois a bhaineann le híosmhéid a shocrófar i ngach Ballstát. Ní fhéadfar an t-íosmhéid a shocrú ag méid is mó ná ECU 50 000.

2. Ar a shon sin, i gcásanna mionchalaoise a bhaineann le méid iomlán nach mó ná ECU 4 000 agus nach bhfuil imthosca tromchúiseacha ar leith i gceist iontu de réir a dhlíthe, féadfaidh Ballstát foráil do phionóis de chineál eile seachas na pionóis dá bhforáiltear i mír 1.

3. Féadfaidh Comhairle an Aontais Eorpaigh, ag gníomhú di d'aon toil, an

méid dá dtagraítear i mír 2 a athrú.

Airteagal 3
Dliteanas coiriú il ceannairí gnóthas

Glacfaidh gach Ballstát na bearta is gá chun gur féidir a dhearbhú, i gcomhréir leis na prionsabail atá sainmhínithe ina dhlí náisiúnta, go bhfuil ceannairí gnóthas nó aon daoine a bhfuil cumhacht chinnteoireachta nó rialaithe acu laistigh de ghnóthas faoi dhliteanas coiriúil i gcásanna calaoise a dhéanann díobháil do leasanna airgeadais na gComhphobal Eorpach, dá dtagraítear in Airteagal 1, arna déanamh ag duine faoina n-údarás thar ceann an ghnóthais.

Airteagal 4
Dlínse

1. Glacfaidh gach Ballstát na bearta is gá chun a dhlínse a bhunú i leith na gcionta atá bunaithe aige de réir Airteagail 1 agus 2(1):
   — nuair is ar a chríoch a dhéantar, go hiomlán nó go páirteach, calaois, rannpháirteachas inti nó iarracht uirthi a dhéanann díobháil do leasanna airgeadais na gComhphobal Eorpach, lena n-áirítear calaois a bhfuarthas a sochar ar an gcríoch sin,
   — nuair a chuidíonn duine ar a chríoch go feasach le calaois a dhéanamh ar chríoch aon Stáit eile nó nuair a aslaíonn sé go feasach é,
   — nuair is náisiúnach den Bhallstát i dtrácht an ciontóir, ar chuntar go bhféadfaidh dlí an Bhallstáit sin foráil go bhfuil an t-iompar inphionóis freisin sa tír inar tharla sé.
2. Tráth an fhógra dá dtagraítear in Airteagal 11(2) a thabhairt, féadfaidh gach Ballstát a dhearbhú nach ndéanfaidh sé an riail á bhforáiltear sa tríú fleasc de mhír 1 den Airteagal seo a chur i bhfeidhm.

Airteagal 5
Eiseachadadh agus ionchúiseamh

1. Aon Bhallstát nach ndéanann a chuid náisiúnach a eiseachadadh faoina dhlí náisiúnta, glacfaidh sé na bearta is gá chun a dhlínse a bhunú i leith na gcionta atá bunaithe aige i gcomhréir le hAirteagail 1 agus 2(1) nuair a dhéanann a chuid náisiúnach iad lasmuigh dá chríoch.
2. Déanfaidh gach Ballstát, nuair a líomhnaítear go ndearna duine dá náisiúnaigh i mBallstát eile cion coiriúil lena mbaineann an t-iompar atá tuairiscithe in Airteagail 1 agus 2(1) agus nuair nach n-eiseachadann sé an duine sin chuig an mBallstát eile de bhíthin a náisiúntachta amháin, an cás a chur faoi bhráid a n-údarás inniúil chun críocha ionchúisimh, más iomchuí. Chun gur féidir an t-ionchúiseamh a thabhairt ar aghaidh, seolfar na comhaid, an fhaisnéis agus ábhar eile a bhaineann leis an gcion de réir na nósanna imeachta dá bhforáiltear in Airteagal 6 den Choinbhinsiún Eorpach um Eiseachadadh.

Coinneofar an Ballstát iarrthach ar an eolas faoin ionchúiseamh a thionscnáitear agus faoin toradh atá air.

3. Ní fhéadfaidh Ballstát an t-eiseachadadh a dhiúltú i gcás calaoise a dhéanann díobháil do leasanna airgeadais na gComhphobal Eorpach toisc amháin gur cion éa bhaineann le cánacha nó dleachtanna custaim.

4. Chun críocha an Airteagail seo, forléireofar 'náisiúnaigh Bhallstáit' i gcomhréir le haon dearbhú arna dhéanamh aige faoi Airteagal 6(1)(*b*) den Choinbhinsiún Eorpach um Eiseachadadh agus le mír 1(*c*) den Airteagal sin.

Airteagal 6

Comhar

1. Má tá calaois mar atá sainmhínithe in Airteagal 1 ina cion coiriúil agus go mbaineann sí le dhá Bhallstát ar a laghad, comhoibreoidh na Ballstáit sin go héifeachtach san imscrúdú, san ionchúiseamh agus i bhforghníomhú an phionóis, mar shampla trí chúnamh dlíthiúil frithpháirteach, eiseachadadh, imeachtaí a aistriú nó pianbhreitheanna arna dtabhairt i mBallstát eile a fhorghníomhú .

2. Nuair atá dlínse ag níos mó ná Ballstát amháin agus caoi acu ionchúiseamh éifeachtach a dhéanamh arna bhunú ar na fíorais chéanna, comhoibreoidh na Ballstáit i dtrácht chun a chinneadh cé acu Ballstát a dhéanfaidh an ciontóir nó na ciontóirí a ionchúiseamh chun an t-ionchúiseamh a lárú i mBallstát amháin más féidir.

Airteagal 7

Ne bis in idem

1. Cuirfidh na Ballstáit an riail *'ne bis in idem'* i bhfeidhm ina ndlíthe coiriúla náisiúnta; faoin riail sin, ní fhéadfar duine a bhfuil a thriail críochnaithe faoi dheireadh i mBallstát amháin a ionchúiseamh i mBallstát eile i leith na bhfíoras céanna, ar chuntar gur forghníomhaíodh aon phionós a gearradh, go bhfuil sé á fhorghníomhú fós nó nach féidir é a fhorghníomhú a thuilleadh faoi dhlíthe Bhallstát a ghearrtha.

2. Féadfaidh Ballstát, tráth an fhógra dá dtagraítear in Airteagal 11(2) a thabhairt, a dhearbhú nach mbeidh sé faoi cheangal ag mír 1 in aon chás amháin nó níos mó de na cásanna seo a leanas:

(*a*) más ar a chríoch féin, go hiomlán nó go páirteach, a tharla na fíorais ab ábhar don bhreithiúnas a tugadh ar an gcoigríoch. Más go páirteach áfach, ní bheidh an eisceacht sin infheidhme má tharla na fíorais sin go páirteach ar chríoch an Bhallstáit inar tugadh an breithiúnas;

(*b*) más é atá sna fíorais ab ábhar don bhreithiúnas a tugadh ar an gcoigríoch cion in éadan shlándáil an Bhallstáit sin nó in éadan leasa chomhriachtanaigh eile dá chuid;

(*c*) más oifigeach den Bhallstát sin a rinne, de shárú ar dhualgais a oifige, na fíorais ab ábhar don bhreithiúnas a tugadh ar an gcoigríoch.

3. Ní bheidh na heisceachtaí is ábhar do dhearbhú faoi mhír 2 infheidhme más rud é go ndearna an Ballstát i dtrácht, i leith na bhfíoras céanna, a iarraidh

ar an mBallstát eile an t-ionchúiseamh a thionscnamh nó go ndearna sé eiseachadadh an duine lena mbaineann a dheonú .

4. Ní dhéanfaidh an tAirteagal seo difear do chomhaontuithe ábhartha déthaobhacha nó iltaobhacha atá curtha i gcrích idir Bhallstáit ná do dhearbhuithe ábhartha.

Airteagal 8

An Chúirt Bhreithiúnais

1. Ní foláir don Chomhairle aon díospóidí idir na Ballstáit maidir le léiriú nó cur i bhfeidhm an Choinbhinsiúin seo a phlé mar chéad chéim i gcomhréir leis an nós imeachta atá leagtha amach i dTeideal VI den Chonradh ar an Aontas Eorpach d'fhonn teacht ar réiteach.
Mura mbeidh réiteach faighte laistigh de thréimhse sé mhí, féadfaidh páirtí sa díospóid í a chur faoi bhráid Chúirt Bhreithiúnais na gComhphobal Eorpach.

2. Féadfar aon díospóid maidir le hAirteagal 1 nó 10 idir Ballstát amháin nó níos mó agus Coimisiún na gComhphobal Eorpach nárbh fhéidir a réiteach trí chaibidlíocht a chur faoi bhráid na Cúirte Breithiúnais.

Airteagal 9

Forálacha inmheánacha

Ní choiscfidh aon fhoráil sa Choinbhinsiún seo na Ballstáit ar fhorálacha dlíthiúla inmheánacha a ghlacadh a théann thar na hoibleagáidí a leanann ón gCoinbhinsiún seo.

Airteagal 10

Páirtiú

1. Páirteoidh na Ballstáit le Coimisiún na gComhphobal Eorpach téacs na bhforálacha ag trasuí ina ndlí inmheánach na n-oibleagáidí a thiteann orthu de bhun fhorálacha an Choinbhinsiúin seo.

2. D'fhonn an Coinbhinsiún seo a chur i bhfeidhm, déanfaidh na hArd-pháirtithe Conarthacha i gComhairle an Aontais Eorpaigh, an fhaisnéis nach mór a pháirtiú nó a mhalartú idir na Ballstáit nó idir na Ballstáit agus an Coimisiún agus rialacha mionsonraithe a pháirtithe a shainiú.

Airteagal 11

Teacht i bhfeidhm

1. Beidh an Coinbhinsiún seo faoi réir a ghlactha ag na Ballstáit i gcomhréir lena rialacha bunreachtúla faoi seach.

2. Cuirfidh na Ballstáit in iúl d'Ardrúnaí Chomhairle an Aontais Eorpaigh go bhfuil na nósanna imeachta is gá faoina rialacha bunreachtúla faoi seach

chun an Coinbhinsiún seo a ghlacadh comhlíonta acu.

3. Tiocfaidh an Coinbhinsiún seo i bhfeidhm 90 lá tar éis don fhógra dá dtagraítear i mír 2 a bheith tugtha ag an mBallstát is déanaí a dhéanfaidh sin.

Airteagal 12

Aontachas

1. Beidh aontachas leis an gCoinbhinsiún seo ar oscailt d'aon Stát a thagann chun bheith ina Bhallstát den Aontas Eorpach.

2. Is téacs údarásach téacs an Choinbhinsiúin seo i dteanga an Stáit aontaigh, arna dhréachtú ag Comhairle an Aontais Eorpaigh.

3. Taiscfear na hionstraimí aontachais leis an taiscí.

4. Tiocfaidh an Coinbhinsiún seo i bhfeidhm maidir le Stát aontach 90 lá tar éis dó a ionstraim aontachais a thaisceadh nó ar dháta an Choinbhinsiúin a theacht i bhfeidhm mura bhfuil sé tagtha i bhfeidhm fós tráth na tréimhse 90 lá sin a dhul in éag.

Airteagal 13

Taiscí

1. Is é Ardrúnaí Chomhairle an Aontais Eorpaidh taiscí an Choinbhinsiúin seo.

2. Foilseoidh an taiscí in Iris Oifigiúil na gComhphobal Eorpach faisnéis maidir leis an gCoinbhinsiún seo a ghlacadh agus aontachais leis, na dearbhuithe, na forchoimeádais agus gach fógra eile a bhaineann leis an gCoinbhinsiún seo.

Section 41   SCHEDULE 4

TEXT IN THE ENGLISH LANGUAGE OF THE PROTOCOL DRAWN UP ON THE BASIS OF
ARTICLE K.3 OF THE TREATY ON EUROPEAN UNION TO THE CONVENTION ON THE
PROTECTION OF THE EUROPEAN COMMUNITIES' FINANCIAL INTERESTS DONE AT
BRUSSELS ON 27 SEPTEMBER 1996

PROTOCOL

**drawn up on the basis of Article K.3 of the Treaty on European Union
to the Convention on the protection of the European Communities'
financial interests**

THE HIGH CONTRACTING PARTIES to this Protocol, Member States of
the European Union,

REFERRING to the Act of the Council of the European Union of 27 September 1996,

DESIRING to ensure that their criminal laws contribute effectively to the protection of the financial interests of the European Communities;

RECOGNIZING the importance of the Convention on the protection of the European Communities' financial interests of 26 July 1995 for combating fraud affecting Community revenue and expenditure;

AWARE that the financial interests of the European Communities may be damaged or threatened by other criminal offences, particularly acts of corruption by or against national and Community officials, responsible for the collection, management or disbursement of Community funds under their control;

CONSIDERING that people of different nationalities, employed by different public agencies or bodies, may be involved in such corruption and that, in the interests of effective action against such corruption with international ramifications, it is important for their reprehensible nature to be perceived in a similar manner under Member States' criminal laws;

NOTING that several Member States' criminal law on crime linked to the exercise of public duties in general and concerning corruption in particular covers only acts committed by or against their national officials and does not cover, or covers only in exceptional cases, conduct involving Community officials or officials of other Member States;

CONVINCED of the need for national law to be adapted where it does not penalize acts of corruption that damage or are likely to damage the financial interests of the European Communities involving Community officials or officials of other Member States;

CONVINCED also that such adaptation of national law should not be confined, in respect of Community officials, to acts of active or passive corruption, but should be extended to other crimes affecting or likely to affect the revenue or expenditure of the European Communities, including crimes committed by or against persons in whom the highest responsibilities are vested;

CONSIDERING that appropriate rules should also be laid down on jurisdiction and mutual cooperation, without prejudice to the legal conditions under which they are to apply in specific cases, including waiver of immunity where appropriate;

CONSIDERING finally that the relevant provisions of the Convention on the protection of the European Communities' financial interests of 26 July 1995 should be made applicable to the criminal acts covered by this Protocol,
HAVE AGREED ON THE FOLLOWING PROVISIONS:

Article 1

Definitions

For the purposes of this Protocol:
1. (*a*) 'official' shall mean any 'Community' or 'national' official, including any national official of another Member State;
   (*b*) the term 'Community official' shall mean:
   — any person who is an official or other contracted employee within the meaning of the Staff Regulations of officials of the European Communities or the Conditions of employment of other servants of the European Communities,
   — any person seconded to the European Communities by the Member States or by any public or private body, who carries out functions equivalent to those performed by European Community officials or other servants.
   Members of bodies set up in accordance with the Treaties establishing the European Communities and the staff of such bodies shall be treated as Community officials, inasmuch as the Staff Regulations of the European Communities or the Conditions of employment of other servants of the European Communities do not apply to them;
   (*c*) the term 'national official' shall be understood by reference to the definition of 'official' or 'public officer' in the national law of the Member State in which the person in question performs that function for the purposes of application of the criminal law of that Member State.
   Nevertheless, in the case of proceedings involving a Member State's official initiated by another Member State the latter shall not be bound to apply the definition of 'national official' except in so far as that definition is compatible with its national law;
2. 'Convention' shall mean the Convention drawn up on the basis of Article K.3 of the Treaty on European Union, on the protection of the European Communities' financial interests, of 26 July 1995.

Article 2

Passive corruption

1. For the purposes of this Protocol, the deliberate action of an official, who, directly or through an intermediary, requests or receives advantages of any kind whatsoever, for himself or for a third party, or accepts a promise of such an advantage, to act or refrain from acting in accordance with his duty or in the exercise of his functions in breach of his official duties in a way which dam-

ages or is likely to damage the European Communities' financial interests shall constitute passive corruption.

2. Each Member State shall take the necessary measures to ensure that conduct of the type referred to in paragraph 1 is made a criminal offence.

Article 3

Active corruption

1. For the purposes of this Protocol, the deliberate action of whosoever promises or gives, directly or through an intermediary, an advantage of any kind whatsoever to an official for himself or for a third party for him to act or refrain from acting in accordance with his duty or in the exercise of his functions in breach of his official duties in a way which damages or is likely to damage the European Communities' financial interests shall constitute active corruption.

2. Each Member State shall take the necessary measures to ensure that conduct of the type referred to in paragraph 1 is made a criminal offence.

Article 4

Assimilation

1. Each Member State shall take the necessary measures to ensure that in its criminal law the descriptions of the offences constituting conduct of the type referred to in Article 1 of the Convention committed by its national officials in the exercise of their functions apply similarly in cases where such offences are committed by Community officials in the exercise of their duties.

2. Each Member State shall take the necessary measures to ensure that in its criminal law the descriptions of the offences referred to in paragraph 1 of this Article and in Articles 2 and 3 committed by or against its Government Ministers, elected members of its parliamentary chambers, the members of its highest Courts or the members of its Court of Auditors in the exercise of their functions apply similarly in cases where such offences are committed by or against members of the Commission of the European Communities, the European Parliament, the Court of Justice and the Court of Auditors of the European Communities respectively in the exercise of their duties.

3. Where a Member State has enacted special legislation concerning acts or omissions for which Government Ministers are responsible by reason of their special political position in that Member State, paragraph 2 of this Article may not apply to such legislation, provided that the Member State ensures that Members of the Commission of the European Community are covered by the criminal legislation implementing Articles 2 and 3 and paragraph 1 of this Article.

4. Paragraphs 1, 2 and 3 shall be without prejudice to the provisions applicable in each Member State concerning criminal proceedings and the determination of the competent court.

5. This Protocol shall apply in full accordance with the relevant provisions of the Treaties establishing the European Communities, the Protocol on the

Privileges and Immunities of the European Communities, the Statutes of the Court of Justice and the texts adopted for the purpose of their implementation, as regards the withdrawal of immunity.

Article 5

Penalties

1. Each Member State shall take the necessary measures to ensure that the conduct referred to in Articles 2 and 3, and participating in and instigating the conduct in question, are punishable by effective, proportionate and dissuasive criminal penalties, including, at least in serious cases, penalties involving deprivation of liberty which can give rise to extradition.

2. Paragraph 1 shall be without prejudice to the exercise of disciplinary powers by the competent authorities against national officials or Community officials. In determining the penalty to be imposed, the national criminal courts may, in accordance with the principles of their national law, take into account any disciplinary penalty already imposed on the same person for the same conduct.

Article 6

Jurisdiction

1. Each Member State shall take the measures necessary to establish its jurisdiction over the offences it has established in accordance with Articles 2, 3 and 4 where:
    (*a*) the offence is committed in whole or in part within its territory;
    (*b*) the offender is one of its nationals or one of its officials;
    (*c*) the offence is committed against one of the persons referred to in Article 1 or a member of one of the institutions referred to in Article 4 (2) who is one of its nationals;
    (*d*) the offender is a Community official working for a European Community institution or a body set up in accordance with the Treaties establishing the European Communities which has its headquarters in the Member State concerned.

2. Each Member State may declare when giving the notification provided for in Article 9 (2) that it will not apply or will apply only in specific cases or conditions one or more of the jurisdiction rules laid down in paragraph 1 (*b*), (*c*), and (*d*).

Article 7

Relation to the Convention

1. Articles 3, 5 (1), (2) and (4) and Article 6 of the Convention shall apply as if there were a reference to the conduct referred to in Articles 2, 3 and 4 of this Protocol.

2. The following provisions of the Convention shall also apply to this Protocol:

— Article 7, on the understanding that, unless otherwise indicated at the time of the notification provided for in Article 9 (2) of this Protocol, any declaration within the meaning of Article 7 (2) of the Convention shall also apply to this Protocol,

— Article 9,

— Article 10.

Article 8

Court of Justice

1. Any dispute between Member States on the interpretation or application of this Protocol must in an initial stage be examined by the Council in accordance with the procedure set out in Title VI of the Treaty on European Union with a view to reaching a solution.
If no solution is found within six months, the matter may be referred to the Court of Justice of the European Communities by a party to the dispute.

2. Any dispute between one or more Member States and the Commission of the European Communities concerning Article 1, with the exception of point 1 (*c*), or Articles 2, 3 and 4, or the third indent of Article 7 (2) of this Protocol which it has proved impossible to settle through negotiation may be submitted to the Court of Justice of the European Communities.

Article 9

Entry into force

1. This Protocol shall be subject to adoption by the Member States in accordance with their respective constitutional requirements.

2. Member States shall notify the Secretary-General of the Council of the European Union of the completion of the procedures required under their respective constitutional rules for adopting this Protocol.

3. This Protocol shall enter into force 90 days after the notification provided for in paragraph 2 has been given by the State which, being a Member of the European Union at the time of adoption by the Council of the Act drawing up this Protocol, is the last to fulfil that formality. If, however, the Convention has not entered into force on that date, this Protocol shall enter into force on the date on which the Convention enters into force.

Article 10

Accession of new Member States

1. This Protocol shall be open to accession by any State that becomes a member of the European Union.

2. The text of this Protocol in the language of the acceding State, drawn up

by the Council of the European Union, shall be authentic.

3. Instruments of accession shall be deposited with the depositary.

4. This Protocol shall enter into force with respect to any State that accedes to it 90 days after the deposit of its instrument of accession or on the date of entry into force of this Protocol if it has not yet entered into force at the time of expiry of the said period of 90 days.

Article 11

Reservations

1. No reservation shall be authorized with the exception of those provided for in Article 6 (2).

2. Any Member State which has entered a reservation may withdraw it at any time in whole or in part by notifying the depositary. Withdrawal shall take effect on the date on which the depositary receives the notification.

Article 12

Depositary

1. The Secretary-General of the Council of the European Union shall act as depositary of this Protocol.

2. The depositary shall publish in the Official Journal of the European Communities information on the progress of adoptions and accessions, declarations and reservations and any other notification concerning this Protocol.

Section 41   SCHEDULE 5

TEXT IN THE IRISH LANGUAGE OF THE PROTOCOL DRAWN UP ON THE BASIS OF
ARTICLE K.3 OF THE TREATY ON EUROPEAN UNION TO THE CONVENTION ON THE
PROTECTION OF THE EUROPEAN COMMUNITIES' FINANCIAL INTERESTS DONE AT
BRUSSELS ON 27 SEPTEMBER 1996

PRÓTACAL

**arna dhréachtú ar bhonn Airteagal K.3 den Chonradh ar an Aontas
Eorpach, a ghabhann leis an gCoinbhinsiún maidir le leasanna
airgeadais na gComhphobal Eorpach a chosaint**

TÁ NA hARDPHÁIRTITHE CONARTHACHA sa Phrótacal seo, Ballstáit
den Aontas Eorpach,

AG TAGAIRT DÓIBH do Ghníomh ó Chomhairle an Aontais Eorpaigh 27
Meán Fómhair 1996,

ÓS MIAN LEO a áirithiú go gcuidíonn a ndlíthe coiriúla go héifeachtach le
leasanna airgeadais na gComhphobal Eorpach a chosaint;

AG AITHINT DÓIBH thábhacht Choinbhinsiún an 26 Iúil 1995 maidir le
leasanna airgeadais na gComhphobal Eorpach a chosaint a mhéid a bhaineann
le calaois a dhéanann difear d'ioncam agus caiteachas Comhphobail a chomhrac;

ÓS FIOS DÓIBH go bhféadfaidh cionta coiriúla eile díobháil a dhéanamh do
leasanna airgeadais na gComhphobal Eorpach nó bheith ina mbagairt orthu,
go háirithe gníomhartha éillitheacha arna ndéanamh ag oifigigh náisiúnta agus
oifigigh Chomhphobail atá freagrach as cistí Comhphobail atá á rialú acu a
bhailiú, a bhainisteoireacht nó a íoc amach, nó gníomhartha éillitheacha arna
ndéanamh ina gcoinne;

DE BHRÍ go bhféadfaidh daoine de náisiúntachtaí éagsúla atá fostaithe ag
gníomhaireachtaí nó comhlachtaí poiblí éagsúla bheith i dtreis san éilliú sin
agus go bhfuil sé tábhachtach, ar mhaithe le gníomhaíocht éifeachtach i gcoinne
an éillithe sin a bhfuil craobhacha idirnáisiúnta aige, dearcadh comhchosúil ar
a gcineál incháinte a bheith ann i ndlíthe coiriúla na mBallstát;

AG TABHAIRT DÁ nAIRE DÓIBH nach gcuimsíonn dlí coiriúil roinnt de na
Ballstáit maidir le coirpeacht atá bainteach le feidhmeanna poiblí a fheidhmiú
i gcoitinne agus maidir le héilliú, ach go háirithe, ach gníomhartha i gcoinne a
n-oifigeach náisiúnta nó arna ndéanamh acu agus nach gcuimsíonn sé iompar a
bhfuil oifigigh Chomhphobail nó oifigigh Bhallstát eile i dtreis ann nó go gcuimsíonn sé é i gcásanna eisceachtúla amháin;

ÓS DEIMHIN LEO gur gá an dlí náisiúnta a oiriúnú nuair nach bpionósaíonn
sé gníomhartha éillitheacha a bhfuil oifigigh Chomhphobail nó oifigigh Bhallstát
eile i dtreis iontu a dhéanann díobháil, nó ar dóigh dóibh díobháil a dhéanamh,
do leasanna airgeadais na gComhphobal Eorpach;

ÓS DEIMHIN LEO freisin nár chóir oiriúnú den sórt sin ar an dlí náisiúnta a
theorannú, i leith oifigeach Comhphobail, do ghníomhartha éillitheacha
gníomhacha nó neamhghníomhacha ach gur chóir é a chur i mbaint le coireanna
eile a dhéanann difear, nó ar dóigh dóibh difear a dhéanamh, d'ioncam nó do
chaiteachas na gComhphobal Eorpach, lena n-áirítear coireanna arna ndéanamh
ag daoine a ndílsítear na freagrachtaí is airde dóibh nó coireanna arna ndéanamh

ina gcoinne;

DE BHRÍ gur chóir freisin rialacha iomchuí a leagan síos maidir le dlínse agus comhar frithpháirteach, gan dochar do na coinníollacha dlíthiúla faoina mbeidh siad infheidhme i gcásanna sonracha, lena n-áirítear díolúine a tharscaoileadh nuair is iomchuí;

DE BHRÍ, ar deireadh, gur chóir forálacha ábhartha Choinbhinsiún an 26 Iúil 1995 maidir le leasanna airgeadais na gComhphobal Eorpach a chosaint a chur i bhfeidhm ar na gníomhartha coiriúla atá folaithe sa Phrótacal seo,

TAR ÉIS COMHAONTÚ AR NA FORÁLACHA SEO A LEANAS:

Airteagal 1

Sainmhínithe

Chun críocha an Phrótacail seo:

(1)(*a*) ciallaíonn 'oifigeach' aon oifigeach Comhphobail nó náisiúnta, lena n-áirítear aon oifigeach náisiúnta de chuid Ballstáit eile;

   (*b*) ciallaíonn 'oifigeach Comhphobail':

— aon duine ar oifigeach nó fostaí eile ar conradh é de réir bhrí Rialachán Foirne oifigigh na gComhphobal Eorpach nó Choinníollacha Fostaíochta sheirbhísigh eile na gComhphobal Eorpach;

— aon duine atá tugtha ar iasacht do na Comhphobail Eorpacha ag na Ballstáit nó ag aon chomhlacht poiblí nó príobháideach agus a fheidhmíonn feidhmeanna is coibhéiseach le feidhmeanna a fheidhmíonn oifigigh nó seirbhísigh eile na gComhphobal Eorpach.

Déileálfar le comhaltaí comhlachtaí arna mbunú i gcomhréir leis na Conarthaí ag bunú na gComhphobal Eorpach agus le foireann na gcomhlachtaí sin mar oifigigh Chomhphobail a mhéid nach bhfuil Rialachán Foirne oifigigh na gComhphobal Eorpach ná Coinníollacha Fostaíochta sheirbhísigh eile na gComhphobal Eorpach infheidhme orthu.

   (*c*) léirítear 'oifigeach náisiúnta' i gcomhréir leis an sainmhíniú ar 'oifigeach' nó 'oifigeach poiblí' atá i ndlí náisiúnta an Bhallstáit ina bhfuil an fheidhm sin á feidhmiú ag an duine i dtrácht chun críocha dlí coiriúil an Bhallstáit sin a chur i bhfeidhm.

Ar a shon sin, i gcás imeachtaí a bhfuil oifigeach de chuid Ballstáit i dtreis iontu agus a thionscain Ballstát eile, ní bheidh de cheangal ar an mBallstát eile sin an sainmhíniú ar "oifigeach náisiúnta" a chur i bhfeidhm ach sa mhéid go bhfuil an sainmhíniú sin ag luí lena dhlí náisiúnta féin.

(2) ciallaíonn "Coinbhinsiún" Coinbhinsiún an 26 Iúil 1995, arna dhréachtú ar bhonn Airteagal K.3 den Chonradh ar an Aontas Eorpach, maidir le leasanna airgeadais na gComhphobal Eorpach a chosaint.

Airteagal 2
Éilliú neamhghníomhach

1. Chun críocha an Phrótacail seo, is éard é éilliú neamhghníomhach gníomh intinneach oifigeach a iarrann nó a fhaigheann, go díreach nó trí idirghabhálaí, buntáistí de chineál ar bith dó féin nó do thríú páirtí, nó a ghlacann gealltanas buntáiste den sórt sin, chun gníomh a dhéanamh nó staonadh ó ghníomh a dhéanamh i gcomhréir lena fheidhmeanna nó i bhfeidhmiú a fheidhmeanna de shárú ar a dhualgais oifigiúla ar dhóigh a dhéanann díobháil, nó ar dóigh di díobháil a dhéanamh, do leasanna airgeadais na gComhphobal Eorpach.

2. Glacfaidh gach Ballstát na bearta is gá chun a áirithiú go ndéanfar cion coiriúil den iompar dá dtagraítear i mír 1.

Airteagal 3
Éilliú gníomhach

1. Chun críocha an Phrótacail seo, is éard é éilliú gníomhach gníomh intinneach aon duine a gheallann nó a thugann, go díreach nó trí idirghabhálaí, buntáiste de chineál ar bith d'oifigeach, dó féin nó do thríú páirtí, chun gníomh a dhéanamh nó staonadh ó ghníomh a dhéanamh i gcomhréir lena fheidhmeanna nó i bhfeidhmiú a fheidhmeanna de shárú ar a dhualgais oifigiúla ar dhóigh a dhéanann díobháil, nó ar dóigh di díobháil a dhéanamh, do leasanna airgeadais na gComhphobal Eorpach.

2. Glacfaidh gach Ballstát na bearta is gá chun a áirithiú go ndéanfar cion coiriúil den iompar dá dtagraítear i mír 1.

Airteagal 4
Comhshamhlú

1. Glacfaidh gach Ballstát na bearta is gá chun a áirithiú go mbeidh tuairiscí na gcionta ina dhlí coiriúil arb éard iad iompar den saghas dá dtagraítear in Airteagal 1 den Choinbhinsiún arna ndéanamh ag a oifigigh náisiúnta i bhfeidhmiú a bhfeidhmeanna infheidhme ar an dóigh chéanna ar chásanna ina ndéanann oifigigh Chomhphobail na cionta sin i bhfeidhmiú a bhfeidhmeanna.

2. Glacfaidh gach Ballstát na bearta is gá chun a áirithiú go mbeidh tuairiscí na gcionta ina dhlí coiriúil dá dtagraítear i mír 1 den Airteagal seo agus in Airteagail 2 agus 3 arna ndéanamh ag a Airí Rialtais, comhaltaí tofa a sheomraí parlaiminteacha, comhaltaí a chúirteanna is airde nó comhaltaí a chúirte iniúchóirí i bhfeidhmiú a bhfeidhmeanna, nó arna ndéanamh ina gcoinne, infheidhme ar an dóigh chéanna ar chásanna ina ndéanann comhaltaí de Choimisiún na gComhphobal Eorpach, de Pharlaimint na hEorpa, de Chúirt Bhreithiúnais nó de Chúirt Iniúchóirí na gComhphobal Eorpach, faoi seach, na cionta sin i bhfeidhmiú a bhfeidhmeanna agus ar chásanna ina ndéantar ina gcoinne iad.

3. Nuair atá reachtaíocht speisialta achtaithe ag Ballstát maidir le gníomhartha

nó neamhghníomhartha a bhfuil Airí Rialtais freagrach astu de bharr a staide polaitiúla speisialta sa Bhallstát sin, féadfar gan mír 2 den Airteagal seo a chur i bhfeidhm ar an reachtaíocht sin, ar chuntar go n-áirithíonn an Ballstát go bhfuil comhaltaí Choimisiún na gComhphobal Eorpach folaithe sa reachtaíocht choiriúil a chuireann Airteagail 2 agus 3 agus mír 1 den Airteagal seo chun feidhme.

4. Beidh míreanna 1, 2 agus 3 gan dochar do na forálacha is infheidhme i ngach Ballstát maidir le himeachtaí coiriúla agus maidir leis an gcúirt a bhfuil dlínse aici a chinneadh.

5. Cuirfear an Prótacal seo i bhfeidhm agus lánurraim á tabhairt d'fhorálacha ábhartha na gConarthaí ag bunú na gComhphobal Eorpach, an Phrótacail ar Phribhléidí agus Díolúintí na gComhphobal Eorpach, Reachtanna na Cúirte Breithiúnais agus na dtéacsanna arna nglacadh chun iad a chur chun feidhme, maidir le díolúine a tharscaoileadh.

Airteagal 5

Pionóis

1. Glacfaidh gach Ballstát na bearta is gá chun a áirithiú go mbeidh an t-iompar dá dtagraítear in Airteagail 2 agus 3, maille le rannpháirteachas ann nó gríosú chuige, inphionóis le pionóis choiriúla atá éifeachtach, comhréireach agus athchomhairleach lena n-áirítear, ar a laghad i gcásanna tromchúiseacha, pionóis lena mbaineann cailleadh saoirse a bhféadfaidh eiseachadadh teacht astu.

2. Beidh mír 1 gan dochar d'fheidhmiú cumhachtaí araíonachta ag na húdaráis inniúla i leith oifigeach náisiúnta nó oifigeach Comhphobail. Agus an pionós atá le forchur á chinneadh acu, féadfaidh na cúirteanna coiriúla náisiúnta, i gcomhréir le prionsabail a ndlí náisiúnta, aonphionós araíonachta arna fhorchur cheana ar an duine céanna i leith an iompair chéanna a chur san áireamh.

Airteagal 6

Dlínse

1. Glacfaidh gach Ballstát na bearta is gá chun a dhlínse a bhunú i leith na gcionta atá bunaithe aige i gcomhréir le hAirteagail 2, 3 agus 4:

 (a) nuair is ar a chríoch a dhéantar an cion, go hiomlán nó go páirteach;

 (b) nuair is náisiúnach nó oifigeach dá chuid an ciontóir;

 (c) nuair a dhéantar an cion i duine de na daoine dá dtagraítear in Airteagal 1 nó i gcoinne comhalta de cheann de na hinstitiúidí dá dtagraítear in Airteagal 4(2) ar náisiúnach dá chuid é;

 (d) nuair is oifigeach Comhphobail atá ag obair d'institiúid de chuid na gComhphobal Eorpach nó do chomhlacht arna bhunú i gcomhréir leis na Conarthaí ag bunú na gComhphobal Eorpach a bhfuil a shuíomh aige sa Bhallstát i dtrácht an ciontóir.

2. Féadfaidh gach Ballstát, agus an fógra dá bhforáiltear in Airteagal 9(2) á thabhairt aige, a dhearbhú nach ndéanfaidh sé ceann amháin nó níos mó de na

rialacha dlínse atá leagtha síos i bpointí (*b*), (*c*) agus (*d*) de mhír 1 a chur i bhfeidhm nó nach gcuirfidh sé i bhfeidhm é nó iad ach i gcásanna nó imthosca sonracha.

Airteagal 7

Gaol leis an gCoinbhinsiún

1. Beidh Airteagail 3, 5(1), (2) agus (4) agus 6 den Choinbhinsiún infheidhme amhail is dá mbeadh tagairt iontu don iompar dá dtagraítear in Airteagail 2, 3 agus 4 den Phrótacal seo.

2. Beidh na forálacha seo a leanas den Choinbhinsiún infheidhme ar an bPrótacal seo freisin:
— Airteagal 7, ar é a bheith le tuiscint go mbeidh aon dearbhú de réir bhrí Airteagal 7(2) den Choinbhinsiún infheidhme ar an bPrótacal seo freisin mura sonrófar a mhalairt tráth an fhógra dá bhforáiltear in Airteagal 9(2) den Phrótacal seo a thabhairt,
— Airteagal 9,
— Airteagal 10.

Airteagal 8

An Chúirt Bhreithiúnais

1. Ní foláir don Chomhairle aon díospóidí idir na Ballstáit maidir le léiriú nó cur i bhfeidhm an Phrótacail seo a phlé mar chéad chéim i gcomhréir leis an nós imeachta atá leagtha amach i dTeideal VI den Chonradh ar an Aontas Eorpach d'fhonn teacht ar réiteach.

Mura mbeidh réiteach faighte laistigh de thréimhse sé mhí féadfaidh páirtí sa díospóid í a chur faoi bhráid Chúirt Bhreithiúnais na gComhphobal Eorpach.

2. Féadfar aon díospóid maidir le hAirteagal 1, seachas pointe 1(*c*) de, nó maidir le hAirteagail 2, 3 agus 4 nó Airteagal 7(2), tríú fleasc, den Phrótacal seo idir Ballstát amháin nó níos mó agus Coimisiún na gComhphobal Eorpach nárbh fhéidir a réiteach trí chaibidlíocht a chur faoi bhráid Chúirt Bhreithiúnais na gComhphobal Eorpach.

Airteagal 9

Teacht i bhfeidhm

1. Beidh an Prótacal seo faoi réir a ghlactha ag na Ballstáit i gcomhréir lena rialacha bunreachtúla faoi seach.

2. Cuirfidh na Ballstáit in iúl d'Ardrúnaí Chomhairle an Aontais Eorpaigh go bhfuil na nósanna imeachta is gá faoina rialacha bunreachtúla faoi seach chun an Prótacal seo a ghlacadh comhlíonta acu.

3. Tiocfaidh an Prótacal seo i bhfeidhm 90 lá tar éis don fhógra dá bhforáiltear i mír 2 a bheith tugtha ag an Stát is Ballstát den Aontas Eorpach an tráth a ghlacfaidh an Chomhairle an Gníomh ag dréachtú an Phrótacail seo is déanaí a

dhéanfaidh an beart sin. Mura mbeidh an Coinbhinsiún tagtha i bhfeidhm ar an dáta sin áfach, tiocfaidh an Prótacal seo i bhfeidhm ar an dáta a thiocfaidh an Coinbhinsiún i bhfeidhm.

Airteagal 10

Aontachas Ballstát nua

1. Beidh an Prótacal seo ar oscailt d'aontachas aon Stáit a thiocfaidh chun bheith ina Bhallstát den Aontas Eorpach.

2. Is téacs údarásach téacs an Phrótacail seo i dteanga an Stáit aontaigh, arna dhréachtú ag Comhairle an Aontais Eorpaigh.

3. Déanfar na hionstraimí aontachais a thaisceadh leis an taiscí.

4. Tiocfaidh an Prótacal seo i bhfeidhm i leith aon Stáit a aontaíonn dó 90 lá tar éis dó a ionstraim aontachais a thaisceadh nó ar dháta an Phrótacail seo a theacht i bhfeidhm mura mbeidh sé tagtha i bhfeidhm fós tráth na tréimhse thuasluaite 90 lá a dhul in éag.

Airteagal 11

Forchoimeádais

1. Ní cheadófar aon fhorchoimeádas seachas na cinn dá bhforáiltear in Airteagal 6(2).

2. Féadfaidh aon Bhallstát a bhfuil forchoimeádas déanta aige é a tharraingt siar go hiomlán nó go páirteach tráth ar bith trí fhógra a chur chuig an taiscí. Gabhfaidh éifeacht leis an tarraingt siar ar an dáta a fhaigheann an taiscí an fógra.

Airteagal 12

Taiscí

1. Is é Ardrúnaí Chomhairle an Aontais Eorpaigh taisc an Phrótacail seo.

2. Foilseoidh an taiscí in Iris Oifigiúil na gComhphobal Eorpach faisnéis maidir leis an bPrótacal seo a ghlacadh agus aontachais leis, na dearbhuithe, na forchoimeádais agus gach fógra eile a bhaineann leis an bPrótacal seo.

Section 41   SCHEDULE 6

TEXT IN THE ENGLISH LANGUAGE OF THE PROTOCOL DRAWN UP ON THE BASIS OF ARTICLE K.3 OF THE TREATY ON EUROPEAN UNION, ON THE INTERPRETATION, BY WAY OF PRELIMINARY RULINGS, BY THE COURT OF JUSTICE OF THE EUROPEAN COMMUNITIES OF THE CONVENTION ON THE PROTECTION OF THE EUROPEAN COMMUNITIES' FINANCIAL INTERESTS DONE AT BRUSSELS ON 29 NOVEMBER 1996

PROTOCOL

drawn up on the basis of Article K.3 of the Treaty on European Union, on the interpretation, by way of preliminary rulings, by the Court of Justice of the European Communities of the Convention on the protection of the European Communities' financial interests

THE HIGH CONTRACTING PARTIES,

HAVE AGREED on the following provisions, which shall be annexed to the Convention:

Article 1

The Court of Justice of the European Communities shall have jurisdiction, pursuant to the conditions laid down in this Protocol, to give preliminary rulings on the interpretation of the Convention on the protection of the European Communities' financial interests and the Protocol to that Convention drawn up on 27 September 1996, hereinafter referred to as 'the first Protocol'.

Article 2

1. By a declaration made at the time of the signing of this Protocol or at any time thereafter, any Member State shall be able to accept the jurisdiction of the Court of Justice of the European Communities to give preliminary rulings on the interpretation of the Convention on the protection of the European Communities' financial interests and the first Protocol to that Convention pursuant to the conditions specified in either paragraph 2(*a*) or paragraph 2(*b*).

2. A Member State making a declaration pursuant to paragraph 1 may specify that either:

    (*a*) any court or tribunal of that State against whose decisions there is no judicial remedy under national law may request the Court of Justice of the European Communities to give a preliminary ruling on a question raised in a case pending before it and concerning the interpretation of the Convention on the protection of the European Communities' financial interests and the first Protocol thereto if that court or tribunal considers that a decision on the question is necessary to enable it to give judgment, or

    (*b*) any court or tribunal of that State may request the Court of Justice of the European Communities to give a preliminary ruling on a question raised in a case pending before it and concerning the interpretation of the Convention on the protection of the European

Communities' financial interests and the first Protocol thereto if that court or tribunal considers that a decision on the question is necessary to enable it to give judgment.

Article 3

1. The Protocol on the Statute of the Court of Justice of the European Communities and the Rules of Procedure of that Court of Justice shall apply.

2. In accordance with the Statute of the Court of Justice of the European Communities, any Member State, whether or not it has made a declaration pursuant to Article 2, shall be entitled to submit statements of case or written observations to the Court of Justice of the European Communities in cases which arise pursuant to Article 1.

Article 4

1. This Protocol shall be subject to adoption by the Member States in accordance with their respective constitutional requirements.

2. Member States shall notify the depositary of the completion of their respective constitutional requirements for adopting this Protocol and communicate to him any declaration made pursuant to Article 2.

3. This Protocol shall enter into force 90 days after the notification, referred to in paragraph 2, by the Member State which, being a member of the European Union on the date of adoption by the Council of the Act drawing up this Protocol, is the last to fulfil that formality. However, it shall at the earliest enter into force at the same time as the Convention on the protection of the European Communities' financial interests.

Article 5

1. This Protocol shall be open to accession by any State that becomes a member of the European Union.

2. Instruments of accession shall be deposited with the depositary.

3. The text of this Protocol in the language of the acceding State, drawn up by the Council of the European Union, shall be authentic.

4. This Protocol shall enter into force with respect to any State that accedes to it 90 days after the date of deposit of its instrument of accession, or on the date of the entry into force of this Protocol if the latter has not yet come into force when the said period of 90 days expires.

Article 6

Any State that becomes a member of the European Union and accedes to the Convention on the protection of the European Communities' financial interests in accordance with Article 12 thereof shall accept the provisions of this Protocol.

Article 7

1. Amendments to this Protocol may be proposed by any Member State, being a High Contracting Party. Any proposal for an amendment shall be sent to the depositary, who shall forward it to the Council.

2. Amendments shall be established by the Council, which shall recommend that they be adopted by the Member States in accordance with their respective constitutional requirements.

3. Amendments thus established shall enter into force in accordance with the provisions of Article 4.

Article 8

1. The Secretary-General of the Council of the European Union shall act depositary of this Protocol.

2. The depositary shall publish in the Official Journal of the European Communities the notifications, instruments or communications concerning this Protocol.

SCHEDULE 7

TEXT IN THE IRISH LANGUAGE OF THE PROTOCOL DRAWN UP ON THE BASIS OF
ARTICLE K.3 OF THE TREATY ON EUROPEAN UNION, ON THE INTERPRETATION, BY WAY
OF PRELIMINARY RULINGS, BY THE COURT OF JUSTICE OF THE EUROPEAN
COMMUNITIES OF THE CONVENTION ON THE PROTECTION OF THE EUROPEAN
COMMUNITIES' FINANCIAL INTERESTS DONE AT BRUSSELS ON 29 NOVEMBER 1996

PRÓTACAL

**arna dhréachtú ar bhonn Airteagal K.3 den chonradh ar an Aontas
Eorpach, maidir le léiriú, trí réamhrialú, ag cúirt bhreithiúnais na
gComhphobal Eorpach ar an gCoinbhinsiún maidir le leasanna
airgeadais na gComhphobal Eorpach a chosaint**

TÁ NA hARDPHÁIRTITHE CONARTHACHA,
TAR ÉIS COMHAONTÚ ar na forálacha seo a leanas a chuirfear i gceangal
leis an gCoinbhinsiún:

Airteagal 1

Beidh dlínse ag Cúirt Bhreithiúnais na gComhphobal Eorpach, faoi na
coinníollacha atá leagtha síos sa Phrótacal seo, chun réamhrialuithe a thabhairt
ar léiriú ar an gCoinbhinsiún maidir le leasanna airgeadais na gComhphobal
Eorpach a chosaint agus ar an bPrótacal a ghabhann leis an gCoinbhinsiún sin
agus a dréachtaíodh ar an 27 Meán Fómhair 1996, dá ngairtear "an chéad
Phrótacal" anseo feasta.

Airteagal 2

1. Féadfaidh aon Bhallstát, trí dhearbhú a dhéanamh tráth sínithe an Phrótacail
seo nó aon tráth eile ina dhiaidh sin, glacadh le dlínse Chúirt Bhreithiúnais na
gComhphobal Eorpach chun réamhrialuithe a thabhairt ar léiriú ar an
gCoinbhinsiún maidir le leasanna airgeadais na gComhphobal Eorpach a
chosaint agus ar an gcéad Phrótacal a ghabhann leis an gCoinbhinsiún sin faoi
na coinníollacha atá sonraithe i bpointe (*a*) nó (*b*) de mhír 2.

2. Féadfaidh Ballstát a dhéanann dearbhú faoi mhír 1 a shonrú:

   (*a*) go bhféadfaidh aon cheann de chúirteanna nó binsí an Bhallstáit sin
          nach bhfuil leigheas breithiú nach faoin dlí náisiúnta in aghaidh a
          bhreitheanna a iarraidh ar Chúirt Bhreithiúnais na gComhphobal
          Eorpach réamhrialú a thabhairt ar cheist a ardaítear i gcás atá ar feith-
          eamh os a chomhair agus a bhaineann le léiriú ar an gCoinbhinsiún
          maidir le leasanna airgeadais na gComhphobal Eorpach a chosaint
          agus ar an gcéad Phrótacal a ghabhann leis má mheasann an chúirt
          nó an binse sin gur gá breith a thabhairt ar an gceist ionas go
          bhféadfaidh sé breithiúnas a thabhairt; nó

   (*b*) go bhféadfaidh aon cheann de chúirteanna nó binsí an Bhallstáit sin
          a iarraidh ar Chúirt Bhreithiúnais na gComhphobal Eorpach

réamhrialú a thabhairt ar cheist a ardaítear i gcás atá ar feitheamh os a chomhair agus a bhaineann le léiriú ar an gCoinbhinsiún maidir le leasanna airgeadais na gComhphobal Eorpach a chosaint agus ar an gcéad Phrótacal a ghabhann leis má mheasann an chúirt nó an binse sin gur gá breith a thabhairt ar an gceist ionas go bhféadfaidh sé breithiúnas a thabhairt.

Airteagal 3

1. Beidh an Prótacal ar Reacht Chúirt Bhreithiúnais na gComhphobal Eorpach agus Rialacha Nós Imeachta na Cúirte Breithiúnais sin infheidhme.

2. I gcomhréir le Reacht Chúirt Bhreithiúnais na gComhphobal Eorpach, beidh gach Ballstát, bíodh nó ná bíodh dearbhú de bhun Airteagal 2 déanta aige, i dteideal ráitis cháis nó barúlacha i scríbhinn a thíolacadh do Chúirt Bhreithiúnais na gComhphobal Eorpach i gcásanna a thagann chun cinn faoi Airteagal 1.

Airteagal 4

1. Beidh an Prótacal seo faoi réir a ghlactha ag na Ballstáit i gcomhréir lena rialacha bunreachtúla faoi seach.

2. Cuirfidh na Ballstáit in iúl don taiscí go bhfuil na nósanna imeachta is gá faoina rialacha bunreachtúla faoi seach chun an Prótacal seo a ghlacadh comhlíonta acu, agus cuirfidh siad in iúl dó freisin aon dearbhú arna dhéanamh de bhun Airteagal 2.

3. Tiocfaidh an Prótacal seo i bhfeidhm 90 tar éis don fhógra dá dtagraítear i mír 2 a bheith tugtha ag an Stát, is Ballstát den Aontas Eorpach tráth na Comhairle do ghlacadh an Ghnímh ag dréachtú an Phrótacail seo, is déanaí a dhéanfaidh an beart sin. Ar a shon sin, tiocfaidh sé i bhfeidhm ar a luaithe san am céanna leis an gCoinbhinsiún maidir le leasanna airgeadais na gComhphobal Eorpach a chosaint.

Airteagal 5

1. Beidh aontachas leis an bPrótacal seo ar oscailt d'aon Stát a thagann chun bheith ina Bhallstát den Aontas Eorpach.

2. Taiscfear na hionstraimí aontachais leis an taiscí.

3. Is téacs údarásach téacs an Phrótacail seo i dteanga an Stáit aontaigh, arna dhréachtú ag Comhairle an Aontais Eorpaigh.

4. Tiocfaidh an Prótacal seo i bhfeidhm i leith aon Stáit aontaigh 90 lá tar éis dó a ionstraim aontachais a thaisceadh nó ar dháta an Phrótacail seo a theacht i bhfeidhm mura mbeidh sé tagtha i bhfeidhm fós tráth na tréimhse 90 lá thuasluaite a dhul in éag.

Airteagal 6

Aon Stát a thagann chun bheith ina Bhallstát den Aontas Eorpach agus a aontaíonn don Choinbhinsiún maidir le leasanna airgeadais na gComhphobal

Eorpach a chosaint i gcomhréir le hAirteagal 12 de, glacfaidh sé le forálacha an Phrótacail seo.

Airteagal 7

1. Féadfaidh gach Ballstát is Ardpháirtí Conarthach leasuithe ar an bPrótacal seo a mholadh. Cuirfear gach togra do leasú chuig an taiscí agus cuirfidh seisean in iúl don Chomhairle é.

2. Glacfaidh an Chomhairle na leasuithe agus molfaidh sí iad lena nglacadh ag na Ballstáit i gcomhréir lena rialacha bunreachtúla faoi seach.

3. Tiocfaidh na leasuithe arna nglacadh amhlaidh i bhfeidhm i gcomhréir le hAirteagal 4.

Airteagal 8

1. Is é Ardrúnaí Chomhairle an Aontais Eorpaigh taiscí an Phrótacail seo.

2. Foilseoidh an taiscí in Iris Oifigiúil na gComhphobal Eorpach fógraí, ionstraimí agus cumarsáidí a bhaineann leis an bPrótacal seo.

SCHEDULE 8

TEXT IN THE ENGLISH LANGUAGE OF THE PROTOCOL DRAWN UP ON THE BASIS OF
ARTICLE K.3 OF THE TREATY ON EUROPEAN UNION, TO THE CONVENTION ON THE
PROTECTION OF THE EUROPEAN COMMUNITIES' FINANCIAL INTERESTS DONE AT
BRUSSELS ON 19 JUNE 1997

SECOND PROTOCOL

**drawn up on the basis of Article K.3 of the treaty on European Union, to
the Convention on the protection of the European Communities'
financial interests**

THE HIGH CONTRACTING PARTIES to this Protocol, Member States of
the European Union,

REFERRING to the Act of the Council of the European Union of 19 June
1997;

DESIRING to ensure that their criminal laws contribute effectively to the protection of the financial interests of the European Communities;

RECOGNIZING the importance of the Convention on the protection of the
European Communities' financial interests of 26 July 1995 in combating fraud
affecting Community revenue and expenditure;

RECOGNIZING the importance of the Protocol of 27 September 1996 to the
said Convention in the fight against corruption damaging or likely to damage
the European Communities' financial interests;

AWARE that the financial interests of the European Communities may be damaged or threatened by acts committed on behalf of legal persons and acts involving money laundering;

CONVINCED of the need for national law to be adapted, where necessary, to
provide that legal persons can be held liable in cases of fraud or active corruption and money laundering committed for their benefit that damage or are likely
to damage the European Communities' financial interests;

CONVINCED of the need for national law to be adapted, where necessary, to
penalize acts of laundering of proceeds of fraud or corruption that damage or
are likely to damage the European Communities' financial interests and to make
it possible to confiscate proceeds of such fraud and corruption;

CONVINCED of the need for national law to be adapted, where necessary, in
order to prevent the refusal of mutual assistance solely because offences covered by this Protocol concern or are considered as tax or customs duty offences;

NOTING that cooperation between Member States is already covered by the
Convention on the protection of the European Communities' financial interests of 26 July 1995, but that there is a need, without prejudice to obligations
under Community law, for appropriate provision also to be made for cooperation between Member States and the Commission to ensure effective action
against fraud, active and passive corruption and related money laundering damaging or likely to damage the European Communities' financial interests, including exchange of information between the Member States and the
Commission;

CONSIDERING that, in order to encourage and facilitate the exchange of in-

formation, it is necessary to ensure adequate protection of personal data;
CONSIDERING that the exchange of information should not hinder ongoing investigations and that it is therefore necessary to provide for the protection of investigation secrecy;
CONSIDERING that appropriate provisions have to be drawn up on the competence of the Court of Justice of the European Communities;
CONSIDERING finally that the relevant provisions of the Convention on the protection of the European Communities' financial interests of 26 July 1995 should be made applicable to certain acts covered by this Protocol,
HAVE AGREED ON THE FOLLOWING PROVISIONS:

Article 1

Definitions

For the purposes of this Protocol:

(*a*) 'Convention' shall mean the Convention drawn up on the basis of Article K.3 of the Treaty on European Union on the protection of the European Communities' financial interests, of 26 July 1995;

(*b*) 'fraud' shall mean the conduct referred to in Article 1 of the Convention;

(*c*) — 'passive corruption' shall mean the conduct referred to in Article 2 of the Protocol drawn up on the basis of Article K.3 of the Treaty on European Union to the convention on the protection of the European Communities' financial interests, of 27 September 1996,

— 'active corruption' shall mean the conduct referred to in Article 3 of the same Protocol;

(*d*) 'legal person' shall mean any entity having such status under the applicable national law, except for States or other public bodies in the exercise of Stateauthority and for public international organizations;

(*e*) 'money laundering' shall mean the conduct as defined n the third indent of Article 1 of Council Directive 91/308/EEC of 10 June 1991 on the prevention of the use of the financial system for the purpose of money laundering, related to the proceeds of fraud, at least in serious cases, and of active and passive corruption.

Article 2

Money laundering

Each Member State shall take the necessary measures to establish money laundering as a criminal offence.

Article 3

Liability of legal persons

1. Each Member State shall take the necessary measures to ensure that legal persons can be held liable for fraud, active corruption and money laundering committed for their benefit by any person, acting either individually or as part of an organ of the legal person, who has a leading position within the legal person, based on

— a power of representation of the legal person, or
— an authority to take decisions on behalf of the legal person, or
— an authority to exercise control within the legal person,

as well as for involvement as accessories or instigators in such fraud, active corruption or money laundering or the attempted commission of such fraud.

2. Apart from the cases already provided for in paragraph 1, each Member State shall take the necessary measures to ensure that a legal person can be held liable where the lack of supervision or control by a person referred to in paragraph 1 has made possible the commission of a fraud or an act of active corruption or money laundering for the benefit of that legal person by a person under its authority.

3. Liability of a legal person under paragraphs 1 and 2 shall not exclude criminal proceedings against natural persons who are perpetrators, instigators or accessories in the fraud, active corruption or money laundering.

Article 4

Sanctions for legal persons

1. Each Member State shall take the necessary measures to ensure that a legal person held liable pursuant to Article 3 (1) is punishable by effective, proportionate and dissuasive sanctions, which shall include criminal or non-criminal fines and may include other sanctions such as:

(*a*) exclusion from entitlement to public benefits or aid;
(*b*) temporary or permanent disqualification from the practice of commercial activities;
(*c*) placing under judicial supervision;
(*d*) a judicial winding-up order.

2. Each Member State shall take the necessary measures to ensure that a legal person held liable pursuant to Article 3 (2) is punishable by effective, proportionate and dissuasive sanctions or measures.

Article 5

Confiscation

Each Member State shall take the necessary measures to enable the seizure and, without prejudice to the rights of bona fide third parties, the confiscation or removal of the instruments and proceeds of fraud, active and passive corruption and money laundering, or property the value of which corresponds to such proceeds. Any instruments, proceeds or other property seized or confiscated shall be dealt with by the Member State in accordance with its national law.

Article 6

Cooperation with the Commission of the European Communities

A Member State may not refuse to provide mutual assistance in respect of fraud, active and passive corruption and money laundering for the sole reason that it concerns or is considered as a tax or customs duty offence.

Article 7

Cooperation with the Commission of the European Communities

1. The Member States and the Commission shall cooperate with each other in the fight against fraud, active and passive corruption and money laundering.

To that end, the Commission shall lend such technical and operational assistance as the competent national authorities may need to facilitate coordination of their investigations.

2. The competent authorities in the Member States may exchange information with the Commission so as to make it easier to establish the facts and to ensure effective action against fraud, active and passive corruption and money laundering. The Commission and the competent national authorities shall take account, in each specific case, of the requirements of investigation secrecy and data protection. To that end, a Member State, when supplying information to the Commission, may set specific conditions covering the use of information, whether by the Commission or by another Member State to which that information may be passed.

Article 8

Data protection responsibility for the Commission

The Commission shall ensure that, in the context of the exchange of information under Article 7 (2), it shall observe, as regards the processing of personal data, a level of protection equivalent to the level of protection set out in Directive 95/46/EC of the European Parliament and of the Council of 24 October 1995 on the protection of individuals with regard to the processing of personal data and on the free movement of such data.

Article 9

Publication of data protection rules

The rules adopted concerning the obligations under Article 8 shall be published in the Official Journal of the European Communities.

Article 10

Transfer of data to other Member States and third countries

1. Subject to any conditions referred to in Article 7 (2), the Commission may transfer personal data obtained from a Member State in the performance of its functions under Article 7 to any other Member State. The Commission shall inform the Member State which supplied the information of its intention to make such as transfer.

2. The Commission may, under the same conditions, transfer personal data obtained from a Member State in the performance of its functions under Article 7 to any third country provided that the Member State which supplied the information has agreed to such transfer.

Article 11

Supervisory authority

Any authority designated or created for the purpose of exercising the function of independent data protection supervision over personal data held by the Commission pursuant to its functions under the Treaty establishing the European Community, shall be competent to exercise the same function with respect to personal data held by the Commission by virtue of this Protocol.

Article 12

Relation to the Convention

1. The provisions of Articles 3, 5 and 6 of the Convention shall also apply to the conduct referred to in Article 2 of this Protocol.

2. The following provisions of the Convention shall also apply to this Protocol:
- — Article 4, on the understanding that, unless otherwise indicated at the time of the notification provided for in Article 16 (2) of this Protocol, any declaration within the meaning of Article 4 (2) of the Convention, shall also apply to this Protocol,
- — Article 7, on the understanding that the *ne bis in idem* principle also applies to legal persons, and that, unless otherwise indicated at the time the notification provided for in Article 16 82) of this Protocol is being given, any declaration within the meaning of Article 7 (2), of the Convention shall also apply to this Protocol,
- — Article 9,
- — Article 10.

Article 13

Court of Justice

1. Any dispute between Member States on the interpretation or application of this Protocol must in an initial stage be examined by the Council in accordance with the procedure set out in Title VI of the Treaty on European Union with a view to reaching a solution.

If no solution is found within six months, the matter may be referred to the Court of Justice by a party to the dispute.

2. Any dispute between one or more Member States and the Commission concerning the application of Article 2 in relation to Article 1 (*e*), and Article 7, 8, 10 and 12 (2), fourth indent of this Protocol which it has proved impossible to settle through negotiation may be submitted to the Court of Justice, after the expiry of a period of six months from the date on which one of the parties has notified the other of the existence of a dispute.

3. The Protocol drawn up on the basis of Article K.3 of the Treaty on European Union, on the interpretation, by way of preliminary rulings, by the Court of Justice of the European Communities of the Convention on the protection of the European Communities' financial interests, of 29 November 1996, shall apply to this Protocol, on the understanding that a declaration made by a Member State pursuant to Article 2 of that Protocol is also valid regarding this Protocol unless the Member State concerned makes a declaration to the contrary when giving the notification provided for in Article 16 (2) of this Protocol.

Article 14

Non-contractual liability

For the purposes of this Protocol, the non-contractual liability of the Community shall be governed by the second paragraph of Article 215 of the Treaty establishing the European Community. Article 178 of the same Treaty shall apply.

Article 15

Judicial control

1. The Court of Justice shall have jurisdiction in proceedings instituted by any natural or legal person against a decision of the Commission addressed to that person or which is of direct and individual concern to that person, on ground of infringement of Article 8 or any rule adopted pursuant thereto, or misuse of powers.

2. Articles 168 a (1) and (2), 173, fifth paragraph, 174, first paragraph, 176, first and second paragraphs, 185 and 186 of the Treaty establishing the European Community, as well as the Statute of the Court of Justice of the European Community, shall apply, *mutatis mutandis*.

Article 16

Entry into force

1. This Protocol shall be subject to adoption by the Member States in accordance with their respective constitutional requirements.

2. Member States shall notify the Secretary-General of the Council of the European Union of the completion of the procedures required under their respective constitutional rules for adopting this Protocol.

3. This Protocol shall enter into force ninety days after the notification provided for in paragraph 2, by the State which, being a member of the European Union on the date of the adoption by the Council of the act drawing up this Protocol, is the last to fulfil that formality. If, however, the Convention has not entered into force on that date, this Protocol shall enter into force on the date on which the Convention enters into force.

4. However, the application of Article 7 (2) shall be suspended if, and for so long as, the relevant institution of the European Communities has not complied with its obligation to publish the data protection rules pursuant to Article 9 or the terms of Article 11 concerning the supervisory authority have not been complied with.

Article 17

Accession of new Member States

1. This Protocol shall be open to accession by any State that becomes a member of the European Union.

2. The text of this Protocol in the language of the acceding State, drawn up by the Council of the European Union, shall be authentic.

3. Instruments of accession shall be deposited with the depositary.

4. This Protocol shall enter into force with respect to any State that accedes to it ninety days after the deposit of its instrument of accession or on the date of entry into force of this Protocol if it has not yet entered into force at the time of expiry of the said period of ninety days.

Article 18

Reservations

1. Each Member State may reserve the right to establish the money laundering related to the proceeds of active and passive corruption as a criminal offence only in serious cases of active and passive corruption. Any Member State making such a reservation shall inform the depositary, giving details of the scope of the reservation, when giving the notification provided for in Article 16 (2). Such a reservation shall be valid for a period of five years after the said notification. It may be renewed once for a further period of five years.

2. The Republic of Austria may, when giving its notification referred to in Article 16 (2), declare that it will not be bound by Articles 3 and 4. Such a

declaration shall cease to have effect five years after the date of the adoption of the act drawing up this Protocol.

3. No other reservations shall be authorized, with the exception of those provided for in Article 12 (2), first and second indent.

Article 19

Depositary

1. The Secretary-General of the Council of the European Union shall act as depositary of this Protocol.

2. The depositary shall publish in the Official Journal of the European Communities information on the progress of adoptions and accessions, declarations and reservations and any other notification concerning this Protocol.

Section 41   SCHEDULE 9

<small>TEXT IN THE IRISH LANGUAGE OF THE PROTOCOL DRAWN UP ON THE BASIS OF ARTICLE K.3 OF THE TREATY ON EUROPEAN UNION, TO THE CONVENTION ON THE PROTECTION OF THE EUROPEAN COMMUNITIES FINANCIAL INTERESTS DONE AT BRUSSELS ON 19 JUNE 1997</small>

AN DARA PRÓTACAL

arna dhréachtú ar bhonn Airteagal K.3 den chonradh ar an Aontas Eorpach, a ghabhann leis an gCoinbhinsiún maidir le leasanna airgeadais na gComhphobal Eorpach a chosaint

TÁ NA hARDPHÁIRTITHE CONARTHACHA sa Phrótacal seo, Ballstáit den Aontas Eorpach,

AG TAGAIRT DÓIBH do Ghníomh ó Chomhairle an Aontais Eorpaigh an 19 Meitheamh 1997;

ÓS MIAN LEO a áirithiú go gcuidíonn a ndlíthe coiriú la go héifeachtúil le leasanna airgeadais na gComhphobal Eorpach a chosaint;

AG AITHINT DÓIBH thábhacht Choinbhinsiún an 26 Iúil 1995 maidir le leasanna airgeadais na gComhphobal Eorpach a chosaint chun calaois a dhéanann dochar d'ioncam agus caiteachas na gComhphobal a chomhrac;

AG AITHINT DÓIBH thábhacht Phrótacal an 27 Meán Fómhair 1996 a ghabhann leis an gCoinbhinsiún sin sa chomhrac i gcoinne éilliú a dhéanann díobháil, nó ar dóigh dó díobháil a dhéanamh, do leasanna airgeadais na gComhphobal Eorpach;

ÓS FIOS DÓIBH go bhféadfaidh gníomhartha arna ndéanamh thar ceann daoine dlítheanacha agus gníomhartha a bhfuil sciúradh airgid i dtreis iontu díobháil a dhéanamh do leasanna airgeadais na gComhphobal Eorpach nó bheith ina mbagairt orthu;

ÓS DEIMHIN LEO gur gá an dlí náisiúnta a oiriúnú, nuair is gá, chun a fhoráil go bhféadfar daoine dlítheanacha a chur faoi dhliteanas i gcásanna calaoise nó éillithe ghníomhaigh agus sciúrtha airgid a dhéanann díobháil, nó ar dóigh dóibh díobháil a dhéanamh, do leasanna airgeadais na gComhphobal Eorpach;

ÓS DEIMHIN LEO gur gá an dlí náisiúnta a oiriúnú, nuair is gá, chun gníomhartha a phionósú lena ndéantar fáltais ón gcalaois nó ón éilliú a sciúradh a dhéanann díobháil, nóar dóigh dóibh díobháil a dhéanamh, do leasanna airgeadais na gComhphobal Eorpach agus chun gur féidir fáltais ó chalaois agus éilliú den sórt sin a choigistiú;

ÓS DEIMHIN LEO gur gá an dlí náisiúnta a oiriúnú, nuair is gá, d'fhonn a chosc go ndéanfar cúnamh frithpháirteach a dhiúltú toisc amháin go bhfuil baint ag na cionta atá folaithe sa Phrótacal seo le cionta a bhaineann le cánacha nó dleachtanna custaim nó go meastar gur cionta den saghas sin iad;

AG TABHAIRT DÁ nAIRE DÓIBH go bhfuil an comhar idir na Ballstáit folaithe cheana i gCoinbhinsiún an 26 Iúil 1995 maidir le leasanna airgeadais na gComhphobal Eorpach a chosaint ach gur gá, gan dochar d'oibleagáidí faoin dlí Comhphobail, a fhoráil go hiomchuí freisin do chomhar idir na Ballstáit agus an Coimisiún d'fhonn gníomhaíocht éifeachtúil a áirithiú i gcoinne na calaoise, an éillithe ghníomhaigh agus neamhghníomhaigh agus sciúradh airgid gaolmhar a dhéanann díobháil, nó ar dóigh dóibh díobháil a dhéanamh, do leasanna airgeadais na gComhphobal Eorpach, lena n-áirítear malartú faisnéise idir na Ballstáit agus an Coimisiún;

DE BHRÍ gur gá, d'fhonn malartú faisnéise a chothú agus a éascú, cosaint leormhaith a áirithiú do shonraí pearsanta;

DE BHRÍ nár chóir go mbeadh an malartú faisnéise ina bhac ar imscrúduithe atá faoi shiúl agus gur gá dá bhrí sin a fhoráil go gcosnófar rúndacht an imscrúdaithe;

DE BHRÍ gur chóir freisin forálacha iomchuí a leagan síos maidir le dlínse Chúirt Bhreithiúnais na gComhphobal Eorpach;

DE BHRÍ, ar deireadh, gur chóir forálacha ábhartha Choinbhinsiún an 26 Iúil 1995 maidir le leasanna airgeadais na gComhphobal Eorpach a chosaint a chur i bhfeidhm ar ghníomhartha áirithe atá folaithe sa Phrótacal seo,

TAR ÉIS COMHAONTÚ AR NA FORÁLACHA SEO A LEANAS:

Airteagal 1

Sainmhínithe

Chun críoch an Phrótacail seo:
- (*a*) ciallaíonn "an Coinbhinsiún" Coinbhinsiún an 26 Iúil 1995, arna dhréachtú ar bhonn Airteagal K.3 den Chonradh ar an Aontas Eorpach, maidir le leasanna airgeadais na gComhphobal Eorpach a chosaint;
- (*b*) ciallaíonn "calaois" an t-iompar dá dtagraítear in Airteagal 1 den Choinbhinsiún;
- (*c*) — ciallaíonn "éilliú neamhghníomhach" an t-iompar dá dtagraítear in Airteagal 2 de Phrótacal an 27 Meán Fómhair 1996, arna dhréachtú ar bhonn Airteagal K.3 den Chonradh ar an Aontas Eorpach, a ghabhann leis an gCoinbhinsiún maidir le leasanna airgeadais na gComhphobal Eorpach a chosaint;
  - — ciallaíonn "éilliú gníomhach" an t-iompar dá dtagraítear in Airteagal 3 den Phrótacal céanna;
- (*d*) ciallaíonn "duine dlítheanach" aon eintiteas a bhfuil stádas den sórt sin aige faoin dlí náisiúnta is infheidhme, amach ó Stáit nó comhlachtaí poiblí eile i bhfeidhmiú údarás an Stáit agus ó eagraíochtaí idirnáisiúnta poiblí;
- (*e*) ciallaíonn "sciúradh airgid" an t-iompar atá sainithe sa tríú fleasc d'Airteagal 1 de Threoir 91/308/CEE ón gComhairle an 10 Meitheamh 1991 maidir le húsáid an chórais airgeadais chun críche sciúradh airgid a chosc, a bhaineann le fáltais ón gcalaois, ar a laghad i gcásanna tromchúiseacha calaoise, agus ón éilliú gníomhach agus neamhghníomhach.

Airteagal 2

Sciúradh airgid

Glacfaidh gach Ballstát na bearta is gá chun sciúradh airgid a bhunú mar chion coiriúil.

Airteagal 3

Dliteanas daoine dlítheanacha

1. Glacfaidh gach Ballstát na bearta is gá chun a áirithiú go bhféadfar daoine dlítheanacha a chur faoi dhliteanas don chalaois, don éilliú gníomhach agus do sciú radh airgid arna ndéanamh ar mhaithe leo ag aon duine, ag gníomhú dó ina aonar nó mar bhall d'orgán de chuid an duine dhlítheanaigh, a bhfuil ardseasamh aige laistigh den duine dlítheanach atá bunaithe:
   — ar chumhacht ionadaíochta don duine dlítheanach, nó
   — ar údarás chun cinntí a ghlacadh thar ceann an duine dhlítheanaigh, nó
   — ar údarás chun rialú a fheidhmiú laistigh den duine dlítheanach,
agus freisin faoi dhliteanas do bheith i dtreis mar chúlpháirtithe nó mar ghríosóirí i gcalaois, in éilliú gníomhach nó i sciúradh airgid den sórt sin nó in iarracht ar chalaois den sórt sin a dhéanamh.

2. Amach ó na cásanna dá bhforáiltear cheana i mír 1, glacfaidh gach Ballstát na bearta is gá chun a áirithiú go bhféadfar duine dlítheanach a chur faoi dhliteanas nuair is é an easpa maoirseachta nó rialaithe de chuid duine dá dtagraítear i mír 1 ba chúis gurbh fhéidir le duine faoina údarás calaois nó gníomh éillithe ghníomhaigh nó sciúradh airgid a dhéanamh ar mhaithe leis an duine dlítheanach sin.

3. Ní eisiafaidh dliteanas duine dhlítheanaigh faoi mhíreanna 1 agus 2 imeachtaí coiriúla i gcoinne daoine nádúrtha is údair nó gríosóirí na calaoise, an éillithe ghníomhaigh nó an sciúrtha airgid nó is cúlpháirtithe iontu.

Airteagal 4

Smachtbhannaí do dhaoine dlítheanacha

1. Glacfaidh gach Ballstát na bearta is gá chun a áirithiú go mbeidh duine dlítheanach arna chur faoi dhliteanas de bhun Airteagal 3(1) inphionóis le smachtbhannaí atá éifeachtúil, comhréireach agus athchomhairleach a chuimseoidh fíneálacha coiriúla nó neamhchoiriúla agus a fhéadfaidh smachtbhannaí eile a chuimsiú amhail:
   (*a*) eisiamh ón teideal chun sochar poiblí nó cúnaimh;
   (*b*) dícháiliú sealadach nó buan chun gníomhaíochtaí tráchtála a chleachtadh;
   (*c*) cur faoi mhaoirseacht bhreithiúnach;
   (*d*) ordú foirceanta breithiúnach.

2. Glacfaidh gach Ballstát na bearta is gá chun a áirithiú go mbeidh duine dlítheanach arna chur faoi dhliteanas de bhun Airteagal 3(2) inphionóis le smachtbhannaí nó bearta atá éifeachtúil, comhréireach agus athchomhairleach.

Airteagal 5

Coigistiú

Glacfaidh gach Ballstát na bearta is gá chun a áirithiú go bhféadfar ionstraimí na calaoise, an éillithe ghníomhaigh agus neamhghníomhaigh agus an sciúrtha airgid, agus fáltais uathu nó maoin a bhfreagraíonn a luach d'fháltais den sórt sin, a urghabháil agus, gan dochar do chearta tríú páirtithe *bona fide*, a choigistiú nó a aistriú. Déileálfaidh an Ballstát, i gcomhréir lena dhlí náisiúnta, le haon ionstraimí, fáltais nó maoin eile arna n-urghabháil nó arna gcoigistiú .

Airteagal 6

Cionta a bhaineann le cánacha agus dleachtanna custaim

Ní fhéadfaidh Ballstát diúltú cúnamh frithpháirteach a sholáthar i ndáil leis an gcalaois, an éilliú gníomhach agus neamhghníomhach agus an sciúradh airgid toisc amháin go bhfuil baint aige le cion a bhaineann le cánacha nó dleachtanna custaim nó go meastar gur cion den saghas sin é.

Airteagal 7

Comhar le Coimisiún na gComhphobal Eorpach

1. Comhoibreoidh na Ballstáit agus Coimisiún na gComhphobal Eorpach le chéile chun an chalaois, an t-éilliú gníomhach agus neamhghníomhach agus sciúradh airgid a chomhrac.

Chuige sin, soláthróidh an Coimisiún aon chúnamh teicniúil agus oibríochtúil a fhéadfaidh a bheith ag teastáil ó na húdaráis náisiúnta inniúla chun comhordú a n-imscrúduithe a éascú.

2. Féadfaidh na húdaráis inniúla sna Ballstáit faisnéis a mhalartú leis an gCoimisiún chun gur fusa na fíorais a shuíomh agus gníomhaíocht éifeachtúil a áirithiú i gcoinne na calaoise, an éillithe ghníomhaigh agus neamhghníomhaigh agus an sciúrtha airgid. Cuirfidh an Coimisiún agus na húdaráis náisiúnta inniúla san áireamh, i ngach cás sonrach, riachtanais rúndacht na n-imscrúduithe agus chosaint na sonraí. Chuige sin, féadfaidh Ballstát, tráth na faisnéise a sholáthar don Choimisiún, coinníollacha sonracha a leagan síos a fholaíonn úsáid na faisnéise ag an gCoimisiún nó ag Ballstát eile a bhféadfar an fhaisnéis sin a chur chuige.

Airteagal 8

Freagracht an Choimisiúin as sonraí a chosaint

Áiritheoidh an Coimisiún, i gcomhthéacs faisnéis a mhalartú faoi Airteagal 7(2), go n-urramóidh sé, i ndáil le próiseáil sonraí pearsanta, leibhéal cosanta is coibhéiseach leis an leibhéal cosanta atá leagtha amach i dTreoir 95/46/CE ó Pharlaimint na hEorpa agus ón gComhairle an 24 Deireadh Fómhair 1995 maidir le daoine aonair a chosaint i dtaca le próiseáil sonraí pearsanta agus saorghluaiseacht sonraí den sórt sin.

Airteagal 9
Rialacha cosanta sonraí a fhoilsiú

Déanfar na rialacha a ghlacfar maidir leis na hoibleagáidí faoi Airteagal 8 a fhoilsiú in Iris Oifigiúil na gComhphobal Eorpach.

Airteagal 10
Sonraí a aistriú chuig Ballstáit eile agus chuig tríú tíortha

1. Faoi réir aon choinníollacha dá dtagraítear in Airteagal 7(2), féadfaidh an Coimisiún sonraí pearsanta a fhaightear ó Ballstát i bhfeidhmiú a fheidhmeanna faoi Airteagal 7 a aistriú chuig aon Bhallstát eile. Cuirfidh an Coimisiún in iúl don Bhallstát a sholáthair an fhaisnéis go bhfuil sé ar intinn aige an t-aistriú sin a dhéanamh.

2. Féadfaidh an Coimisiún, faoi na coinníollacha céanna, sonraí pearsanta a fhaightear ó Bhallstát i bhfeidhmiú a fheidhmeanna faoi Airteagal 7 a aistriú chuig aon tríú tír ar chuntar go bhfuil an Ballstát a sholáthair an fhaisnéis tar éis comhaontú leis an aistriú sin.

Airteagal 11
Údarás maoirseachta

Aon údarás arna cheapadh nó arna chruthú d'fhonn feidhm na maoirseachta neamhspleáiche ar chosaint sonraí a fheidhmiú maidir le sonraí pearsanta arna sealbhú ag an gCoimisiún de bhun a fheidhmeanna faoin gConradh ag bunú an Chomhphobail Eorpaigh, beidh sé inniúil chun an fheidhm chéanna a fheidhmiú i leith sonraí pearsanta arna sealbhú ag an gCoimisiún de bhua an Phrótacail seo.

Airteagal 12
Gaol leis an gCoinbhinsiún

1. Beidh forálacha Airteagail 3, 5 agus 6 den Choinbhinsiún infheidhme freisin ar an iompar dá dtagraítear in Airteagal 2 den Phrótacal seo.

2. Beidh na forálacha seo a leanas den Choinbhinsiún infheidhme freisin ar an bPrótacal seo:
    — Airteagal 4, ar é a bheith le tuiscint go mbeidh aon dearbhú de réir bhrí Airteagal 4(2) den Choinbhinsiún infheidhme freisin ar an bPrótacal seo mura sonrófar a mhalairt tráth an fhógra dá bhforáiltear in Airteagal 16(2) den Phrótacal seo a thabhairt,
    — Airteagal 7, ar é a bheith le tuiscint go mbeidh prionsabal "ne bis in

idem" infheidhme freisin ar dhaoine dlítheanacha agus go mbeidh aon dearbhú de réir bhrí Airteagal 7(2) den Choinbhinsiún infheidhme freisin ar an bPrótacal seo mura sonrófar a mhalairt tráth an fhógra dá bhforáiltear in Airteagal 16(2) den Phrótacal seo a thabhairt,

— Airteagal 9,
— Airteagal 10.

Airteagal 13

An Chúirt Bhreithiúnais

1. Ní foláir don Chomhairle aon díospóid idir na Ballstáit maidir le léiriú nó cur i bhfeidhm an Phrótacail seo a phlé mar chéad chéim i gcomhréir leis an nós imeachta atá leagtha amach i dTeideal VI den Chonradh ar an Aontas Eorpach d'fhonn teacht ar réiteach.

Mura mbeidh réiteach faighte laistigh de thréimhse sé mhí, féadfaidh páirtí sa díospóid í a chur faoi bhráid na Cúirte Breithiúnais.

2. Aon díospóid idir Ballstát amháin nó níos mó agus an Coimisiún maidir le hAirteagal 2, i ndáil le pointe (*e*) d'Airteagal 1, agus le hAirteagail 7, 8 agus 10 agus leis an gceathrú fleasc d'Airteagal 12(2) den Phrótacal seo a chur i bhfeidhm nárbh fhéidir a réiteach trí chaibidlíocht, féadfar í a chur faoi bhráid na Cúirte Breithiúnais tar éis do thréimhse sé mhí ón dáta a thug ceann de na páirtithe fógra don pháirtí eile go raibh díospóid ann dul in éag.

3. Beidh Prótacal an 29 Samhain 1996, arna dhréachtú ar bhonn Airteagal K.3 den Chonradh ar an Aontas Eorpach, maidir le léiriú, trí réamhrialú, ag Cúirt Bhreithiúnais na gComhphobal Eorpach ar an gCoinbhinsiún maidir le leasanna airgeadais na gComhphobal Eorpach a chosaint, infheidhme ar an bPrótacal seo, ar é a bheith le tuiscint go mbeidh dearbhú arna dhéanamh ag Ballstát de bhun Airteagal 2 den Phrótacal sin bailí freisin i leith an Phrótacail seo mura ndéanfaidh an Ballstát i dtrácht dearbhú dá mhalairt tráth an fhógra dá bhforáiltear in Airteagal 16(2) den Phrótacal seo a thabhairt.

Airteagal 14

Dliteanas neamhchonarthach

Chun críoch an Phrótacail seo, beidh dliteanas neamhchonarthach an Chomhphobail faoi rialú ag an dara mír d'Airteagal 215 den Chonradh ag bunú an Chomhphobail Eorpaigh. Beidh Airteagal 178 den Chonradh céanna infheidhme.

Airteagal 15

Rialú breithiúnach

1. Beidh dlínse ag an gCúirt Bhreithiúnais in imeachtaí arna dtionscnamh ag aon duine ná dúrtha nó dlítheanach in aghaidh cinneadh ón gCoimisiún a díríodh chuig an duine sin nó is dá chúram go díreach agus go leithleach, mar

gheall ar shárú Airteagal 8 nó aon riail arna glacadh dá bhun nó mar gheall ar mhíú-sáid cumhachtaí.

2. Beidh Airteagail 168a(1) agus (2), an cúigiú mír d'Airteagal 173, an chéad mhír d'Airteagal 174, an chéad mhír agus an dara mír d'Airteagal 176, agus Airteagail 185 agus 186 den Chonradh ag bunú an Chomhphobail Eorpach, maille le Reacht Chúirt Bhreithiúnais na gComhphobal Eorpach, infheidhme *mutatis mutandis*.

Airteagal 16

Teacht i bhfeidhm

1. Beidh an Prótacal seo faoi réir a ghlactha ag na Ballstáit i gcomhréir lena rialacha bunreachtúla faoi seach.

2. Cuirfidh na Ballstáit in iúl d'Ardrúnaí Chomhairle an Aontais Eorpaigh go bhfuil na nósanna imeachta is gá faoina rialacha bunreachtúla faoi seach chun an Prótacal seo a ghlacadh comhlíonta acu.

3. Tiocfaidh an Prótacal seo i bhfeidhm 90 lá tar éis don fhógra dá bhforáiltear i mír 2 a bheith tugtha ag an Stát is Ballstát den Aontas Eorpach ar an dáta a ghlac an Chomhairle an Gníomh ag dréachtú an Phrótacail seo is déanaí a dhéanfaidh an beart sin. Mura mbeidh an Coinbhinsiún tagtha i bhfeidhm ar an dáta sin áfach, tiocfaidh an Prótacal seo i bhfeidhm ar an dáta a thiocfaidh an Choinbhinsiún i bhfeidhm.

4. Ar a shon sin, déanfar cuir i bhfeidhm Airteagal 7(2) a fhionraí mura mbeidh, agus fad nach mbeidh, an institiúid ábhartha de chuid na gComhphobal Eorpach tar éis a hoibleagáid na rialacha cosanta sonraí a fhoilsiú de bhun Airteagal 9 a chomhlíonadh nó mura mbeifear, agus fad nach mbeifear, tar éis téarmaí Airteagal 11 maidir leis an údarás maoirseachta a chomhlíonadh.

Airteagal 17

Aontachas Ballstát nua

1. Beidh an Prótacal seo ar oscailt d'aontachas aon Stát a thiocfaidh chun bheith ina Bhallstát den Aontas Eorpach.

2. Is téacs údarásach téacs an Phrótacail seo i dteanga an Stáit aontaigh, arna dhréachtú ag Comhairle an Aontais Eorpaigh.

3. Déanfar ionstraimí aontachais a thaisceadh leis an taiscí.

4. Tiocfaidh an Prótacal seo i bhfeidhm i leith aon Stát a aontaíonn dó 90 lá tar éis dó a ionstraim aontachais a thaisceadh nó ar dháta an Phrótacail seo a theacht i bhfeidhm mura mbeidh sé tagtha i bhfeidhm fós tráth na tréimhse thuasluaite 90 lá a dhul in éag.

Airteagal 18

Forchoimeádais

1. Féadfaidh gach Ballstát an ceart a fhorchoimeád gan sciúradh airgid a

bhaineann leis na fáltais ón éilliú gníomhach agus neamhghníomhach a bhunú mar chion coiriúil ach i gcásanna tromchúiseacha éillithe ghníomhaigh agus neamhghníomhaigh. Aon Bhallstát a dhéanann forchoimeádas den sórt sin, cuirfidh sé an taiscí ar an eolas tráth an fhógra dá bhforáiltear in Airteagal 16(2) a thabhairt, agus tabharfaidh sé na mionsonraí dó maidir le raon feidhme an fhorchoimeádais. Beidh forchoimeádas den sórt sin bailí go ceann tréimhse cúig bliana ón bhfógra sin. Féadfar é a athnuachan uair amháin go ceann tréimhse eile cúig bliana.

2. Féadfaidh Poblacht na hOstaire a dhearbhú, tráth an fhógra dá dtagraítear in Airteagal 16(2) a thabhairt, nach mbeidh sí faoi cheangal ag Airteagail 3 agus 4. Scoirfidh dearbhú den sórt sin d'éifeacht a bheith leis cúig bliana tar éis dháta glactha an Ghnímh ag dréachtú an Phrótacail seo.

3. Ní cheadófar aon fhorchoimeádas eile amach ó na cinn dá bhforáiltear sa chéad fhleasc agus sa dara fleasc d'Airteagal 12(2).

Airteagal 19

Taiscí

1. Is é Ardrúnaí Chomhairle an Aontais Eorpaigh taiscí an Phrótacail seo.

2. Foilseoidh an taiscí in Iris Oifigiúil na gComhphobal Eorpach faisnéis maidir leis an bPrótacal seo a ghlacadh agus aontachais leis, na dearbhuithe, na forchoimeádais agus gach fógra eile a bhaineann leis an bPrótacal seo.